Almost Naked

Almost Naked

"A Personal Journey"

By Bob Porter
August 2003

iUniverse, Inc.
New York Lincoln Shanghai

Almost Naked
"A Personal Journey"

iUniverse, Inc.

For information address:
iUniverse, Inc.
2021 Pine Lake Road, Suite 100
Lincoln, NE 68512
www.iuniverse.com

ISBN: 0-595-29685-8 (Pbk)
ISBN: 0-595-75199-7 (Cloth)

Printed in the United States of America

To Lee, who lived most of this with me.

I wish to acknowledge and thank Mary Lou Guandolo for her editorial expertise and Terri Miller for her administrative support.

Table of Contents

*1 reprinted from <u>My Friends & Mentors</u> (1994)
*2 reprinted from the <u>Moscow Contrivance</u> (2000)
*3 reprinted from <u>Strictly Personal</u> (1996)
*4 reprinted from <u>Sooner Born</u> (1997)

Introduction

If one's lucky, some day he reaches age 60. My sixtieth birthday occurred February 27, 1995. While many view birthdays with mixed emotions I have greeted each one with enthusiasm and optimism. "Appreciation" is one word that described my feelings on my sixtieth. I had survived several illnesses including Parkinson's disease, first diagnosed in 1980, and an operation for cancer in early 1992. Although these seemed life threatening at the time they were diagnosed, I still enjoy a good, if reduced, quality of life. I guess I identify with comedian Tom Lehr's observation, "When I compare myself to Mozart, I take very little comfort that by the time he reached my age, he had already been dead 20 years."

In fact, I was so enthusiastic about my good fortune that I wrote a book entitled, My Friends and Mentors, The First Sixty Years to share some experiences with friends and family. The process of writing the book was its own reward. It was sheer delight to recount anecdotes about good times that I had shared with people whom I had been able to claim as friends for twenty years or more. I recommend everybody try it. Naturally I sent copies of my book to the thirty-nine living "friends and mentors" featured in the book. I also invited them to join me to celebrate my Sixtieth. To my amazement thirty-three actual made it, including my third grade girlfriend, my high-school girlfriend, and a college girlfriend. What a fantastic evening! What Mozart missed!

At NASA, I had the good fortune to work closely with James E. Webb, the Administrator who directed the programs that put man on the moon. He was an unconventional thinker who gave unconventional assignments. One of my assignments was to ask several wise men what they had done right in their careers. I asked this question to myself as well. I've concluded that everything gets done through people and that interaction with my mentors has been my greatest blessing.

This is my sixth book. It is a collection of short pieces I wrote from December 1990 to the present. It is autobiographical and relates mostly humorous events but I recognize that if truth is his stated objective, an autobiographer is usually his own worst enemy.

1

The challenge of biography and autobiography is presented well in a story about Voltaire in which a friend bares his soul to him. Voltaire listens and then roars in laughter. The friend is crestfallen and ask him how he could just laugh at such a vulnerable disclosure. Voltaire replied, "First there is you as you think you are. Then there is you as I think you are. Then there is you as you really are. Then there is me as you think I am. Then there is me as I think I am. Then there is me as I really am. I laughed because I couldn't tell which two of us were speaking at any moment in time."

This is autobiographic in the form of anthology. It has three principal elements. The first contains material I have written but not published over the past ten years. The second is made up of pieces I wrote on my mentors in 1992. my Christmas letters since 1987. The third part contains Christmas letters since 1987. Many of our habits are derived from messages we learn from everyday events. When an anecdote provides us a basis for giving advice I have noted this.

In real life, the truth, the whole truth and nothing but the truth can be called "the naked truth." When we put on vestments, we protect the ugly from prying eyes. If you can still see the outlines of reality but not the sharp edges you have what I call "almost naked" truth. This is as much as I can aspire to deliver, thus, the name of this book.

Our pathways to survival take many routes including science, religion, war, medicine, and sex. They are all paths from a poorly-understood beginning to an equally baffling end. Some would say it's fortuitous that there are carrots, as well as sticks, on the road leading to this end. Others would say it's a gift that we're programmed to enjoy carrots!

PREFACE
Sex, Mentoring and
"The Search for a Higher Power"
December, 1995

I've asked people to tell me about their mentors. One female friend whom I've known for almost forty years said, "I don't think I can. It's too personal. All my mentors have been men, and most of them wanted to go to bed with me." I wondered, but I didn't ask: how many did or didn't. It really didn't matter. No answer would threaten our relationship. We're friends, and yet, on reflection we have emotional bonds like lovers. We grew up together and have been mentors to each other about life.

I found her answer thought-provoking. Before talking to her, I hadn't thought of mentoring as having sexual overtones. Procreation is an obvious prerequisite to species survival. Mothers of many species will sacrifice their lives to preserve their prodigy. Our priorities are clearly set with "preservation of the species."

Where does being or having a mentor fit in our struggle to survive? The answer is simple: Mentoring expedites the passage of vital survival information from one generation to the next. Only the fittest survive. "A little edge" can make a great difference over a couple of million years. Mentoring and sex are two complementary routes to species survival.

Some people have many mentors. To my surprise, many claim none.
One can't mentor alone. It takes at least two. The analogy to love relationships is overwhelming. Society condones, in fact, blesses menoring relationships between people of the same sex or opposite sex and without age or marital constraints. Nonetheless, these relationships can be very intensive in that they can require greater personal disarming, exposing more vulnerabilities than physically having sex. Being honest is not always a good survival mechanism.

3

The words of two mentors come back at this moment. The first from a college professor: "Frigidity is the inability to disarm." Breaking down barriers is critical to both sex and mentoring. Frigidity in mentoring means that communication fails. How many marriages have come apart when we hear, "I just can't talk to him," or "She won't listen?"

The second thought was from a psychiatrist who, when I asked him if he really believed that women had a "penis envy complex," smiled and said, "We all want it all." Ideally, one would like perfect love making and perfect mentoring abilities to merge in one person. But that's unlikely. Expecting too much is a close competitor to demanding too little.

Probably, "we all want it all." But when both parties value their existing relationships and conflicts arise, their survival instincts invoke a biological command, "save the most valuable." Thus, one subconsciously chooses between which one he, or she, perceives as more meaningful.

But man needs at least one more survival mechanism. His life must have value to justify the effort to survive. Life is both a gift and a labor. At a biological level, we receive, our commands, our instincts, through "genetic codes." But man's intellect demands he give his life value.

The world does not provide sufficient answers. Often this search requires a sharing of ancient mentors' wisdom: the Bible, the Talmud, the Koran, the Tanakh. We take different paths, but we're on the same journey. Sharing it prepares us to accept our mortality. This direction reinforces the belief that our struggle to live appears to be part of a purposeful plan. All our instincts cry out, "Survive and evolve."

"Ridiculous," you say. How can I seriously rate "mentoring" with sex, much less relegate the "search for a higher power" to being a mere "survival mechanism." Of the former, I would argue that species survival is competitive. If you have an advantage others don't, you are more likely to win. All animals and humans have a sex drive, but only humans can pass on the lessons of history. Mentoring may be our most undervalued survival mechanism.

Comment: To meet real characters just climb your own family tree

Every family has "defining moments" which are passed on, usually by word of mouth, to shape that character's place in family history. My family has its share of characters that I remember fondly.

The Rest of the Story
December 16, 1998

This is really three stories related to a single book. The book, *101 Ranch* by Ellsworth Collings and Alma Miller England, was part of my father's library. I knew that my parents had taken the two hour drive due north of Oklahoma city to visit it on many occasions and believed that it earned its name by boasting more than 101, 000 acres (157 square miles). But I had not thought of it as particularly special, rather it was one of those books I "planned to read someday," and it barely escaped being thrown out in each of five house moves. When I finally read it this summer, I found it to be very special indeed. In fact, it initiated a personal adventure which took me into what the announcer for the Lone Ranger called, "those gold days of yesteryear."

As I thought about "yesteryears," I also reflected on the extraordinary nineteen twenties. This was my father's world in his thirties, and I added some anecdotes about him and his times. It was a time in the oil business of big monopolies and exploitation of Indians; of a great economic crescendo which was soon to culminate in the "Crash" and the "Great Depression." It was a time when his life crossed paths and fortunes with the legendary and outrageous 101 Ranch.

Next, I'd like to peek under 101's big top (as recorded in the book) to see what's going on and who's there. Finally, I'd like to tell you about some coincidences which make the 101 Ranch particularly special to three generations of our family.

The Twenties and the Oil Business

My father was a "wildcatter" who drilled for oil on the frontier (where the "wild cats" roamed). Looking for oil in Oklahoma in the 1920's was a larger-than-life experience. Those who lived through this era had to be rugged to survive. For example, when Dad broke his leg in seven places, there was no doctor for fifty miles. But it wasn't an insurmountable problem. They just tied him to the head board of a sturdy bed, found a strong "roughneck" (the name for men who worked on the oil rigs) and had him stretch the leg while his friends manipulated the bones back into line. It was a compound fracture and a bottle of gin was the only available anesthesia. But in the "oil patch," everything had its risk.

There were a lot of hard days even if your legs were whole. My father drove 50,000 miles a year in a succession of faithful Buicks. A good spare tire was the oil man's best friend. A jack, tire patch kit, and bicycle pump weren't many votes behind. Much travel was over "section lines" on dirt roads which were built to define a one mile grid. These were the early Dust Bowl days. In the summer when the "wind came sweeping down the plains," it blew over the red clay, dried it up to form black, choking dust clouds which cut visibility to a few feet. When it rained, the roads became "slicker than a peeled grape" and even more dangerous than the winter snows. Imagine trying to change a tire when it was 110 degrees (before air conditioning) in the middle of a dust storm, and you have part of the picture. Imagine sitting in your car in a ditch hoping a car with a chain will come along, and you have another part. Dad spent many nights in his car at the rig and then drove into the town of Perry or Pawnee, Oklahoma, where he could order fresh eggs and home grown bacon for breakfast.

He had to carry the payroll, in cash, of course; consequently, he also carried a .38 caliber semiautomatic pistol in his car's glove compartment. A lot of people carried guns. In fact, in 1939, my Dad was shot and almost killed by a deranged man who came into his office to talk about "my land." The man thought he had sold Dad some worthless land and became irritated when Dad discovered oil on it. He sat down across the desk and kept messing with something in his right pocket. Dad walked over towards him as he pulled out a .38 caliber pistol, which Dad managed to get a weak grip on. The man fired and the bullet passed so close to his heart that the doctor said he only lived because his heart was contracting. It hit a rib, left his body, then ricocheted off the air conditioner and hit his secretary, Willa Mae Simmons, in her breast bone. Dad seized the gun and hit the man in the jaw, knocking him cold. As his strength bled away, he resolutely sat on him until the police came. Not your everyday experience, even in the wild west.

Even horse play sometimes involved gun play. For example, there was the day in the little town of Watchorn (if you consider six houses, a warehouse, and a country store "a town"). There was a store with a sign painted on its side of an eight foot in diameter gold pocket watch with two six foot horns protruding out of the top. My "Uncle Robert," who was chairman of the company, had sent a telegram saying that two English friends would be paying the town a visit and they should be entertained. Now there wasn't much entertainment in Watchorn so Andy Krow, a legend for inventiveness in his own time, set about to arrange some entertainment. He took the Englishmen into the store for dinner. Just after sitting down, he calmly advised them, "If there's any gunfights, get down on the floor as fast as you can." Then he gave the signal to his friends to come in shooting. The Englishmen hit the floor and tried to "think themselves invisible." The only problem was that in the ruckus a kerosene lamp was knocked over which burned the building down.

You had to be smart and wily to survive as well. Many big companies drilled offsets adjacent to new discoveries draining the discovery well's reserves while taking a "stop me if you can, sell to me cheap if you can't" attitude. Furthermore, as soon as the news got out that oil had been discovered, the land around it became much more valuable and hundreds of men hustled out to the area to buy up land around the discovery. This required an accurate survey so the legal description was correct. There is a famous story about one of the largest fields in Texas which was surveyed incorrectly leaving a strip open right down the center.

It was very difficult for a small company to obtain rights to the entire field which it discovered, or even the immediate offsets, because they lacked the manpower to react on short notice and seldom had enough cash on hand. Further, one faced larger company competition which had both. Earl Slick, a relative of my friend Rod Frates, pulled a great maneuver which outfoxed his competition and assured him of a place in Oklahoma history. He discovered what was later known as the Cement (?) Field in central Oklahoma. He knew that as soon as the word got out that he had struck oil, "land men" (the name for professional lease buyers) with their survey crews would blanket the area and gobble up all available land. Sure enough, for the next few days the trains arriving at the railroad station were loaded with land men and their support teams. But Earl had outsmarted them. For you see, there were very few cars at that time and very few roads, and it was a long, long way from the railroad station to the discovery site. Transportation to the well discovery area was difficult and depended on horse and buggies. The first thing Earl did was to hire all the available transportation in the area near the railway station and move it to a protected place until he brought in his own land men who went out to rather casually lease all the land he needed. He had been well named.

After the first week, business transactions and lease brokering moved into the hotels. I vividly remember three of the classics which survived into my lifetime. The Huckens in Oklahoma City; the Mayo in Tulsa; and the Brown Palace in Denver. They all exhibited a multistory central lobby so one "could see who was in town" and a mezzanine with big stuffed chairs that one could sink into so deeply he felt walled off in privacy to negotiate. Each chair had a highly polished brass spittoon next to it where a gentleman could spit his chewing tobacco if he so desired. The most serious hotel problem in the twenties was fires. As long as he lived, whenever our family would go to a hotel, the first thing Dad would do was locate the fire exits and point them out to us.

Oil well fires were a real threat too. The oil industry was pushing the limits technologically and the pressure of the gas and oil reservoirs was often much greater than the state-of-the-art valves intended to contain them. Dad had several close friends killed in oil well fires and underground mine explosions.

The difference between success and disaster was a matter of inches at the bottom of a 2,700 foot hole. If you went in too far or too fast, the gas cap might blow you away. If you were successful in drilling the gas cap but drilled too deep and penetrated into the water below the gas and oil, you could decimate the quality of production. In brief, even though they had found oil and gas, the success of the well was still in doubt. Among the newspaper clippings, I found references to two fires at Watchorn wells over a period of six years; one caused by a cigarette and the other attributed to lightning.

The Watchorn wells on the 101 Ranch all avoided fire. But, my father's fears were realized when, four years later in south central Kansas, Watchorn Oil's biggest new discovery well caught fire. It was drilled to a record one mile depth. It had an estimated open flow of 225 million cubic feet a day. This would challenge even today's safety equipment. A large fortune literally burned up before its owner's very eyes.

The 101 Ranch

When one thinks about the 101 Ranch extravaganza today, it seems very strange, particularly considering the subject matter, to have a show depicting events in which the actors play themselves. For example, Buffalo Bill and Geronimo actually killing real buffalo (while Geronimo was on leave from a military prison), or participation in mock re-enactment of battles or massacres between former enemies using as actors the actual combatants who originally fought each other. The Calvary continued to win, perpetuating a myth, and the poor Indians continued to relive their humiliation, with no mention (I'll bet) of the white man's perfidious trickery with the treaty.

One of the show stoppers was the Terrapin Day. According to the 101 Ranch book, "*Thus the second derby was run in 1925 with 1,679 entries; the third in 1926 with 2,373 entries, and down through the following years, always with increasing entries. Only land terrapins were permitted in the derby—the kind common throughout the Southwest.*" (The section on Terrapin Day starts on page 148 in the book.)

"The many diversified resources of the 101 Ranch made it the natural show place of the Southwest. There was ranching with all its old-time picturesqueness. There were thousands of cattle and horses, the unblocked trails and the cattle pastures, the unchanged cowboys, the round-up camps, the rodeo, the corrals, the buffalo, and many tribes of Indians, living undisturbed in wigwams, lodges, or rough houses."

"*It was,*" says Corb Sarchet, "*one continuous entertainment of guests, social, political, business leaders, writers, explorers, actors, the prominent men and women in every line. Presidents of giant railway systems mingled with the cowboys and donned their regalia, pleased at the chance. Admiral Byrd rode the elephants; John Philip Sousa joined the Ponca Indian tribe; Mrs. Mary Roberts Rinehart came for atmosphere when she was ready to write her Lost Ecstasy; Walter Teagle sat on the floor with a bust of Geronimo, the Apache chief, in his arms to be enlightened on the price of crude oil; Will Irwin and his wife, Inez Haynes Irwin, came for a day and remained a week; Williams Jennings Bryan shook hands with Tony, the monkey; Sidney Smith drew Andy Gump on the White House walls; Teddy Roosevelt was delighted; Will Rogers sang cowboy songs all night long with Mrs. Pawnee Bill at the piano; Fred Bonfils came to see the terrapin derby; Jack Mulhall was on hand to star in the moving picture–Nancy Astor, John Ringling, Randolph Hearst, William S. Hart, Irvin Cobb, Rex Beach, Richard Bennett, General Bullard, Charles Curtis, William F. Cody*

(Buffalo Bill), William Allen White, Helen Gibson, Bacon Rind, Art Gobel, Will Hayes, General Savitsky, John D. Rockerfeller, Jr., James E. Garman, Warren G. Harding, Roy Howard, Ezra Meeker, Colonel Zack Mulhall—what an array! Unceasingly they came–each found the same welcome, each was enchanted, each had seen a fairyland." [From <u>Daily Oklahoma</u>, December 16, 1934]

Furthermore, their values were evidently shared by a lot of people. It is remarkable that although it was located in the middle of nowhere, they still had large attendances. They depended heavily on the railroads. The 101 Ranch was founded in the 1890's and ran strong into the mid-nineteen thirties. They put on the first "roadeo," which they preferred to call a "roundup" and originated the event called "bulldogging" in which a cowboy leaps from his horse onto the steer and then wrestles it to the ground and ties three feet together. The cowboy wins who accomplishes this in the shortest time. This is a standard event in today's rodeos.

The "Wild West Show" traveled to Europe and entertained an estimated 800,000 people in London alone, but when the British declared war in 1914, they confiscated their horses. The book itself is a fascinating portrait of entertainment on the American frontier. It was a true extravaganza, disproportionately larger than the larger-than-life daily toils of the wildcatter. Whether a creator or product of the twenties, it was a noteworthy part of the scene. It was a "circus" in many senses.

Reflections on our Family and the 101 Ranch

The 101 Ranch book served as a stimulus for me to think about the 1920's, to think about my father's life, and to realize how different it was from my own. I wondered why this period seemed unknown to me previously. The 101 Ranch was playing on the public's romanticizing of the "wildest" as it might have been earlier, e.g. when Buffalo Bill and Geronimo were in their prime, that is, before the Indians surrendered and suffered through their "trail of tears." Outside the circus, in the real west of the 1920's, there was still a high risk environment. If not for the Calvary and Indians, then for the wildcatter. Frontiers always exist somewhere. Each decade has, within its numbers, people who survive and even thrive on the frontiers. People able to "live by their wits." Why is this ranch and this book special to me? Let me tell you the "rest of the story."

Perhaps some of the readers have heard me talk about my "Uncle Robert" Watchorn of whom I am very proud (even if his stated goal in life was to provide "a Bible for every Chinaman"). Actually, he was my father's uncle and my great uncle. My wife calls him the "family relative," meaning the one whose relatives tend to brag about. In 1920, he visited my father in Mt. Hope, West Virginia. Uncle Robert was characteristically direct. "The future's in oil, not coal, John. I'm going into oil. Are you with me or against me?" Needless to say, Dad went "with him." "Uncle Robert," as I called him, was very tough and very principled. He had strict rules, set forth in signs on his oil rigs, such as "There will be no cussing nor spitting on the drill rig floor." Another sign, which survived to my day from a warehouse, stated simply, "Nothing for sale—don't ask." That was Uncle Robert; moralistic, no nonsense, with a strong belief that God had a mission for him.

The 101 Ranch was important to him, as he was to it, because it was where he first discovered oil. The "Watchorn Field" changed his financial situation. It was what oil men refer to as a "company maker." It also became the principal source of assets for The Watchorn Foundation. In turn, this gave him the opportunity to repay his debt to the community where he was born. He bought that part of the town where he had lived in abject poverty and built each family a separate house. This was important to the Miller brothers who owned the 101 Ranch because it financed their zenith.

When I opened the book, I discovered a letter, written seventy-five years ago. I hadn't realized until this summer that the Watchorn field was actually on the 101 Ranch, or that my dad had leased the land from its owners, the Miller brothers, or that he almost lost it at the last minute. It is said that "everything gets done through people" and the truth of that statement in this case was revealed in the next to last paragraph of the letter contract I found dated August 10, 1922, written to my great uncle by the owner of the 101 Ranch. I discovered it inside the cover of the 101 Ranch book! The paragraph reads as follows:

"I could have made a deal yesterday with a man from St. Joseph, MO. to have a well drilled immediately on their's but I prefer to give our people a square deal and the first opportunity on anything I am letting out down there, and I realized after talking with your Mr. Porter that it would work an injustice on you to let one of these wildcatters come in on that 10 acres, and force about three off-sets from you people."

This is a telling reflection on the ethics of Mr. Miller. It shows how much one depends on friendships, particularly in frontier environments where legal protections are few. He is recognizing that if he sold to the outside group that they would have forced Dad to drill immediately which would have put him at a severe disadvantage of "drill now or be drained."(The laws have changed now so as to control spacing in order not to lose oil by producing it too fast.) Needless to say, had this turned out otherwise, my family's history in the oil business may have read much differently.

My father's reputation, and that of his company, clearly made a difference in their business dealings. I came across a story in the October 28, 1928 edition of the Wichita Eagle. The first part was a conventional report of a new gas discovery concerning flow rates and geology on a new Watchorn discovery. The story had large pictures of Dad and his associate, Frank Harper. What amazed me was the next to the last paragraph which reads as follows:

"The public, unacquainted with the oil man, has long held the belief that they are crooks. Protection and Ashland haven't got this idea. They hold John Porter and Frank Harper in the highest esteem and as expressed on the streets of Protection Saturday." *"Should a fellow make a statement like that in this section of Kansas he had better qualify it by excepting the Watchorn company."*

(It's evident the man who shot my father 20 years later never read this article.)

What did this book mean to me? It showed me a perspective of the twenties my father had shared with me but which had not been examined until this moment. It stimulated me to open old envelopes, letters, trunks and books which led to new discoveries about my father which attested to his modesty. As we approach the end of this millennium, I wonder if our sense of political correctness will change as much in the next century as it has over the past seventy-five years? And how will it change in another thousand? The 101 Ranch was a monument to a few moments in the history of our country. The book captures these almost forgotten moments, their spirit, and I wanted to obtain copies I could share with some friends. Naturally, I called my daughter, Amy, "the book sleuth." To my great surprise, the responses started coming within a few hours from William F. Daily's rare book store in Los Angeles. By skillfully applying a tool of her generation, the Internet, she turned up five copies of different editions.

Finally, not all stories make it to the printed page. Uncle Tut was married to one of Dad's sisters. He invited Dad to go to a convention in Chicago. Tut was a great shot with a rifle or pistol and valued his own reputation at this accomplishment highly. It turned out there was a shooting gallery on the convention floor. Before long, Uncle Tut was showing off and had a pretty large audience. Dad commented that one of the girls who was watching was a pretty good shot herself. He said he would even bet ten dollars that she could out shoot Tut who roared defiantly and leaped at the proposition. After he lost, Dad introduced him to Annie Oakley, "an old friend from the 101 Ranch."

Comment: "Likes" Are Boring— Pick A Spouse Who's Different

I traveled a great deal. Lee and the children on rare occasion made these trips with me. It was tiring for all parties and there were, at least in retrospect, some really funny occurrences.

Journeys

19 August 1996

Journeys take many forms: some are physical, some are psychological. Moving residences is often both. Whether two miles or two thousand miles, the words "change, uncertainty, and adjustment" always apply. Recently, Lee and I moved a short mile from our home into an apartment. My New Yorker wife was ecstatic. She was losing the nursing responsibilities for fifty-four varieties of plants, a swimming pool, two unneeded floors of space to clean, and my daughter's dog. Further, she was gaining a "staff" of her very own: a reception desk, and best of all, a responsive maintenance crew. "I feel that I've had a great burden removed," she said.

Actually, I kind of liked my "old person" personae. This move took me away from my Oklahoma single housing roots and back yard. I miss my driveway. I miss Amy's dog (Apartment Rule: "No pets allowed!"). But what affected me most was the symbolism of perhaps moving into my "last home" and the interaction with pending lifestyle changes related to health and job.

Some people make moving seem as routine as an Olympic diver who simply goes to the end of the board, commits him or herself quickly, then makes a perfect execution look easy. I can't. Rather, I agonized and deliberate, "Why now?" This plunge took about four years looking before leaving the security of my familiar, stable platform.

There's a parlor game in which each participant is asked to describe his or her "dream house." After all the uninitiated answer questions about each room and living space, its location in town, and have indicated their priorities, they are informed that what they have really done is describe themselves. Some postulate that the size of the front yard indicates the distance one wants from the stranger on the street; it also represents the "public image" one wishes to project, while one's back yard represents private space for insiders within the gates. Correspondingly, the relative emphasis placed on one's bedroom, kitchen, living room (more formal entertaining) or den/study for personal matters, depends on one's personal priorities and preferences. So deep are the psychological roots of our living quarters, and I was apprehensive going at it from the direction of space I had seldom experienced except when I was banished during the periods Lee and I were separated. On further reflection, "reduced space" may have translated to "unwelcome constraints," maybe even, subconsciously, "reduced personal control." So much for my candidacy as "parlor game psychologist."

Then there's the business of packing. Before I was married I did not know there was a right or wrong way to pack a car. Naively, I just put what I'd want on the trip in the back seat and stuff the rest in the trunk. It was one of the first lessons of marriage. Lee's father faithfully followed a non-interventionist policy and usually bit his lip rather than interfere, but every rule must have its exceptions and not packing the car correctly would have violated the "Cleanliness Next to Godliness Act." John would hold back as long as he could and then amble up and say, "Can I help you? I used to load ships during the war." (This ritual unfolded on every visit just as though it was the first time.) Lee must have been trained by him, because I could always count on her repacking the car after quietly casting a disapproving glance at my mindless endeavors. I felt the pressure was on.

"Three moves equal one fire" is a pretty good rule of thumb to estimate the material one throws away when one changes residences. Everyone knows in the great battles of life, like moving, rule number one is, "Travel light. Take no prisoners." This is easy to say, but almost impossible to do. Before one can execute a known enemy, such as an old tax file, one is obligated to at least hold a summary trial which can stimulate affectionate reflection recollected after reading my expense accounts. For example an attempt to enjoy a business dinner in Paris while battling the "London flu." (The doctor cost more than the dinner.)

I found many letters between my father and mother, newspaper clippings and photos about oil wells my father drilled in the nineteen twenties, letters I had written my parents from a bicycle trip to Europe and from Dartmouth. I found my mother's diary, written when she was 16, as well as my own from childhood trips with my parents. These brought many smiles, but took time.

Finally, there's the unpacking phase. It's another kind of journey, a journey to all the wrong places. At least when we were packing, I knew where things were supposed to be. I could find a spoon, a bowl, or a dish. Now, every snack is an adventure. I think the previous tenant must have come from a "mirror image" universe. Maybe she was just left handed, but the kitchen seems backwards to me. I find all my intuitive moves are wrong, and I have to reorient myself, or risk hitting my shins on the open dish-washer door. (I'll learn. I'll learn.)

The biggest problem of unpacking is that Lee and I just think differently. When we were first married, we moved into a small house in New Jersey. I was looking for a bottle of aspirin. I looked in the medicine cabinet, under the bathroom sink, and even in the ice box. Finally, I asked my beloved if she had any suggestions. She replied nonchalantly, "It's in with all the other two inch bottles."

Of course. Why hadn't I thought of that?

Comment: Make sure you don't laugh at the wrong time

En Route to Tehran
19 August 1996

It was the time Lee accompanied me to Paris in 1974 when she acquired a case of the London flu. She was vomiting violently every three hours like "Old Faithful." I had scheduled a business dinner at one of the finest four star restaurants with Joe Fox, an IBM vice President, which, of course, I "had to attend." Lee may have been sick but she knew that the Tour d'Argent was worthy of almost any risk so, after a suitable bout with the flu, we hastened to the restaurant to take advantage of the next three hour interval.

Planning paid off. The pressed duck lived up to its reputation. It could be accurately reported that, "Dinner went down well." After returning to the hotel, the reverse occurred. However excellent the duck may have been, it will never replace chicken soup as a medical cure.

Then the situation went from bad to worse. Suffice it to say that her condition worsened to the point she passed out and the "hotel doctor" arrived and proceeded to test her vital signs, Humphrey Bogart style, by slapping her face to bring her to her senses.

Finally, he left. Lee was draped over the corner of the bed like a wet rag. It was two in the morning. Most of Paris was in bed. I heard a commotion in the hall so I dragged myself up and opened the door. The hallway was full of smoke. I looked at my "dish rag" and muttered the final insult of the evening, "I don't know how to tell you this honey, but I think the hotel's on fire."

My turn came in Tehran where the London flu caught up with me. It was two in the morning and I was really sick. Lee was asleep and I staggered by her bed on my rush to the bathroom. After having left most of me behind, I was too weak to stand, so I crawled past the end of Lee's bed towards my own when I heard a firm voice say, "You forgot to wash your hands." Too weak to argue, I crawled on my hands and knees and while still kneeling put my hands in the washbowl and performed my duties before crawling back past my semi-comatose wife.

Rough Drafts
12 August 1996

My phone rang brazenly. It was 5:30 in the morning, Paris time. That made it 11:30 Washington time—not the right time for a proper wake up call on either continent. It was Lee, and she was very much awake.

"Robert," she said, "Jennifer and Judith [our 16 year old daughter and her friend] have gone into the wine cellar and gotten drunk."

I admit I was concerned more over which vintage they had violated than their medical or psychological condition. To me, their lack of craft spoke to their lack of experience and could even be viewed as failing their first course in "clandestine consumption of alcoholic beverages." Not an entirely bad sign.

I shared this insight with Lee and was sharply informed that my perspective from 5,000 miles away was not nearly as vivid as it was to one who had just pushed, pulled, twisted, and tugged a loose-limbed teenage tippler up three flights of stairs, only to have her slip and slide her way partially down again. Nor was I there at midnight to help scrub her thick blue bedroom carpet.

"Can't you come home immediately?" she pleaded. Sympathy was needed and remote assurances weren't substantive enough. In fact, they just exacerbated the situation. She was challenging a whole style of life and business travel with its prolonged absences. I had just arrived and said I really didn't think I should change my plans, nor would I. My predictable answer fueled the fire further.

Thirty minutes later I received another tearful call. "It's worse than I thought," she said. "Jennifer fell and hurt her head. She's in the bathtub but can only speak French!"
At the end of the week I went home. I opened the door and saw Jennifer. "Well, kid, how are you doing?" I asked jauntily.

"Not too well, Dad, "she said, through tightly clenched teeth. "When I got drunk I must have fallen down the stairs and broken my jaw. It's wired shut now."

"Well, Amy," I said, turning to my younger daughter for a piece of encouragement, "How about you?"

"Not too good," she replied. "The doctor says I have an extra bone in my foot and I have to have an operation."

Silently, not daring to risk any further questions, I crossed the room and bent down to give my wife a friendly peck on the lips. She turned her head away, and answered my unspoken question. "Ben [our dog[was run over by a truck this morning. He's hanging on."

At that moment I understood what my father meant when I was young and he used to call in from a trip and ask me to go in the kitchen and report if the stove's still there.

Well, our dog survived; Amy now has one less bone in her foot; Jennifer's jaw stiffens occasionally, reminding her of her miscalculated escapade. (She will someday share this with her children, no doubt including editorial comment.)

POST SCRIPT TO ROUGH DRAFTS:
THE MAIN POINT

25 August 1996

To be perfectly honest, our marriage occasionally shows the scars of those traveling days 15 years ago—like the night when I showed my wife a light-hearted draft of this paper. We all write in a certain voice. The same voice may be pleasant to one and harsh to another depending on context and experience. Communication, especially on personal subjects, is highly subjective. The author cannot speak with a single voice to a varied audience. For example, when I first wrote a very short anecdote, "Rough Draft." I was attending a writer's class at Dartmouth. I thought it was pretty light stuff.

I casually showed it to my wife. We have been married 34 years. However, during this time we were separated twice for six months each. The first time was soon after the event described in "Rough Draft" though never tied directly to this event. The second, a year later. The second reconciliation took, and we have been back together for 14 years. Years we have both valued and enjoyed. For me the story line was one of life's "grin and bear it" situations (raising children), to be shared with fellow human beings who have all had struggles and usually become a part of the character building process."

But for my wife, Lee, it brought back bitter memories of those cases of my unavailability when she needed me. For her, it too vividly recalled the emotions of the "final strokes" in a crumbling marriage. A crime forgiven, but not forgotten.

I took the initiative in showing it to Lee. This raises the general question for writers as to whether and when to discuss a memoir in draft form, especially if the reader was party to the event. After much reflection, I consider this particular case an example of the second benefits of memoir writing because this event caused me to understand a point I had not fully understood about the depth of my wife's emotions, even today, on this subject.

Initially, I felt a great deal of anger on my part towards Lee for her reaction to this. To my mind, I had been judged "guilty" of crimes of omission where no mal intent was present. I still believe in my innocence although I must also admit to my guilt. I wasn't in Paris because I wanted to escape—but I wasn't home when I was needed.

Who's the victim? We were both defendants and plaintiffs in a sense. No doubt it depends on jury selection. This event will ultimately have some beneficial effect because it caused me to understand an important wound of Lee's which has not yet, and probably will never, completely heal. I've also concluded that just because it has a very special impact, for a very specific person, I will nonetheless publish it both for the reasons I had originally and as a point to share with other writers of memoirs. I think Lee would approve but I'm not going to ask her.

There is the broad question as to how much to share with one's spouse, on any subject of a memoir or short remembrance. It also matters whether it is shown in draft and the size and nature of the audience. When I wrote my books on friends and mentors, I intentionally avoided issues of judgement. In general, I recounted events which were either pleasant, humorous, or positively critical. I did not write about any close members of my family except for my parents, both of whom are deceased. I also excluded people I didn't consider friends. I think this was wise. When there were questions of historical fact in my own mind, I did ask for the opinion from others. In retrospect, I believe this suited my purposes very well, but I was consistent in inserting the caveat that these were not intended to judge, "reveal great truths," or persuade, but rather to celebrate friendships and share personal thoughts.

In summary, writing memoirs usually serves many agenda items for the author, some of which he or she probably doesn't recognize. Divine revelation usually requires divine sources or the message seems to get muddled and/or serve some purpose not intended by the communicator. Certainly, that's true in my case. We humans frequently think of ourselves as being very complex and everyone else as obvious. In fact, I think we are all much more transparent to others and opaque to ourselves than we will ever believe or admit. Writers beware.

Comment: A good room is hard to find

Our travel agent was normally quite good, but she "goofed up" in placing me in the London West Hotel. Two letters follow:

LETTER TO TRAVEL AGENT

LONDON WEST HOTEL

LILLIE ROAD LONDON SW6 1UQ ENGLAND
Telephone: 01-385-1255 Telex: 917728

Don't send me boy to London West, my dying mother said.
Don't send me boy to London West, I'd rather see him dead.
Send him to the Cannaught, the Dorchester or Browne,
But save him please from London West and others so renown.

—Old English Ballad

October 15, 1984

Dearest Nadia:

You are now and shall ever be a part of my memories because of "our" London experience. I say "our" because I never could have done it myself. No, don't be modest. Share the limelight. You played a Hellenic role in choosing the London West Hotel (LWH). Thus I am writing this letter so "we" can savor this experience together.

It's hard to know where to start. Location? Clientele? Alarm clocks? Windows? Bed? Ted service? Room size? Expense? or Elevators? Let's start with the big picture.

Its <u>location</u> is within the greater London area, somewhere west of Earl's Court and south of East Jesus. Its <u>clientele</u> falls, as best as I can tell, into two groups: first, Americans and Germans who are mobilized every morning and evening for transport in juggernaut sized armored personnel carriers which are slightly smaller than a 747 but require almost as much runway (woe to the unwary taxi driver or pedestrian); and second, poor Arabs or rich Americans who can afford long taxi rides to town. Of course, for the less fortunate folks there's always the "tube." This may be satisfactory during the day—I did it at night, and I don't recommend it then <u>unless</u> you are looking for gay, male, punk prostitutes sporting black or green motorcycle togs and pink or white hair ("Hi there, luv," he said expectantly. "Looks like we've got a soft one out shopping."). Further, they become very testy once they discover you haven't come to the area to "shop." If this is one's idea of having fun, then the LWH, on Lillie Lane, is the place to have it.

The <u>room design</u> is really a modern commercial miracle. <u>No</u> space is wasted and I understand the Institute of German Yoga Instructors granted it a "4 twist" rating. Not even having a yellow belt in Yoga myself, I found it impossible to find the space to complete an exercise which required only that I lie on the floor, draw my knees to my chest and rotate once to my right and once to my left.

Waking up is a scintillating experience. There is a built in <u>alarm clock</u> which dramatically goes off between 4 and 6 AM and continues ringing until it's good and ready to stop. It didn't bother me nearly as much as it did the occupants next door who never understood why they couldn't turn it off by pounding on the wall.

Like the alarm clock, the <u>elevators</u> also had minds of their own. Sometimes they would respond to a button push, sometimes not. Sometimes they would travel part of the distance and let you off, so you could take the stairs; other times they could stop between floors, or at a floor, but not open the door, thus giving one the opportunity to press the "come and get me" button. Fortunately, I was never incarcerated for long in this way, but I was awakened repeatedly by the plaintive, persistent ringing by early morning risers who had not yet learned that an 8 floor pre-breakfast walk down the stairs was <u>really</u> good for your health.

<u>Taking a bath</u> is worth a short mention, although it took a long time. The hot water, it seemed, was rationed so you had to fill the tub 1 inch at a time while carefully monitoring its progress lest the cold water rush in and nullify all your diligent labor. In fairness, this condition probably correlates with the post-arrival and pre-departure of the beleaguered tourist groups and should not be blamed on the architect. Unfortunately, however, a new group arrives or departs every couple minutes so I suspect that if one had X-ray vision and looked down the hotel, Superman style, at any given moment he would see 150 people of various shapes

and colors sitting naked in their partially filled bathtubs with one hand on the handle and the other under the faucet measuring the water temperature.

Any of those not in the bathtub were no doubt trying to solve the teapot prob-lem, Breakfast, you see, is brought to the room sans hot water. It makes it chal-lenging, jet lag and all, to (1) find the hiding spot for the teapot, then (2) find the right setting on the plug switch which services the teapot plug, then (3) find the proper wall switch to turn on the teapot plug, and finally, (4) activate the teapot switch to heat the water. (Hint: When the red light is lit on the teapot, the teapot is off!) Once you have switches (1) through (4) set properly, the rest is a piece of cake. (Comment: Only 1 of 24 possible permutations will work.)

Opening the window was another household chore I'll just touch on. At first glance one would jump to the conclusion that you could slide it more than 1-1/2 inches. Further inspection of its design would support this assumption, a very logical one considering it was the only means of ventilation for the room. After breaking one fingernail trying to move the broken plastic catch, I called the desk clerk who assure me "maintenance" would repair it the next day. When I checked the next night, it wasn't fixed but there was a dried spot of blood where "mainte-nance" apparently tried.

Did I like anything you ask? The answer is a resounding *yes*! I really like this sta-tionery and "matching" envelope they gave me. Also, I found I had something in common with all other guests. We were all sent there by travel agents who weren't there themselves.

Much love,

J. Robert Porter, Jr.
Beleaguered Traveler

LETTER FROM TRAVEL AGENT

Text of letter from Utell International in response to my letter to Globe Travel Service

Utell International

Utell International (UK) Limited...119 West 57th Street, New York, NY 10019

Telephone (212) 397-1560, U.S. WATS 800-223-9869. Cable TRANSO-TEL. Telex 424716

December 5, 1984

Dear Nadia:

Re: <u>The most amusing letter we have ever received</u>

J. Robert Porter, Jr.—Beleaguered traveler is a genius. First, let me assure you, he has forever implanted an absolutely indelible vision of both the LWH (as he so affectionately dubbed "her" and his memorable travel experience.)

Mr. Porter's letter has received a wide readership—from the hallowed yet hectic halls of our New York office to the bustling and austere corridors of our corporate headquarters in London.

For days the talk among managers included a discreet "have you read Nadia's London West letter?" Mr. Porter has, without knowing it, made me even more "infamous by association" than I had managed to make myself prior to his letter.

Oh to brush literary elbows with such an astute and clever observer of London in high season! I keep his letter on my desk to re-read when my everyday correspondence gets too tedious, too mundane.

What can I say? When the London Embassy didn't come through, we did our best. Of course none of us could have guessed that Mr. Porter would have returned to the U.S. with chills from the bath, tea-withdrawal symptoms, cramped legs, elevator-phobia, and a bruised thumb...not to mention a list of unwanted, unsolicited phone numbers from gentlemen with fluorescent hair.

Please assure Mr. Porter that although we regret the unpleasant experience he had at the London West, we loved his letter!

Actually, Nadia, we have as a result of Mr. Porter's letter made changes in the descriptive information of this hotel which would enable us to have a more accurate assessment of the property.

Thanks for sending on the letter, and happy holidays to you and Mr. Porter!

Best regards,
Airline Manager

P.S.
God Rest You J. R. Porter
Let Nothing Ye Dismay
(At least the London West Hotel
Is Very Far Away).

We Did Our Best To Help You In
The Booking Of Your Stay.

We Are Sorry
Forgive Us We Pray
(Forgive Us We Pray)
We Are Sorry
Forgive Us We Pray.

> Comment: Every 34 years,
> let your wife go on
> vacation by herself

"Oh it's a long, long time from dusk 'til the dawning, but the night grows long, when its three and I'm yawning."

—an old Porter refrain

Basic House-Sitting 101

Every thirty-four years or so, Lee insists on taking a trip at a time that fits her schedule, not mine. OK, so this was the year, and I willingly accepted it. In fact, I secretly welcomed it, because it gave me an opportunity to prove to myself, and a world of doubting Thomases, that I could survive for 30 days with just a small army of nervous friends and well-wishers to nurture and support me. "Over the hill? Hell no, Mark Twain, 'damn the torpedoes,'" and all that.

Lee is in a field course in Israel as part of her curriculum at Wesley Seminary. All I've had to do was water the plants once a week and eat TV dinners or share the table of others, and at the same time, keep breathing.

"Piece of cake." You say. Not quite. Let me give you my perspective.

First, watering three plants, co-located in the kitchen and four cacti located in the greenhouse may sound easy, but there are more job stresses than are apparent at first. Lee recognized this, and rather than just telling me to "water the plants twice a week," insisted on giving a short course on "plant care and nurturing." It featured a lesson on "Plant positioning," including personal tips on sun angle, external meteorology, and climate control ("Oh, yes, it helps to leave the door between the kitchen and the greenhouse a little bit open.") Naturally, a short text accompanied it, but inevitably some questions I had later were not anticipated. For example, balancing Lee's wishes for healthy plants against the real-estate agent's admonition, "Keep the house cool at all times." I concluded it's the decisions, not the work, that kills the dedicated housekeeper. Second, being a part-time social butterfly is a harder job than one might suppose. The opportunity was provided by many caring friends who no doubt recognized the burden of being left with three plants and four cacti to water. What they didn't appreciate was that my wings were initially out of shape from under-utilization. This was quickly remedied by increasing the pace of my usual three-day-a-week 7 a.m. pre-work chess game with Larry Heilman (along with a continental breakfast served by Ann) to full week-long septathalon. Other friends, the Lamberts, the Grieses, the Boasbergs, the Montgomerys, and Silberts, all helped whip me into fighting form with invitations to fill my days and evenings. Even Lee's church members called to see if I was alright. I had a vision of their hanging up the phone, then jotting down a note to fax Lee, "Subject and all plants doing well."

We had recently closed on a co-op apartment. Lee's final instruction before beginning her trip into the wilderness was, "Sell the house." It was said as simply as the way Mrs. Job must have said, "Where's the lottery ticket?" Normally this wouldn't be a particularly challenging task for a combat hardened, part-time housekeeper like me. What was daunting was the implication that in order to sell it, I needed to maintain and present it according to the standards Lee had previously set for herself. Further, I feared the implication that if it didn't sell, my "inability to follow a simple set of instructions" would be brought into question.

A wise general also plans a route for his retreat, so when I accepted my "mission impossible" assignment I had thought about my options if the worst case scenario occurred,. For example, I could even replace the plants with look-a-likes, empty all the wastebaskets, and make the bed before Lee walked in the door. But no, now I had to have my duties open to surprise inspection by unsympathetic house hunters. This meant that my original, secret fall back plan had been pre-empted by cruel fortune.

Well, now it's almost four in the morning. This is one of the times I miss Lee most. The plants have been watered religiously, except for one plant in my second floor study (which I swear was omitted from my briefing.) It is now just three days until Lee's return. The house is sold. (Praise the Lord and my real-estate agent.) My social wings are in better condition. I fully expect to survive to celebrate our thirty-fourth anniversary on June 2. This year, at least, I know what to get her for "Take 34": a plant for the second floor study.

COMMENT: Choose your seat-mate carefully

Don't check your bags, Don't land at JFK after nine PM. This was one of the most traumatic incidents in my life. Everything that I've reported is true.

Yes, but….
July 4, 2000

When I'm asked. "Did you enjoy your "dream trip" on the QE2? Did it revive pleasant childhood memories from your youth when you crossed the Atlantic with your parents?" The answer is "Yes, but to realize my dreams it required I confront a few nightmares.

As background let me explain I have just returned from an ocean voyage with my oldest daughter, Jennifer, and her three children, Vincent, age 11, Alex, age 8, and Porter. age 7 aboard the QE2. This was followed by a two day sight seeing tour of London and a flight home. Lee stayed home so as to better personalize the experience for me and complete vital quilt art works for upcoming shows. Although our trip on the whole exceeded every positive pre-trip hype. In truth, the last 28 hours returning to Washington far exceeded all negative expectations as well. What follows is a distillation of the worst of these last moments viewed in the most comic perspective.

If these events were being presented cinematically, the soundtrack might include an unmetered, discordant cough, punctuated by occasional atonal hoots that took me off the quarter-deck and made sleeping in my cabin very attractive when, that is, I wasn't eating, reading, writing journals with Alex or playing chess with Vincent and Porter. The ship portion of the trip was in every way fulfilling and my cough was, at that time, more an annoyance than crisis. Building to a crisis didn't begin until I started my journey home. Furthermore, I learned a "perfect crisis," like a "perfect storm" requires several events to earn "historic" status. These events, as it turned out, had short gestation periods.

Event 1. I missed my British Airways flight to Washington by two minutes. It was my own fault. I accept responsibility but, in retrospect, a telling omen.

Event 2. "The good news/ bad news gambit" in which the victim, me, happily takes a seat on a later British Airways flight to New York City's JFK airport thinking that he will be delayed only by a couple hours, but instead is summarily informed when he arrives that "all flights to Washington will be delayed for two hours because of the weather." This raises the age old question, "If the Titanic had landed safely would management have found another way to lose all the luggage?"

In this case I naively thought, "No sweat, my big bag had been checked through to Washington on American Eagle." I admit I was concerned that it held all my medications. Unfortunately, because of the extended day associated with the time change, I had already used up the daily supply I carried on my person and my "briefcase backup" had not been transferred to my computer-carrier briefcase which replaced my everyday briefcase on some trips. It was five-thirty PM EST. I have to take medication for Parkinson's every two hours or undergo werewolf magnitude changes.

Event 3. I'm tired. I can't find the American Eagle desk until nine-thirty. It was then I found out that my bag was missing. I know it seems impossible that it could take four hours to find the right American Eagle counter but I swear it's true. The reasons include: I was told to go to three **wrong** terminals, each requiring a twenty to thirty minute bus commute in ninety plus degree heat. The computer bag/briefcase I retained with books and working papers actually weighed about twenty pounds. It felt like fifty as I trudged with decreasing hope though furnace temperatured terminals. It took at least ten minutes search time in each terminal to reach the **wrong** gate, and another 15-30 minutes, sweating profusely, waiting to find the **wrong** person.

(If anyone really wants to know, the initial cause for the confusion had resulted from an adjustment the girl in London made to "properly" prepare the ticket change from Washington to New York. In retrospect she knew too much: American Eagle was acting as a partner with Sabena; consequently, to the London ticket modifier, I should be officially transferring to a Sabena flight. In this environment it is to be expected that they had no idea where my baggage was and also, this regrettably explains how I took an extra thirty minute delay as a result of being given a boarding pass onto a Sabena flight to Zurich instead of Washington! In short, they were speaking different languages in London and New York and no one could translate.

Event 4. On my first visit to terminal 4. I leaped off the bus and moved with all deliberate speed to a door a little bit to the side of the main entrance. Four very muscular black men dressed in expensive, black, tailored business suits stood at the door. I was moving like I knew where I was going and started to walk through the side door. They looked at me like I was expected. One stepped forward and said, "Are you from CIA?" I said, "No, is this the entrance to American Eagle?" I wanted to say, "No, is this the way to Air America (an infamous CIA owned airlines) but judgement prevailed over humor. This took on a new significance thirty minutes later on my way back to the bus about a hundred feet away where I saw a large white man in his late forties being lifted into an ambulance. He was ashen and had blood all over his face and shirt. I asked one of the people standing around what happened. He replied, "some government guy got stabbed." That's all I know. I found nothing in the papers the next day. **This is not a joke** nor had my night of living dangerously ended.

Event 5. Here was the scene: It was 11 PM EST. I'd gone without sleep for 24 hours. I hadn't taken my medication for five hours which meant I was overdue three hours. With my bag missing I knew I couldn't have any medication until the next morning. My cough from the ship had come back with frightening malice. All flights to Washington had been canceled for the night. I asked about a hotel and was told by an airline clerk that they don't accept guests after 10 o'clock in that area. Suddenly, the terminals were empty. A cop commented that they opened the terminals up for street people to sleep implying that he wouldn't go into the nether regions until first light. I had diarrhea and needed to go to the bathroom badly. It clearly wasn't my day, and I had no intention of being the only person vulnerably perched on a toilet in an otherwise empty twenty-stall layout. This would be the ultimate test of mind over matter. The emptiness and silence were spine tingling. Every shuffled footstep, every sound, was ominous and foreboding. I retreated to the ticket counters which were now shutting down. There seemed to be a crescendo of shared panic to get out before the world wound down and yielded with barely a whimper to the darker forces of late night JFK. The black woman at American Eagle had a heart of gold. I must have looked pathetic. She listened to a part of my story (I skipped the CIA bit). Then she arranged to get me on a special bus with other damned souls headed for Reagan National airport in Washington, DC. **And so began the scariest part of the trip!**

Event 6. I was seated in the second row of the bus. On our bus the driver was seated down front on a lower level. This disconnected him audibly from the rest of the bus. Immediately behind him in my row on the other side of the aisle was a supply of soft drinks and pretzels. I had my side of the row to myself but the other passengers were packed closely enough together that it was more like slow dancing than riding in a public conveyance. The two gentlemen sitting in front of me were probably in their thirties. One, from Mexico, spoke Spanish, The other, from Brazil, spoke Portuguese. They chose to speak in English. They were nice looking. As I sat there staring blankly as if mentally challanged, I could hear enough of their conversation to believe that these were two fairly senior drug lords or at least regional distributors. Quite clearly they planned this first meeting on the plane to Washington and used this opportunity alone on the first row with no one in front to talk business. I was an unwilling listener whom they hadn't yet realized had been included in their conversation. Questions: When would they figure it out? What would they do then?

Scenes from Hitchcock's "The Man Who Knew Too Much" flashed before my mind in real life. A low point came when one suggested they go out when they got to Washington and have a friend, Louis, fix them up with a couple of "bitches" from his "pound."

"How do we know they don't have some disease?" His associate responded thoughtfully. To which he replied, "Louis holds his women responsible for not infecting any of his friends. A few years ago one of them gave a case of the clap to one of our boys. We made an example out of her and since then,—no problem."

"I wonder how they treat eavesdroppers and witnesses?" I thought as I feigned sleep. Surely it was only a matter of time until they noticed a loose end—me. Needless to say I didn't want to hear any of their conversation. Even more importantly, I didn't want to appear capable of hearing anything. I tried to think myself invisible. That didn't work. Have you ever noticed that when someone asks you to "act naturally," it's impossible? Well, so it seemed that night. Add to that trying be inconspicious with untreated Parkinson's, much less with a hooting cough. Suddenly I realized, that's it, the answer. I never thought that being forced to slur my speech, clear my throat, in a primitive, bestial way could ever be an advantage, but that was the real me, cast in a role I could never have faked consciously, as our bus pulled into Reagan National Airport at 4 AM with me appearing to be a mentally challenged, coughing, hooting, wheezing, clearly to the onlooker, a terminally ill person, a totally non-threatening witness.

I felt I was the luckiest guy alive.

COMMENT: Everything gets done through people

I met some great people im my travels and made some good friends and a few disappointments.

HIGH SOCIETY

Iran was my principal focus from 1974 to 1979. I was commuting eight and half time zones on an eighteen to twenty hour flight every other month. From the outside it looked too good to be true: eating at four star restaurants. Viewed from the inside it was a study in high pressure marketing which often required that we work through the night only getting by on three or four hours sleep. On the other hand I met a number of memorable people, some famous, some infamous:

Lord Jellico

Lord George Jellico was the leader of the conservative party in the House of Lords. He was also a senior partner at Paribas Warburg, a British investment banking house. I had met him when I was raising some capital and his firm invested. Lord Jellico had made the acquaintance of a young lady under contract to KGB. At that time he was Minister of the British Civil Service. He resigned and rejoined Paribas Warburg.

Lee, Jennifer, myself, Amy and my mother decided on the spur of the moment to fly to Tehran. I didn't like flying, particularly with skyjackers so I insisted that we travel in two groups. Jennifer, age 10, flew with me. Lee ended up with Amy, age 8 and a half and my mother, age 75, who didn't hesitate to give her free, but usually, unneeded travel advice. Lord Jellico invited Lee, my mother and myself to dinner at the Intercontinental. I had told Lee of his claim to fame, but not my mother. He was the first major figure in a sex scandal we had ever met and the scene was a little bit like the episode of Fawlty Towers in which John Cleese tries very hard not to mention "the war" at a table of Germans. Of course, Cleese made mistakes such as asking, "What would you like on your huns," when he meant to say 'buns.' Correspondingly, I felt awkward raising the subject of "religious sects." Lee was also consciously avoiding any conversation line that would refer to "sex or scandal." She succeeded admirably although I suspect Lord Jellico rather enjoyed his notoriety and secretly laughed at the efforts to avoid any related subjects. After dinner as we walked down to the lobby. Lord Jellico said to me, "Now Bob, you and your lovely wife and mother will have to come visit us at our country house outside of London," then turned to Lee and asked, "When will you be returning to London?" Lee replied, "I'll be there next Friday, but Robert and Jennifer are stopping in Paris so they won't get in until Saturday." (While Lee thought this implied that neither of us would be available, Jellico saw another interpretation, or at least pretended so). He put his hand under her chin and said, "Ah, that just makes you all the more interesting, my dear." Lee blushed a deep red. Jellico's eyes had a good natured twinkle.

I arrived on Saturday, and Sunday we went out to his country house for a typical British garden party.

Sir Sigmund Warburg

"Sir Sigmund" as he was called, was probably the most prestigious figure in British banking. He was a Renaissance man and Latin scholar, with a reputation throughout the Western world of finance. If I had known then what I later learned about him, I would have been very intimidated. He was well into his eighties and had clear blue eyes which required no glasses. He asked me where my company did business, and I mentioned Brazil, among others. "I remember the first time I went to Brazil. I was met by the head of our accounting firm, and I asked him, "How do you do business in Brazil?" He replied, "You must always remembers the four "w's". First, who do you need to influence? That is who controls the decision you care about. Second, what commodity will you pay them in? For example, cash, women or position? Third, where will you pay them? In Brazil? In London? Finally, when will you pay them? Now or later? Before or after the transaction?" The CIA couldn't have said it better.

Kim Roosevelt

Kim Roosevelt, grandson of Theodore Roosevelt, had been the head of the Middle East desk for CIA and the person who was given most of the credit for the counter-coup by the Shah of Iran against Mossadeqh. Kim befriended EarthSat and played an enormous role in introducing us into Iranian society. Perhaps the most noteworthy single event was arranged by one of his friends, Chahine Agahayan, who was probably Prime Minister Hoveda's best friend. We met the Prime Minister on a Thursday afternoon (their equivalant to a Saturday afternoon.) I was proposing that Iran would build a ground receiving station and there was a delicate question as to who should be the lead government agency. I had not expected to have more than 15 minutes of his time and consequently, did not prepare a formal briefing. It caught me by surprise as he led us in to an enormous Cabinet room and said, "I have convened the entire Cabinet, and you have two hours to make your presentation." Subsequently, this led to a series of additional meetings with individual ministers. It mattered greatly to us which minister was chosen because each minister had its own favorite contractor. We were relieved when the Minister of Agriculture was chosen because EarthSat was held in high regard by him.

Unknowingly, our presentation to the Cabinet and our subsequent private meetings took us over a forbidden line. General Smart, a retired four-star general, was our Executive Vice President and was traveling with me. He contacted the top military people in Iran and their security service (SAVAK) paid very close attention indeed to anyone who had direct access to both the top civilian and military leaders. Furthermore, I was the frequent guest at the Embassy socially, where the former Director of CIA, Mr. Helms, was Ambassador. Also, it was probably known that I had been with CIA. In short to a paranoiac counter intelligence officer we might have looked different than we really were. The fact that we were under surveillance was pointed out vividly in an event that occurred in our hotel room. General Smart asked to see the specially enhanced satellite pictures I had brought with me. He looked at them and commented that they were so good he wasn't going to show them to any generals for fear "they might classify the whole program." A short time later we left our room for thirty minutes to have a cup of tea in the lobby. When we returned the pictures were gone from inside my locked briefcase. We subsequently became quite friendly with a number of Cabinet ministers and were greatly saddened when the first two ministers shot when the Ayatollah took over were the Prime Minister and the Minister of Agriculture.

On another trip, Kim Roosevelt and his son, Jonathan met us in Paris and we went together to meet the famous Saudi arms agent, Adnan Khosoggi at his apartment across from the Hotel Paris Athena. Khosoggi had a number of former Lockheed people on his staff who had experience with U2's and were interested in the application of photo interpretation to civilian objectives. Jennifer accompanied us to what was to be her first business meeting. She sat perfectly on a settee with her hands crossed and, much to my surprise, not squirming at all. She was the perfect young lady. Afterwards, Khosoggi went over and said to her, "You are enchanting, mademoiselle. I think I will let one of my sons ask you out." Jennifer responded with the perfect curtsey. The first and last, I think, in her life, and I have no idea where she learned it.

Kim's sons, Jonathan and Kermit, had become good personal friends, and we have spent many hours sharing the consultant's bond of waiting endlessly in hotel rooms for some event to take place.

Prince Sharam

Prince Sharam was the son of the Shah's twin sister, Ashraf. We were invited to join him for lunch at one of his palaces outside Tehran. I was accompanied by Professor Lee Arnold, of NYU and Mr. Frank Godsey, who was formerly a group vice president for Westinghouse. He and Dr. Arnold had both previously been consultants to the Administrator of NASA and the Secretary of Transportation. Both were investors in EarthSat. Prince Sharam was Harvard educated and was interested in playing a role in the development of remote sensing in Iran. At lunch, I noted the wine was very good and asked what it was. Professor Arnold put me on the spot by saying, "Bob is an expert on wines, so why don't you tell us what it is." I couldn't back out at that point so I suggested that it might be a 1957 Bordeaux. Godsey, who was a no nonsense, plain spoken Texan, who seldom entered a conversation, interjected in a matter-of-fact manner, "1963 Chateau-neuf-du-Pape." This would have been a lesser wine, but I foolishly asked the waiter to show us the label. Sure enough, it was 1963 Chateau-neuf-du-Pape. It was the wine that Frank Godsey drank every day at home, and he knew it when he tasted it. I kept very quite.

Minions

When one travels as much as I do, you meet a number of people who have to be admired for their coping skills, i.e. survivability. Here are two who shall remain nameless.

The first managed to beat the "reservation problem." It is a fact that all planes traveling from Europe arrive at approximately midnight in Tehran. If you look in the lobby of any of the big hotels at 1:30 AM, you will see about 100 people sitting in chairs in the lobby holding their reservation slips in their hand, armed with the recent knowledge that there is no room for them. I met a Frenchman who solved this problem. While others waited, he simply tipped the concierge and knowing that Air France has a block of rooms available for the stewardess', asked if he could be put in a room with an Air France stewardess. The answer was, "Certainement Monsieur."

The second story starred an Italian and an Iranian who worked for one of our partners. We had a voluptuous secretary named Vicky, who had a crush on Charles Sheffield. Vicky brought in homemade cookies for tea at the office. Charles thanked her and invited her to lunch. On reflection, he wondered what he had implied, so he asked his cohort if this was tantamount to a proposal for marriage. The man assured him that it was not. Charles asked a second question. "Will she bring her mother with her?" His friend contemplated the situation and, observing that the secretary was an attractive 20 year old, and her mother was probably an attractive 40 year old, answered, "No, but if she does, invite me to join you."

COMMENT: Don't think you're going to out-negotiate an Iranian who's been trading rugs in his family for 3,000 years.

Tehran Remembered

I can honestly say that EarthSat never paid a bribe any place in the world. "Teaming arrangements" between companies were infamous in Iran. We were given a contract with the Minister of Agriculture to select their computers. We were working with the Farminfarmingyan company and Azassiz Farminfarmingyan was our partner. Azassiz asked me if I would meet with probably the wealthiest agent in Iran. His name was Mahvi. I reluctantly agreed and went out to his palatial home in the Tehran suburbs. It was summer, and he was dressed casually with a thin, beige turtleneck sweater, and he sat in an oversized chair with enormous gold-plated arms. He spoke to me in a subdued voice, "Mr. Porter, you seem very nervous as though you would expect me to try and influence you. Let me tell you. There are eight potential contractors, including Lockheed, Honeywell, TRW, Bendix, just to name a few. I represent all of them. But I also own 50% of Honeywell's operation in Iran, and I can assure you that Honeywell will be the computer which will be selected. So relax, I have no need to influence you." It reminded me of a joke:

There was a competition to select an astronaut to go to the moon to search for minerals. The job was dangerous and specialized, so commercial proposals were undertaken. The field was narrowed to three finalists. In the interviews each was asked how much he wanted to be paid and what he would do with the money. The first, a German, replied, "I want three million dollars. I will give one million to the fatherland, one million to my family, and keep one million for myself." Next they interviewed an Englishman who replied, "I want six million pounds. First, there's two million for me, than two million for my mistress, and then two million for family."
Next, they interviewed an Iranian. "I want nine million dollars in gold. First, there's three million for you. Then there's three million for me. Finally, there's three million for that crazy German we're going to send to the moon." (This explains why we lost those jobs in Iran, except for the times we ended up as subcontractor.)

Learning to do business in Iran was a major educational experience. We had some unexpected advantages. I asked a lawyer who represented a great many prestigious American and European companies which he preferred to represent. He responded that the American companies made their managers into Chief Executive Officers so the president of a major auto company would likely have come from one of the divisions. He was not schooled in International trade and frequently his lack of sophistication was an embarrassment to his host. By contrast, Europeans picked their senior officers because of their diplomatic skills and international *savoir faire*. EarthSat had a very impressive team which combined technical expertise and very presentable people. We had another advantage. The Ministers preferred to work with the CEO of a small company rather than the Vice President of a large company. The CEO could make faster decisions. It was far easier to introduce the president and CEO of a company to a Minister than it was a vice president.

I was double crossed in Iran by a false friend. I was expressing my rage when his cousin asked me, "Do you know the farsi word *ketman*?" I replied I didn't. He informed me that it referred to a policy developed by the Shiites in their conflict with the Sumi when asked, "Who is the true disciple of Mohamed?" The wrong answer frequently resulted in death, but the Koran says it is wrong to lie. It also says that "Preserving the faith" was man's highest obligation and consequently the policy of ketman forgave telling a lie to preserve the faith. Naturally, one should be as honest as the situation permits, i.e. telling a half truth is better than telling a quarter truth, etc. According to my Iranian friend, "95% of the Iranians *ketman* all but three people, typically one parent (seldom both); one other relative such as an uncle or cousin; and one friend with whom he went through school and life. As for the others he tells them what they want to hear.

"I ask myself if I am one of these three people," he said "and if I conclude I'm not, then I expect to be ketmaned. Americans seem to think they have "two hundred best friends" and then are surprised when they get hurt."

But keeping too many secrets impairs one's ability to mentor or to be mentored. Indeed these are survival mechanisms for success in running a government or a business. Maybe this explains why Iran suffers radical changes in governments so frequently. Three trusted friends may be too few to lower your guard and still provide adequate communication. Two hundred may include too many distrustful friends. What is the right number? Its is important to share life experiences but—.

COMMENT: "You can go from heaven to hell, from honor to dishonor, but you'll never find anything that's dead, solid perfect."

This statement, made by a character of the author, Dan Jenkins, deserves a high place among the truest quotes. It is very close to the advice, "Don't let the best be the enemy of the good."

Even if you can't think like Einstein or sing like Sinatra that doesn't mean you can't get in the game.

Insights at On Site
March 9, 2000

My family boarded planes on Friday, February 18, 2000, and flew to Nashville, Tennessee to attend On Site. This program has been developing the Experiential Family Therapy Method, a process to bring out the sources of pain in one's life, especially pain that originates in family systems. Our specific program was a format with our family and two therapists with very heavy duty probing over a four day period. I didn't know what we were getting into, I just knew that Amy had gone to a different On Site workshop where she learned about this one, and thought that a four day review of our collective experiences might be instructive, even beneficial. The first hint of possible stress was when I went to breakfast the first morning and received hearty congratulations and the admiring statement, "God, you're brave, I'm really proud to meet you." I wasn't brave but ignorant and, not being able to walk out, I just gave him my best Ben Hur, "We who are about to die, salute you" look and kept on walking to find my destiny.

DESTINY 101, SATURDAY, THE FIRST DAY: After working out some rules which included no radio, TV or alcohol, the views of each participant, including the supervisors, were expressed as to his/her goals and what reservations one may have had. Then we rotated chairs one by one until everyone had re-stated the goals of each other. Afterwards, the person who had made the original statement would critique and correct the listener-speaker. Inasmuch as everyone put his personal spin on what he or she wanted, it proved that no one hears without imparting some personal spin to what one thinks one hears. We each came to this program thinking that someone else would learn quite a bit. It was a real shock that we each found ourselves challenged and sometimes exhausted. The first night we all wondered if the course would really be worthwhile and whether it would bring both resolution and closure to the problems we identified. The next days showed us what two experienced professional therapists can do with four people in four full days in an isolated environment.

In the afternoon, we sculpted our relationships. In this process we placed one another around the room pointing out who was closest and the most distant, and who provided the most energy. We all found this exercise traumatic. I went to bed at 7:15 pm the first night and Lee at 8:00. We were interrupted in the middle of the night by one of the children who couldn't sleep, and climbed into bed with us like a five year old.

SUNDAY, THE SECOND DAY: Family histories were taken with everyone participating. Emphasis was put on the pain other family members had felt coincident with events they had identified to be of note. From this I concluded that members of a family almost always share the pain felt by others. Stated otherwise, you can't hurt alone even if you try. My generation called it "toughing it out." Psychologists today call it "denial." This approach of associating pain is somewhat unique to this program. None of us slept well that night, but we all had changed our minds and thought this was a very valuable experience.

On THE THIRD DAY we probed deeper into the family histories, which included the histories of Lee's and my parents and our reactions to growing up with our siblings. We also worked on how to argue. We took some of the most sensitive issues and argued them out using this technique. The approach would be that one person would state the issue and how he/she felt about it. Then the other participant would reflect what he/she heard the first person say. Then the first person would correct, if necessary, the second person. Then the second person would say how that made him or her feel, and the process would be repeated in reverse. Then one adds, "and what I need from you," and the other reflects this back and then responds "what I can do for you?" This technique was very effective. Normally when people argue they don't have to acknowledge hearing what the other person says, nor explicitly say what he/she wants you to do, but rather just ignores the strong points and/or gets up and goes away. One of the big advantages of having these meetings is that enough time is provided to allow these discussions to go to conclusion resulting in true closure. We all slept well that night, and all felt the course was very useful.

DAY FOUR was a surprise. We thought we had touched on all the pain and were doing something as a fun relief exercise. We went into a big lecture hall that had a vertical wall about 25 feet high. Artificial rocks were placed on the wall. We were hitched up in harnesses and offered an opportunity to climb the wall <u>blindfolded</u>. Naturally none of us wanted to pass up a limited time offer like this, so we all volunteered. We climbed one person at a time. The non-climbing members were taught how to hold the ropes attached to the safety harness and were responsible for the climber's safety. One person served as a guide who would direct the blinded climber where to put his or her hands and feet. Each person took a turn at being the climber and would assign the roles to the back up team members. There was a special therapist in this segment who asked perceptive questions which brought out hidden information about the way we made decisions. This taught us about the managerial relationships between group members. We found this to be surprisingly revealing.

My description does not do justice to the On Site program. So much depends on the quality of the therapists. They were excellent. **One worries that it might just open wounds and not get to closure. In our case, we felt exhausted but relieved. I can honestly report that no issue was more painful when we left than when it was when first introduced. Stated otherwise: Some healing took place in every case.** We probably exited the program a lot less ignorant and a little more brave. I would particularly recommend it to people with adult children. We wondered what it would have been like to have attended a program like this with our parents. We concluded that it would have probably been fantastic…. but almost inconceivable.

Evensong

I met him for the first time that evening. He mentioned he was "Class of Fifty"; 1950 I assumed. That made him about 69. "I think of myself in my twenties, except when age catches up with parts of me," he said.

They were recently married. Each for the second time. Both had been deeply committed to their first marriages. When he was losing his wife to cancer, he retired early so they could "share some time," but as one learns, "Things change." Now he's working again, and here he stands: a lifetime behind, a lifetime ahead. She lost her first husband to a prolonged mid-life crisis. Each of the newlyweds have tasted life's vintage and non-vintage years.

When I watch two young people starting out on their first marriage, I think to myself, "What do they know?" I answer with an involuntary shake of my head. Meg and Bob are "survivors." Their bonds are forged with knowledge of humankind's limits, private snapshots, which defy articulation: a child's angst, a grandchild's joy, an illness, the loss of a friend, the realization of each other's mortality and time's swift hand.

Thanksgiving Day Reflections
1997

On New Years Eve 1992, I first noticed a lump on my neck which was subsequently diagnosed to be squamous cell cancer. After the operation, the doctors said they had gotten "almost all" of it, but that a round of radiation therapy was necessary. We would have to wait three years to find out if high technology, prayers, and luck would keep me going. I had been diagnosed to have Parkinson's Disease in 1981, and that had turned out much more tolerable than I ever expected, so after the usual bouts of denial, depression and acceptance, I was willing to consider the positive alternatives. Now, almost five years later, without any recurrence, my prognosis is good, and I humbly appreciate all the more the many gifts I still enjoy.

Although, theoretically, one doesn't need a killer disease to value his friendships, this is a frequent side effect. I "think anecdotally," that is, my thought processes are sprinkled with recognizable anecdotes, words of advice from friends, *apercus* from the past. Consequently, about twenty years ago, I took my personal phone book and systematically reflected on every name, asking myself, "What did I learn from this person?" I also looked at it the other way around, noting whose name was associated when an anecdote came to mind during the course of a day. I concluded that some mentors were more effective than others, in part because of special characteristics they possessed, and because I was expecting to learn more from some than from others; consequently, I was more receptive. It also made me contemplate how much more I might have learned if I had been even more open to new ideas.

But I digress. The point I want to make is all this became the stimulus to write a book I titled <u>My Friends and Mentors, The First Sixty Years</u>. It was based on remembrances of **good** times I had shared with friends. This was not intended as a biography, nor did I try to represent a balanced overview or judgement. In brief, it was an expression of thanksgiving which I highly recommend as therapy and sheer joy.

Thanksgiving is my favorite holiday. There are no mandatory gifts, no religious protocols, and we always have something to be thankful for no matter how many problems we face. Just thinking about past good times makes the present go better.

Comment: Things change

It was a surrealistic scene. Lee was sitting on one side of the room looking at her checkbook to see what her requirements would be during the trial separation. I was on the other side of the room, running a VISICALC spreadsheet, weighing the effect of different permutations on my available funds. It suddenly struck me that this scene was being repeated in houses all over the country. Indeed, enough to justify an apple computer commercial.

Event: Our separation—Circa January 1980

A proposed TV commercial by Robert Porter

SPLITTING THE APPLE

Within the inner sanctum of the judge's chambers a hushed mood prevails. Finally, the plaintiff, a typical perky American divorcee (played by Sandy Duncan) speaks, "I'm just a plain southwest farm girl myself, but if it wasn't for my APPLE III I'd probably still be married to that no account city slicker sitting across the desk (she points an accusatory finger). He used to have me so tied down with chores, I just didn't have any free time! Then APPLE III came to the rescue! It helped me reschedule milking the cows, slopping the hogs, plan all the shopping, even writing the checks. Why, it even gave me enough free time to go to town. (That's when I caught Romeo there with his secretary, Betty Sue!)"

The defendant (played by Dick Cavett) turns to face the TV audience, revealing a loveable, boyish grin. "I owe a lot to APPLE III also," he said. "When Peggy Lee caught me dead to rights, I thought financial ruin would be my only friend. That was before my friendly APPLE III dealer and accountant introduced me to VISI-CALC and turned my life around. They showed me how to reduce the assets my ex-wife could claim by depreciating my cows and hogs, using an EASY DOUBLE DECLINING BALANCE SUBROUTINE and then recompute my taxes (getting a big tax credit for that new car I bought Betty Sue) and keep track of all the little details (like business mileage to town). That paid the lawyer's fees by itself and left a pretty penny for Peggy Lee (camera focuses on her smiling).

Finally, the judge, (played by Wilt Chamberlain) speaks as he places his massive hand on a compact computer console in front of him, "Divorce used to be complicated and expensive before APPLE III came along, but when this piece of space age technology is matched with TWO DISC DRIVES AND A NEC SPIN-WRITER, who am I to argue?"

At this time, the announcer (played by Robert Young) steps on stage. "Well, ha ha, your honor, now all you have to decide is who is entitled to the APPLE III under the community property settlement." (Everybody laughs.)

COMMENT: Don't join the CIA

Will the Real Robert Porter Please Duck!

January 9, 1995

To tell you the truth, when I was with the CIA, I was not James Bond. I had no "license to kill." I was a scientist in R&D. It was quite all right when I worked as an "overt" Agency employee to say I worked for the Agency—except when I traveled abroad, where the threat is personal. Someone not on the government's payroll, i.e., a terrorist, will figure that "getting" a former employee is a close second best thing to "getting" a nice fresh one. He then takes matters into his own hands and creates an incident. The Chief of Station in Greece was assassinated during one of my visits to Greece because a newspaper identified him. Thus, when one's a businessman abroad, if he's wise, he keeps a low profile. This was particularly true in the mid-seventies when skyjacking and kidnapping was in high fashion.

A very scary "coincidence" occurred when I flew to Athens in 1975 to visit friends on my way to the Middle East. I happened to pick up a book at the airport titled on the Bay of Pigs titled "Betrayal," before getting on the plane. I looked at it because I wanted to see if it had any comments about General Cabell, who was a close friend of mine and a "mentor" in my book. On the first page, I read the author's opening, *"The ID card in my wallet read: Robert Porter; sex, male; hair, brown; eyes, blue; height, 6'0"; weight, 176 lbs.; age, 26 (in 1961); employer, Comcor, Inc."* It's me I thought! As I read further, this guy was on his way to Athens to buy arms, and he was involved in some very rough stuff, i.e., brutal murders, money laundering, and no doubt still had enemies in many of the areas I was visiting routinely.

Ordinarily, one would expect someone with the same name to look completely different, certainly not exactly the same. In this case, our ages were the same, and the only difference was one inch in height. coincidence? Anyway you score it, I was veryHe even had an electronics background, and I had just finished a tour at the Signal Corp research lab in Ft. Monmouth. Even so, you would normally expect that you wouldn't be confused because you wouldn't have the same life style. Not so in this case. I had been traveling to Athens for two years and often

59

visited with CIA friends there. Why hadn't they said something? Maybe they had never met the other Porter—maybe they had! Very spooky!

This book caused a flashback to a day in 1966, when I was unexpectedly called to the office of the Deputy Director for Science and Technology (DDS&T). I thought it was a little unusual that I didn't know any of the other four men waiting to go into the office, but I was currently heading a fairly hot project and just figured "I'd been recognized." I introduced myself to each one of them, "Bob Porter, Office of Research and Development." They responded with a simple name but no organization. This didn't surprise me. The meeting started, and the DDS&T started briefing us on a very sensitive subject. After ten minutes, it became clear to me that they had the wrong Robert Porter! I politely interjected that they had made a mistake and asked to be excused, but **I had heard enough then, to realize now, that this "Robert Porter" in the book was the one I had been "mistaken for" in 1966 at the CIA.**

If the other people had known the other Bob Porter, you would expect them to do a double take when they met me, and I claimed his name—unless they knew in advance. If they weren't surprised, and I was the only unwitting person in the meeting, then were they looking me over? Was it sheer unlucky. Someone at CIA had obviously been assigned my name for cover purposes before I joined the Agency, but after I applied.

I was concerned at the time that my name would have been tagged at Greek customs, and my behavioral pattern would have fit his profile. If action had been taken against me by anyone, the mistake would be "understandable" if the mistake became known; if it wasn't known, and I was a decoy, then the locals would have thought that the book's "Robert Porter" was gone from this world. If he had active enemies, my death or kidnapping would take his place. That was my "most pessimistic case," but the one I thought most about on the long plane ride to Athens.

In spy stories you can imagine almost anything! Real life has its opportunities too. Was the man I was staying with an evil spymaster? **Who are your friends?** I was an innocent party in a very unlikely and uncomfortable coincidence. I have no idea what happened to the other "Robert Porter." The whole matter is a puzzlement which may have more to it than I know! But I think I'll skip Greece next vacation.

A New C&W Hit by R. Porter

I'M TOO HUNG UP TO EVER HANGUP ON YOU

Now I was alone in my bed last night.
My mind was empty, my eyes closed tight.
When I heard a sound, I could clearly tell.
Was the frightful call of old Ma Bell.

I fumbled around and reached for the phone.
When it fell on the floor, I let out a groan.
The voice I knew, no but's or maybe's
It was the 4:30 phantom, my ex-old lady.

"Now, Robert," she said, "I hope you're not busy
But I couldn't sleep, my mind's in a tizzy.
I've been thinking about all the things you do bad
And to tell you the truth, right now I'm real mad!"

Well, I stammered and stuttered and muttered and moaned.
While she vented her rage through that old telephone.
Now I didn't hear everything, but I'd heard enough.
To know I was tired of taking her guff.

So I reached for the button to end it all.
But a voice in my head asked, "Why did she call?"
And I smiled as I answered from deep in my heart.
That I knew she still cared, even though we're apart.

So I guess I just don't care what you do.
You can call me in the day and the nighttime too.
You can call when you're happy or feeling blue.
Cause I'm too hung up to ever hang up on you.

COMMENT: Honor anniversaries

I have the habit of writing poems to my children for their birthdays and anecdotes to my wife on our anniversaries. In retrospect, this is one of the best things I have done. They are appreciated at the time and serve to provide a snapshot of the way you are thinking at any moment of time which you would never have otherwise.

Take 16

When the Minister said to the bride, "Will you, Lee, love, honor and obey," she should have asked some questions. <u>Love</u> what? <u>Honor</u> whom? And, <u>obey</u> for what reason? On the other hand, no one ever asked, and even if she had, the Minister could never have seen clearly what was ahead for her, and even if he had, it is doubtful she would have believed him, and, even if she did, she probably would have gone along with it anyway.

Where is it written that she should <u>love</u> the "damned dog"? Or <u>honor</u> a surly adolescent? Or <u>obey</u> a "lazy" husband? No, surely that's not what the Minister intended. On the other hand, the Minister asked that question of both parties, and that poses another problem: Where is it written that he should love gardening? Or honor a rhetorical question? Or obey a wife's "compulsive" whim?

Some say it's in the stars. After all, she is a Virgo, born 24 August, and he is a Pisces, born 27 February. They were married June 2nd in a leap year when Saturn was high in the sky (just after the stock market fell). Any astrologer could tell you, "problems ahead." What if they waited till June 10, when Venus became more visible in the early evening sky and Mars had settled below the horizon— just one week? Maybe he'd hate the dog, or prefer cats, and she'd hate the garden. Who knows? But that wasn't possible anyway. Fate had precluded that alternative: The Minister was already committed to another wedding the 10th. I wonder if the couple married that day asked any questions, got any answers, lasted 16 years, and own a dog or a garden?

Take 30

She's in the bedroom doing yoga.
He just got back from 30 minutes of mostly walking and a short run.

She's about to go to her studio and work on her fabric art.
He's taking the morning off to work at home and write this.

Tonight, she attends her course on "Addictions."
Tonight, he's going to one of those "violent cop movies" with a friend.
The kind she wishes he "wouldn't support with his ticket."

Tomorrow they'll celebrate their 30th with a couple close friends at a restaurant.
One day's delay is hardly an issue.

They've been up since 4:30 AM when their 26 year old daughter told them she couldn't sleep and had to finish packing at her last residence for today's move. This, following a break up with her almost-fiancee of two years. A tough week for all parties!

Changes over 30 years? Yes and no. Some genetic imprints persist and so do some environmentally acquired patterns. Last night they had an argument over <u>how</u> to tell their 26 year old she hasn't yet learned what they have over the past 30 years. (Wouldn't it be nice if she didn't have to go through the pain her parents experienced? But, as his father used to say, "Nobody ever learns from history!")

Blessedly, the way they argued was different than the way they did 30 years ago, which was different than the <u>way</u> they did 20 years ago, which was different than they did 10 years ago. But the <u>reason</u> for the argument is the same: different people, different styles! Genetic or environmental, the interaction of any two people is unique, and its roots are deep. They've certainly learned that.

Marriage and tennis are a lot alike: There are a lot of close calls, every referee has his own point of view, and it's the moves you make when the ball's not in your court that separates the winner and the also-ran!

Take 35

"Did you enjoy the party?" she had asked yesterday in the elevator.

"Yes, very much. I was down a bit earlier this afternoon," he replied, anxious to say more.

"I really wish you'd get out and try new things. I wish you'd just try that Sunday yoga class **once**. You'd like it. I know. Why are **some** people always afraid to try new things?"

"Why can't **other** people listen and not judge so quickly?" he thought.

They were both right and wrong. Self-discipline was never his strong suite, and it's depressing to hear about depression. On the other hand, if she had been more patient, he was trying to say that what he had noticed that afternoon was how quickly his mood had shifted up, which makes the point that one needs to remind oneself when they're down that mood reversals occur in both directions. Now his mood had shifted down again.

Tomorrow is their 35th Anniversary. When the minister had said "for richer or poorer, in sickness and in health," neither of them could anticipate reality this far ahead, much less the specifics. They'd just "do the right thing" if difficult times came, and so far they had.

Damn, the future seems simple! One problem is people don't just live or die. In fact, it's not easy to tell if someone's sick or not, much less how sick, even if you're the person or his/her doctor. I've never met a patient who doesn't prefer wild speculation to an autopsy's certainty.
Sometimes when he said, "I love you," she would smile and say, "This moment you do." She was right of course. He didn't love her in the elevator or for some time after, yet he knew he really did the whole time. Hours later, he thinks how to rephrase his statement so it would be both accurate and truthful. Perhaps," I

still love you," he muttered to himself. But then he paused, realizing that wasn't quite right either because his concept of "love" had grown over 35 years. Maybe adding "warts and all" would pass. Actually, it was surviving "warts and all" that made their marriage special. But no, "I love you, warts and all" still needed some fine tuning. Anyway, her touch said enough.

Thirty-five years of marriage. Just think of it. There isn't any way to contemplate 35 years of marriage except through living a particular 35 years with a particular person. The meaning of "I love you" constantly grows.

When I see a couple exchanging vows, I admit the first thought that comes to mind is, "What do they know now?" "Nothing." "Factual not cynical," he'd assert. For ahead of them will lie the greatest educational challenge of their lives. After 35 years, they may share or disagree with my views on many things, but agreement on this one point is almost a certainty: one's grades in marriage and parenting are the most important marks of his/her life.

So, it wasn't all wedding night champagne. He had once asked her what was her greatest asset. She answered, "Commitment." She asked him his. He replied, "Love of truth." The first 35 years had tested both.

Take 38

It's been 38 years since we said, "I do."Of course, neither of us knew what we were signing up for but, after 38 years we realize that it was a pretty heavy commitment. The other night I went to a garden party. After wandering a while, I noticed the guests had divided into "affinity groups," based on their most pressing illnesses, e.g. "The prostate group, the by-pass group, the implant group," etc. Surprisingly, the conversations were upbeat. These were groups of individuals, who either believed they had beaten the challenge and/or, were advising someone on what steps to take to beat his/her current problem. I exaggerate to make a point. The guests didn't spend the evening talking about their illnesses, but there were a lot of 35th to 40th anniversary people who a shared the survivor's bond of adversities.

I honestly don't know whether I can realistically plan on thirty minutes or thirty years of life expectancy. I know those who have had serious illnesses would agree with me that "planning to die is no way to live." The good news is that **doing counts. Right now is the only time you can count as real.** I decided to make up a list of real options for this moment. It is the following:

1. Write this story
2. Go to bed
3. Think of something else to do
4. Call or visit a friend
5. Organize something, e.g.-"to do" list
6. Work on book
7. Watch television
8. Write an essay; participate in Dartmouth class 57 online activity
9. Read something
10. Go shopping
11. Play chess
12. Exercise

I don't know anyone personally who got divorced after 38 years. It certainly isn't on my "to do" list. Rather, I've become more appreciative of unheralded experiences: help in buttoning a cuff, moving into the guest bedroom on a particularly restless night, shared moments with family, trying to help one another through life's shoals and narrows, an occasional pat on the back, or praise for a well written piece. This is not to say that Lee and I have declared a moratorium on trying to change the other, but we accept more year by year. Thirty eight's a pretty good number. It's a time when you realize that soon, whether in thirty minutes or thirty years, you will "part," and you accept that, but with an enhanced appreciation for the kindnesses you've shared.

Take 40

If I believed in horoscopes, which I don't, I'd be in serious trouble because I don't know when I was born. This was insensitively revealed to me when I went to register for Social Security at the age of 65. The government guy looked at all the papers I'd brought with me that he had requested and, after shuffling through them, asked casually as he gesticulated towards a pile of my papers and said, "Who is this guy?" I responded it was me. He then pointed to another pile of papers and said, "Then who is this other guy? You said your birthday was February 27, 1935, and this birth certificate says you were born on March 2, 1935. What's the story?" I was getting the idea that he had been through this routine before. He certified me because in either case, I was old enough to qualify, and that was his only interest. I have thought about it, because I feel rather silly having celebrated my birthday on the wrong date for 65 years. I concluded that this wasn't an accident, but rather, a plan by my father to designate February 27th as my official birthday in order to be the same as his sister, a widowed lady without children who shared that date and always thought of me as "her child." What difference did 3 days make anyway?

I have a different but similar problem in establishing when to celebrate our 40th Wedding Anniversary. Lee and I were separated twice for approximately 6 months each time, so if you subtract that time, it becomes difficult to arrive at the precise date to celebrate. I would contend this is truly our 40th anniversary and those interludes when we lived apart were no different than respites in marital quality that many people have, but don't consider counting. Surely, it would open Pandora's box if one were to try to "score" marital time. For example, it would be difficult to agree on what constitutes "good time" versus "bad time." Further, pain is a frequent party to periods of growth. Indeed, one of the greatest functions marriage performs is keeping you honest. If we only counted the years that were pain free, we'd only be left with a few honeymoons and, they wouldn't be good marriages. It's not all pain either; there's soothing and sharing and loving too. And those times you just barely survived were transformed by a hug or a touch. In brief, one earns his/her time for each year of marriage, and I believe we've earned credit for a full forty. Happy 40th, Lee.

Take 41

(On the occasion of our 41st Anniversary)
(June 2, 2003)

He had looked for a wife who would be a lover, a mother, and a friend. She had looked for a husband who would provide security, be a responsible parent and possessed reasonably high intellectual capacity. Each got part of what he/she wanted as well as some traits for which they hadn't bargained. While most of the criteria they had sought forty years ago were still valid, the biggest one, if one were to search today would be "caregiver" and "partner." When he thinks back to the wedding ceremony, the phrases, "For richer, for poorer, in sickness and in health" resound loudly. It seemed like fine print detail at the time. Now its specter casts a shadow over the entire marriage. The rules change when you reach this time of life. It's not fair who is chosen to give or take more. Roles can be reversed in minutes. Further, it's even more difficult when one's care giving penalizes the caregiver, often to the extreme of impacting his or her own ability to survive. This evokes anger and depression. How many people can one's emotional and financial safety-net hold? We are fortunate to have sufficient resources to broaden our support base, but divorces are the construct of lesser crises than these. Winston Churchill was harassed about his drinking by a female Member of Parliament. He replied, "You, madam, are ugly." To which she replied, "And you Mr. Prime Minister, are drunk." To which he replied, "Yes, but I'll be sober in the morning." Life threatening diseases and chronic fatigue seldom get better in the morning.

When was the last time anyone got life on his/her own terms? We all have to draw some "pain cards" along with the "pleasure cards." Before we discard all of our "pain cards," we should realize that life demands we would have to face the luck of the draw and choose from other people's discards. If we are not willing to risk worse, we ought to hold onto the cards we have currently. Over the past 40 years, we have learned that pleasure often comes out of pain and providing comfort to the truly vulnerable can be one of life's most rewarding experiences. "Compromise but set your limits" is the mantra of our time of life.

71

There is a sadness that comes with old age and that's the naked truth, but there also comes opportunity for true empathy and the realization of different pleasures than we originally contemplated. I think I'll appreciate my present cards.

Tersh and Sally—The Big 40
June 16, 2000

When I was asked to say a few words about Tersh and Sally on the occasion of their fortieth anniversary I was not surprised. For many years I have faithfully served as his official, "Only Republican friend." This entitled me to attend selected Boasberg galas. Naturally, this required certain Boswellian tasks on my part, which, considering his tennis game didn't make this task easy. In short, in my part-time role as biographer of the Boasberg family. I earned every canape.

Oh, there are many Boasberg stories over the years that are light hearted and pleasant: The famous "bird in the chimney," the day my life passed before my eyes in Sally's pool after a twenty mile bike ride in high heat, or the ski trip to Vermont on which Tersh and I actually cried with laughter and pain when we were misfitted with rental ski boots but persisted while looking for our kids, last seen trying to carry their skis to the car a tortuous mile away. So much for our attempts at single parenting grade school kids.

While it's impossible to make Tersh appear the stalwart tennis player he imagines himself, Sally, as we all know, has quietly accumulated many well deserved honors without caveats or any analogs to Tersh's "tennis blemishes". On the contrary, Sally's problem is that she knows the facts about almost everything and is occasionally called on to suffer fools lightly.

We also know Sally possesses an encyclopedic memory and vocabulary, but for some reason, I have discovered that you can key on only two of those many words to tell you what she's really thinking. The two words are "Yes" and "yeah."

A "yes"is simple. It means that she wasn't listening to your question, didn't hear a word your said, but acknowledges she knows you exist, and she might listen to you in a minute. This is the opposite of *"hai"* in Japanese.

"Yeah" on the other hand is like one of Sally's gardens, or Tersh's wines: full of subtleties and complexities which challenges all ones senses to appreciate the moment. For example:

There's the "yeah" that's inflection in cut off sharply at the end. This means, "I really disagree with everything you just said, but you're a friend so we'll just carry on."

Then there's the "yeah" that rises at the end. This means :I completely disagree with what you just said, and I'm going to tell you so, after a short pause, to give you time to reverse your position.

Third, there's the long drawn out, questioning, "Yeah" which means, "I wish you would stop agreeing with me when you really don't understand my point."

Finally, there's the "yeah," followed by a forced laugh, I heard when I almost spilled a second bottle of wine in the same day watching football. Miraculously, I caught it in mid-air without spilling a drop. Someone said "great

In conclusion, whether "yes" or "yeah" the ayes have it for the Boasberg's after 40 years. Piece of cake, eh?

My 58th Birthday

February 27, 1993

Dear Friends,

If you're wondering what you've just received, it is a letter which reflects three streams of thought I had while recovering from removal of a neck cancer last week. Many of you have shown interest and great support. For your purposes, this is sort of a battle report. This may be of special interest to a second group of friends with Parkinson's disease and those who may wonder what special twists also having PD provided in my case. Finally, today is my 58th birthday, and I have some reflections I want to share on this occasion if you are interested.

Let me be clear from the outset: I hate hospitals and for the first three nights, I lay awake complaining to myself and anyone who'd listen, "How idiotic it was to design a sick bed in an Ear, Nose and Throat (ENT) recovery ward which could only be utilized by either sitting up and rotating 90 degrees in bed or turning your neck 90 degrees." (Impossible if you have just had neck surgery.) Further, this maneuver leaves you facing a direction where you have to rotate painfully back again to the first position if you want to see the TV set. Change channels-same operation. "The Hospital Bed From Hell," I call it. There's more, but you get the idea.

So it was that at 4 AM on Saturday, February 19, 1993, four nights after seven hours of surgery on my neck, I awakened in my hospital bed trying to cope with the sleep cycle perturbations that inevitably occur after long anesthesia. I had not taken any sleeping pills and had slept well since 8:30. My wife had suggested that to get back to sleep I should try slow, deep breathing rather than counting, I had decided on the refrain from the <u>Battle Hymn of the Republic</u> to pace my breathing.

Sometime at about the third "Hallelujah" of the second verse, my mind wandered, and I focused on the strong, but unusual smell of perspiration. I wondered if patients under sedation perspired more because they didn't move about as much. Certainly, my pajamas were cemented firmly to the sheets, and I was sweating up a storm at those points where there had been little movement. In fact, I recalled what the doctor's first command yesterday morning had been, "Have the nurse help you take a shower!" He repeated it twice again before he left the room. "I must really smell," I thought.

I also remembered from my running days that perspiration smells differently depending on whether one is metabolizing mostly carbohydrates and sugars (the body's preferred choice) or, after they ran low, fats and proteins. The perspiration product from the latter, ketones, smell quite differently, and is what I would expect to smell in an ENT recovery ward where people had not been eating for some time.

Not that there weren't other points of scientific interest. For example, that afternoon I had developed an apparent allergy to something. When my internist was making his rounds, we had feverishly looked for an explanation in medications but found none. That mystery was still an open agenda item.

Most intriguing of all to me were the hallucinogenic sessions I had experienced on numerous occasions since the long operation. These are more common in people who have either Parkinson's disease (and with the associated PD medications), as well as with patients who have undertaken long periods of anesthesia. Although I had never previously experienced hallucinations with PD, I was not surprised since I knew I was made a good candidate by adding the long operation.

I had already characterized them into five categories: <u>realistic</u>, such as the repeat of one pass play (about 2 seconds in length) in what seemed to be the SF 49ers against some unrecognizable team; <u>botanical exotica</u>, such as long, exotic plants and flowers in three dimensions; <u>animation of inanimate objects</u>, such as patterns in the curtains; <u>hair growth</u>, such as beards and mustaches on women and men's faces; and, finally, <u>networks of brilliant colored bars of light</u> which sometimes looked like luminous daddy long-legs spiders. None of these hallucinations seemed real or threatening, but rather "benignly curious."

At the time my attention was focused on a particularly interesting looking plant that was "growing" in my hospital room, the smell of sweat became particularly overwhelming, and I recalled some articles I had read about the changes in olfactory response (either increased or decreased) for short periods after surgery. The possibility also occurred to me that a hypersensitive response to the sweaty smell might be a factor. With this in mind, I became interested in identifying the particular smell of my sweat, and I needed an objective observer to contribute to my newest research project.

Nurse Wende seemed to be a promising "make-shift spectrometer," whose good nature and professionalism permitted me to ask her the somewhat atypical questions, "Wende, would you come in my room for a minute and smell me?" I couldn't tell by her muted, but supportive reaction whether she thought I was delirious but harmless, or if I had just become the ninth patient that night to ask the same question. She came in, stood near, and cautiously inhaled. "All I can smell are all the beautiful flowers in this room!"

EUREKA (or, more appropriately, ACHOO). Everything suddenly came together: the allergy, the hallucinations, and the smell of sweat. Even though a new theory had just been born, I acknowledged a few additional questions might need to be addressed before I picked up my Nobel Prize:

First, not every patient was having these hallucinations; therefore, a reasonable explanation must fit the diversity of conditions present in this specific situation. In fact, when I mentioned this to my doctors, I interpreted their reaction to indicate it was quite unusual. Therefore, I initially explained it to myself as a rather unique combination of Parkinson's, medication and anesthesia.

Second, reflection on the times in which I experienced these hallucinations had not been carefully documented. However, several recollections came to mind: I first remembered these occurring after about the second day into the recovery process and intensifying with time. This suggestion that the hallucinations were stimulated by <u>post-operative events</u>, such as (a) return to PD medication, and/or (b) the introduction of flowers, and/or (c) the introduction of extreme perspiration, and/or (d) miscellaneous events, such as the increased consumption of chocolate or other gifts.

To resolve this issue further, I performed two micro-studies in my "mini-lab." The first centered on the logic that if the flowers, or any other environmental agent, was one of the culprits, then when I was having a hallucination, I should have been able to enhance its intensity by breathing more deeply. Two minutes later, as I fixed my gaze on a bath sponge that lit up like a computer-generated network of blue and white luminescent bars, I had my next opportunity to test this approach. I took a deep breath and <u>just the opposite happened</u>—the hallucination went away as if I turned off the computer display! When I breathed normally again, it reappeared! I repeated this sequence four times with identical results in the next two minutes! I was absolutely convinced this was not an irrelevant artifact (and I still am).

My first explanation was that deep breathing had displaced the mucous from my olfactory sensor temporarily, and that it had slid back as soon as I breathed normally. It could also be related to the oxygen/carbon dioxide balance.

My second micro-study was to have the flowers removed and see what happened. My hallucination symptoms decreased markedly, but not completely.

Third, several other questions still needed to be resolved: for example, "Why wasn't the nurse overwhelmed by the pervasive smell of perspiration," or, stated conversely, "Why was I?" A possible explanation for this was provided in the *NY*

Times (article attached) this week. It reports on some new data regarding olfactory receptor blockers called Bark2 which orchestrate the perception of smells by telling your receptors when to "shut off" on one smell and "move on" to be alert for others. This chemical isn't present in the right amounts in PD patients and could be diminished in patients experiencing anesthesia. Perhaps, with "normal staff" like nurse Wende, her brain tells itself to ignore the smell and move on to search for other smells, or it may work the way our audio sensor ignores passing freight trains when we're conditioned to expect them. Although I'd excitedly confided my theories to nurse Wende, I am sure she will not disclose them to anyone else.

And now, a few serious words

Today is my 58th birthday, and I would be remiss if I didn't say a few serious words to place our blessings in perspective.

The question that matters when you come out of the hospital is not, "How was your trip?" But rather, "How's your surgery doing?" In this case, the answer is, "It's too early to know." Ask me on my 60th and 65th birthdays. Now, I have a good shot at an optimistic outcome. Radiation follow-up is required and will begin in about a week. I am back at work, but will keep my schedule light for the next 6-8 weeks. I know you care, and I appreciate it.

It's amazing how seldom we look at our lives in perspective. It is a bit jarring to see, in close proximity as in the hospital, how many real life dramas are in progress daily to which we are normally oblivious. How quickly life can change. How inexplicable life is. How many unrecognized dependencies we have. It makes me reflect on our vanities and how little we choose to know and appreciate those who address these realities daily and still maintain some modicum of normality when among the rest of us.

Finally, I want to thank you again for all your support. Your commitment to play an active part to solve life's problems, to share our burdens, is what I value most. What have I learned in 58 years? "If you think you accomplish anything all by yourself, you're wrong." You need all the help you can get.

Sincerely,

Robert Porter

Lee's 60th Birthday

Dear Lee,

Tomorrow is your 60th birthday. Tonight you will be returning from a bicycle trip from Prague to Vienna with Jennifer. I'd just like to share a very few thoughts about your first 60 years which are special to me.

Your laugh. I bet this surprises you, but it's one of my fondest memories. Your laugh starts down very deep in your psyche and bursts in steps to the surface like a spring sneeze, out of control, until it seizes your facial muscles, threatening to discharge the drink your hand has just taken. It's wonderful to witness such an all consuming sharing of joy, to share your secret thoughts like your memory of conning your 4 year old brother into wearing the high topped sneakers he hated.

Your tears. It's taken me a long time to understand those; to understand they weren't called out to evoke my need to "rescue you," but to appreciate the pain you felt, the relief you needed. Nonetheless that "rescue button" is real to me, and I know I must bear the added responsibility to protect my button. Maybe I should invent a button which says, "Hands off—this is MY button."

I respect your commitment to friends, the disenfranchised, to Jennifer and Amy and me.

Much love,

COMMENT: Beware of medical doctors who sound like medicine men and and medicine men who sound like medical doctors.

This section recalls a humorous look at my real-life antics struggling to extend my stay on Earth. the only positive effect was the placebo effect. This story is a corollary to the admonition, "Never trust a blind ambulance driver."

Last Rights

In July 1997, I took an ambulance ride to the hospital, but instead of my life flashing before me, preparing me for the final judgement, I only saw a limited selection of reruns which could have been out-takes off the editing room floor of the TV shows "This Is Your Life," "ER" and "Worlds Worst Home Videos." "In "concert,"they provided a therapeutic comedic relief, and stark terror. Let me start at the beginning:

For various reasons I conceived of the possibility that I might be having a heart attack. Even real doctors belabor the point that "the first few minutes are critical."The previous night, I had spoken with my doctor on the phone and received the instructions that although he wasn't greatly worried, if my symptoms (extreme tightness in left shoulder and neck) intensified I should go to the Emergency Room of the nearest hospital.

Some of the truest words ever spoken by Will Rogers were, "Man is an animal who would rather die than make an ass of himself." What if I cornered the market on "The world will end on June 8th" signs and it didn't? hee haw." Then there were the "boy who cried wolf" stories. Then there are all the supportive people who will be unconvinced by even a false alarm, especially if a false alarm was justified. Let's face it, there's not much sympathy for the guy who confuses the boat to cross the river Styx with the ferry to Staten Island. When, and if, one reaches the point that he/she is willing to risk "asshood," I can assure you he/she will want to make that trip as inconspicuously as possible.

Finally, at a time when the tightness escalated I called 911. I was prepared to accept the humiliation of an ignoble ambulance exit from my apartment house and put myself in the hands of a crack, experienced, alert, ER team. Instead let me tell you what really happened. 15 to 20 minutes after I called, a fire engine arrived. Yes I mean one of those giant trucks with loud horns and blaring sirens. It pulled into our quiet haven as unintrusively as the Queen Elizabeth II on her maiden voyage. Five minutes later, after I had received a call from the desk to see, "if it's alright to let them come up" (never fall for the old "burglar in a fire truck".

Four Fire Dept. employees arrived carrying a stethoscope and first aid kit. One of them explained since the ambulance hadn't arrived yet, they would take my vital signs. In another 15 minutes the "A team" arrived. I sat in a chair which took me to the lobby and out the front door as a small congregation of curious well wishers gathered.

The trip to the hospital was a health test far more demanding than any I received at the hospital. It's five minutes by car to Sibley hospital. My ambulance took 15 minutes, because the driver was lost. I had three clues this was the case. First, I felt us turn the wrong way. Let me tell you, this gets a patient's attention. Second, I saw us pass the same building twice. (Subsequent reflection would reveal that my heart must have been strong.) Third, I heard the good natured assistant loudly jibbing him, "Hey, man, ha ha, you're really lost." To which the driver replied, "Aren't we going to hospital #12." The only consolation I felt was that a DC taxi driver might have gotten more lost.

After we arrived they got right to the heart of the issue. "Was this a code 3 or code 4?" and "look at that B-CC ambulance over there." "Wow, I wonder how much it cost?" I felt like telling them that B-CC "probably skimped on fire trucks."

In brief, I survived. They saved the *piece de la resistance* for two weeks later when I got an envelope from the DC government suggesting that I send them "a voluntary contribution for $225 rather than wait for normal processing." Good old DC!

COMMENT: Death's so damned final

One was in his seventies; two were in their sixties; one was in her fifties; and one in his forties. This section remembers five people who added much to the quality of my life, whose recent loss hurts, and whose friendships I sorely miss.

Carolyn Young Hodnett
A Remembrance
March 8, 1997

Tuesday, March 5, wasn't an ordinary day in my life. It was the day Carolyn Young Hodnett left this world. Carolyn has truly been "a friend for life."

An early story comes to mind: She was the smartest, cutest girl in my third grade class. I was a holy terror, and she regarded me appropriately. In the third grade, she was the femme fatale of all third grade boys. She would not return my affection no matter how many times I pulled her pigtails and menaced her. In retaliation for her unpredictable behavior (as seen by me), I obtained the assistance of an older girl who was a family friend and had her write a note professing her great love to Charles Mee. She signed Carolyn's name to it. Charles responded to the unwitting Carolyn, stating in his best third grade prose that he reciprocated her affection. Carolyn tore up the note and threw it in the wastebasket where the third grade irregulars found it, pieced it back together, and teased poor Charles unmercifully.

Nichols Hills School justice was quick and sure. The principal, Miss Richardson, said simply to me, "You signed a girl's name, therefore, your punishment will be that you will wear a girl's dress for one day and be called Roberta." So there I was wearing blue jeans and a dress. Naturally, the boys reasoned that it was all Carolyn's fault and tried to bury her in the sandpile. Miss Richardson once again pronounced a fearsome sentence, this time on **Philip Griffing, Charles Mee and Clive Clark**. "You played with a girl, so you will also dress like one and, for one day, you shall be called Phyllis, Charlotte and Clementine."

By high school, I had gotten my act together, and Carolyn and I were good friends. We spent many hours talking on the phone about teenage subjects. This friendship carried through college, and her life in NY and Washington. I was in Carolyn's wedding.

When you have seen or talked on the phone with someone at least once a year ever since the third grade, you have a lot of remembrance. I think I called her on every birthday (May 2) for the last 25 years. I know I thought of her on that day from the age of ten, and will as long as I live.

When I think of Carolyn, I think first of her voice and the hundreds of hours we spent on the telephone, mostly before the eighth grade. Recently, I commented that she was a damn good phone conversationist, and in her most immodest statement ever, she giggled, "Yes, I really am, aren't I?" This was a milestone.

Actually, the thing that surprised me most was her lack of confidence about herself. I commented on this observation and told her I was amazed that she didn't know that the only reason she was chased at every opportunity by third and fourth grade boys was because they liked her. She said she knew it at some level, but, she shuddered at her remembrance of those days.

I think a love for truth and a great sense of humor were her two traits I found most endearing. These compliment one another because seeking truth necessitates a lot of disappointment, and a sense of humor is almost mandatory just to survive. Certainly, her most important role in my life was as a "co-investigator" in attempting to solve the crime of the century: Cancer. Let me explain in an unusual way. In 1992, I wrote a piece on Parkinson's Disease and the pro-active patient. Carolyn was certainly pro-active, and she liked the final chapter very much. It was a bond we shared. Part of it went as follows:

5:15 AM—The Solution

*Imagine you were listening to **Mystery Theater** on PBS.*

"Of course, Hastings, how can I be so stupid? It was right before our eyes all the time!" *Agatha Christie's great detective, Hercule Poirot, continues as we strain our ears and lean forward in our chairs to hear the solution of the "crime of the century." And, we love it, because we love a mystery, especially if it relates to "death." How much more would we be involved if we were **both** the victim and the detective?*

And so it was with me. It was 5:15 in the morning. What gave me the clue was a flashback to a conversation which occurred 29 years ago in Fort Monmouth, NJ. Some friends (actually Carolyn and her family) were visiting us, and we came upon their two young children merrily throwing gravel from our driveway at the side of our car! After a strong reprimand, their mother turned to me, and, as though it was the full explanation, sighed, "It's different when it's your own children!"

The great detective continues talking to his associate in my mind:

*"What kind of **being**, Hastings, can be so obsessed with finding his tormenter that he can ignore much of the pain from his own wound?"*

"Under what conditions, Hastings, can a man truly accept his fate while, at the same time, challenge it?"

"How can one love a disease, Hastings? How can someone become so engrossed with an insult, a threat to his very life, that he can turn this negative event into positive energy?"

*"In response to the first question, Hastings, 'only a **human** being' is the answer! In response to the second, 'only a human being who believes his actions will prevent further harm to others.' Finally, in the third case, 'only a human being who is capable of love/hate relationships!' There are many suspects, Hastings."*

*"That's the secret! It could be anyone with PD or cancer," I thought, and **a whole new insight opened up with this analogy.***

Cancer is the perfect card for a true mystery fan to draw and both Carolyn and I were sharing a real-time fight for life. In her case, she fought for about 15 years.

After I learned about my cancer of a lymph node in my neck, Carolyn was one of the first people I spoke to about it. I compared doctors' lists with her and modified my selection based on her experience.

We both sensed a bizarre love/hate relationship with cancer. I had noticed the same when I first found out I had Parkinson's Disease twelve years earlier. My story continued: *Although I hated what PD does to me and others, **I love a mystery and both PD and cancer are classics**. There is a relentless, evil force which terrorizes its victim; the high tech gadgetry to find ever more subtle clues; the feeling that the victim is running out of time; the bonding that occurs between investigator and victim; the dashed hopes and fears that come with the discovery of false leads; there are hypotheses to be tested and traps to be set; each alibi must be tested, each theory explored; new theories must be postulated. In fact, I realized I love playing the role of the detective so much that it lessens the pain of being the victim! To play, you must be pro-active. The process of "understanding your own" helped me accept my fate while, at the same time, I am rationally challenging it. It took my mind off the negative and shifted the emphasis positively to try to solve the problem. It draws on insights which only the victim's unique perspective allows him to see. I felt I could contribute to the solution of one of the "mysteries" of the century!*

*In my case, I actually derived some enjoyment from some of these moments. I took real pleasure in becoming an expert on me. I enjoyed setting forth theories (right or wrong) on possible relations between PD and jet lag, biorhythms, "smart cells," "frozen ideas," "bursts of thought," life-long problems with spelling, poor handwriting as a kid, dreams at night, the different roles of the left and right sides of the brain, the selectivity of neural-toxins, the diversity of symptoms, the commonality of symptoms, and the sharing of life drams. **Because I had been pro-active, Parkinson's and cancer have actually enriched my life in a significant way. If I hadn't been pro-active, played the detective, they would have been a complete loss! It's as simple as that!***

I believe Carolyn saw her life as a challenge to be met without regard to "fairness." Her sister had died in her thirties from breast cancer; she knew the odds, and without undo trepidation, faced that challenge. We knew only fictional detectives could avoid death, but being victimized didn't mean you had to behave as a victim. Further, even if hope was the elixir of Ozymandias, it must be consumed in its own time, even if historical perspective shows it to be part of the march of folly and human vanity. Surely, Shelly's Ozymandias was either a fictional king who lacked any sense of humor, or a real king who had a great one.

I believe Carolyn also shared my conclusions in that paper which bear very much in my thoughts on this, her funeral day.

Conclusions

I am awed by a human's ability to think, to have bursts of thoughts, to extract labels from the subconscious, each one with its attached story. I am awed by my mind's ability to amplify fear and depression so that seconds seem like years, and how quickly I can have full recovery with everything back in calm, orderly perspective. But what amazes me most of all is the uniqueness of each individual's <u>brain</u>, neurochemically, as is testified to by the wide variance in PD symptoms and varied responses to different drugs. Once again, it reminds us that there will never be one, single, pharmacological solution to all PD or Cancer symptoms. Further, when this incredible organ, our brain, is juxtaposed to the power of our <u>minds</u>, consciously and/or subconsciously, to mediate between conflicting genetically transferred survival instincts and information acquired through experience, one can only shake his head in appreciation of a higher order in nature than we will ever understand.

We shared a sense of adventure from being pro-active with our illnesses. We shared the awe of seeking higher truths than humankind can ever understand, much less articulate. Although she was a Renaissance woman with that special gift to attain new insights whether from a good book, a Bach fugue or a friend's problem. I am very thankful to have known her.

Joe Morford, R.I.P.
September 14, 1995

I can still visualize the first time I met Joe Morford. It was at the University of Oklahoma's geology field camp in Canon City, Colorado. He drove up in his Austin Healey with a big school boy smile and trim muscular body. He always retained his easy smile. Joe always reasoned that if one out of eight was good for oil wells, one out of two's not bad for physical conditioning.

Serendipity played a role in our next meeting. I was sitting next to Peter Debucher on a plane. We didn't know each other, but started talking. For some reason, he mentioned that Joe was his partner and gave me his number. We got together that night and had a helluva reunion. That was in about 1971, and I probably spent the night at Joe's home in San Francisco forty times after that and came to know Joe III and Mike as they grew up

Joe was one of a kind. He had an irrepressible generosity of spirit. He loved his family, he loved his friends. He enlivened everyone with whom he came in contact. His sense of humor was reflected in the name of his company, OFT, which he said stood for "Oil Field Trash." Nonetheless, he was a serious and innovative geologist who was happiest when he was up in his office working on a prospect.

He had fond memories of his bar tending days in Aspen. Despite an increase in weight, he would boldly venture down the Back Diamond trails at Vail. He would never admit that a trail existed he couldn't go straight down (this was important because he couldn't turn like he used to), and he nearly killed himself trying to keep up with my fourteen year old daughter on "Roger's Run." "Denial" was his middle name when it came to his "senior citizen skiing."

One of the funniest stories I've ever heard was about the time he and Bobby Hefner tried to sell their first big deal to a major oil company. His wife's father helped them get the introduction. They were dead broke and wanted to make a good impression. Unfortunately, they met a man at the bar they owed money so they stayed up all night drinking with him, giving him their first 200 best reasons he would have to wait a "few weeks to be paid." An hour before the meeting, Hefner reasoned that he needed "30 minutes of sleep to fine tune my game," and met Joe at the meeting. Joe went first, and he thought his presentation was, "OK except for the distraction caused by Hefner." Bob had his hands under the table and was moaning continuously while struggling with something unseen. Finally, Joe said, in a matter of fact fashion, "Mr Hefner will show you the specifics of our deal." Sheepishly Hefner produced a long ropy piece of paper that had been wound tight. He rolled it out on the table with fully 10 million wrinkles. The problem it turned out was he had left his briefcase key at his apartment and was tearing a hole in the soft corner of the brief case and then pulling the map through the hole while Joe was talking. They didn't get the job.

Joe's passing leaves a real void in my life. He was truly a good friend. Some of our most enjoyable moments were spent joking or talking seriously. He had a knack for reliving every moment of his life so as to share them with his friends. He never laughed at some one, always with them. Personal friendships were rated first in his value system. I remember his telling me about a friend who borrowed some money he never paid back. What bothered Joe most about it was, "I can understand the SOB wanting to spend my money on something else, but that's no excuse for not returning my phone calls."

This is not to say he didn't have some rough times, some sad times. He survived having less, and having more.

I don't know whether or not there's a heaven or hell, but I hope that whichever place I go, Joe's waiting to greet me, because it will be just a little bit better than it would have been otherwise, at least for me.

Robert Hastings
R.I.P.

A Remembrance

Bob Hastings died on October 23, 1996 at the age of 73. We met in 1963, soon after I joined the Agency. Bob Hastings was certainly "uncommon": An uncommon pursuer of truth; a man with a hearty yet wry sense of humor; a Renaissance man who appreciated both logic and the absurd. A man with one glass eye. To share an appreciation of Hastings, and his friendship, was reason enough to create a common bond between people otherwise only slightly known to one another. To some he was almost a cult figure although he would be abashed by the suggestion that he was even a good role model.

His favorite liquor was Armagnac. His favorite wine Clos de Tart. Both choices reflected careful deliberation based on empirical testing in the classic Aristotlean tradition. He believed man could enhance any moment if he "seized the day" whether that moment involved discussing the merits of a good Burgundy or debating the implications of the "J-booster." He disliked self-righteous pomposity whether it was on the part of the intelligence community or those who would abolish the intelligence community. He had a Jonathan Swift quality which showed both his amusement and dismay about the human condition. Recently, I shared a favorite cartoon with him. It pictured two old geezers sitting in enormous overstuffed chairs playing checkers in a fancy club. The caption read, "Call me a philosopher if you will, Harry, but I say if we weren't supposed to be on top, we wouldn't be on top." He liked it.

Then there was Beethoven whom he believed should be savored like all revelations of higher truths (and great ports) whose complexity was expressed in consummate simplicity

I can only remember upsetting Hastings one time. We had one employee who was Bob's opposite. While Hastings was logical and understated, this guy often

91

rushed to judgement, and took every point personally. One night I untruthfully said, "By the way, Bob, I hear Frank has a fantastic collection of Beethoven." There was silence as though he had just had a vision of Armageddon. After a long pause, he queried, in the voice of a mortally wounded man, "You're kidding, aren't you?"

His "library" (if "library" includes stacks of books he left behind, which far exceeded the capacity of his book shelves) documented deep interest in a pot-pourri of subjects including intelligence, cosmology, animals, travel, food, and sports lore.

His argumentative skills were legendary. He was a counter-puncher who didn't suffer fools lightly. Rather, he let them walk their own gangplanks, then, at the propitious moment would give a heaving laugh (followed by a deep chesty cough) and say, "I don't think so." The whys followed. Woe to him who was anxious to judge.

Dietary self-discipline was unquestionably his weakest suit, while eating and drinking were two of his greatest joys. He smoked like a chimney for many years. In 1972, in a futile attempt to get him to quit, I took his own estimate for the number of cigarettes he had consumed to date and multiplied it by the number of milligrams of tar in each cigarette. I submitted that if he had retained 20% of the tars, over half his body weight today could be attributed to that source. He sub-mitted in return that it just proved you can't believe everything a scientist says.

I didn't even try to dissuade him to reduce his culinary extravaganzas. I don't know anyone who enjoyed cholesterol as much as Bob, especially lobster with butter followed by a thick chocolate dessert. Clearly, he had a secret technique, for although he refuted all establishment medical advice, he far exceeded the life span of his closest friends by exploiting every opportunity to indulge himself in a quality feast. Clear also was the fact that exercise wasn't his secret weapon. If he had been a cult figure, it's amusing to visualize the appearance of his followers and contemplate how long they could have survived.

This is written primarily as a remembrance, not as an obituary. The latter would mention Audrey, his wife of 40 years, without mentioning her collection of over 3,000 crystal and ceramic rabbits. It probably would not take note of his deep sentiments toward Princeton '45 (to which he leaves the bulk of his estate). Finally, it would appropriately recognize the substantive contribution he made to CIA during the height of the Cold War when he served as one of the most respected and influential analysts of Soviet missile capabilities, particularly at the time of the Cuban Missile Crisis, when a mis-calculation could have changed the history of man.

In 1970 he joined EarthSat. He saw a great potential to apply technology developed in the intelligence community for civilian purposes. Although he suffered a pulmonary embolism, he valiantly tried to continue work. His health failed him again in 1972 when he suffered a stroke, and he finally retired. EarthSat did not have long-term disability insurance. I introduced him to my friend, and attorney, Tersh Boasberg, who won a landmark case in the U.S. Supreme Court in which Bob was awarded coverage under Workman's Compensation. A close friendship developed between them, and Tersh now serves as executor of his estate.

Bob's life after his retirement was a true challenge. His estate, and the award from workman's compensation combined, were only enough to provide for very modest living. While always scholarly in habits, he liked people. He had a close, loving relationship with his wife. But unfortunately, Audrey had long-standing medical and emotional problems so she depended on him. This made his work all the more gratifying, and his inability to work all the more painful. This situation may have deterred the development of a broader community support system.

His medical confrontations limited his stamina and restricted his ability to go out to museums or socialize. Although his mind remained generally clear, his speech was often slurred, and he became reclusive except for those brief moments he cherished with a few good friends for an occasional lunch. The vision in his one remaining eye was limited so that driving himself at night was impossible and a risk during the day. Even with all his medical and financial problems, he placed no burden on his friends or society; he maintained his mental gifts as well as he could through reading and listening to music. Unlike Job, I never once heard Bob curse his lot, express any self-pity, personal bitterness, nor envy of his fellow man. Rather, he pursued his love of life and the joys it allowed him until the very end.

One problem remains. Bob has no heirs or living relatives. What can be done with a house full of books and fine old wines? Books can wait, but wine has a finality that demands immediate attention and what are old friends for if not to save good wine from unfamiliar lips. I'm sure Bob will appreciate our help. Join us at 1 PM Saturday, 1 November 1996, at Tersh Boasberg's, 3136 Newark Street, NW, Washington, D.C., and raise a glass in memory of an uncommon man, Bob Hastings.

Mike Place

To Whom It May Concern:

Mike Place died of an unknown cancer today at age 46. He hypothesized it was caused by the times he spent riding his bike behind the pesticide truck to keep cool in the summer.

Wednesday, October 18, 2000

This is addressed primarily to the younger employees at EarthSat who didn't have an opportunity to know Mike Place because they are just too new. More specifically, it's about why Mike concerns you whether you knew him or not.

First, a thought: Isn't it interesting how many of the most valuable parts of our lives are affected by institutions or actions by people we never knew. Consider EarthSat and Mike Place. Certainly Mike "set the bar" for the industry as the author/programmer of image processing software. His mastery and understanding of mathematics, his insight into applications models, his ability to conceptualize models and invent short cuts which would literally cut orders of magnitudes off our competitor's fastest speed, was demonstrated time after time.

But Mike also "set the bar" in several other ways. For example, he was the soul of integrity and professional ethics. In recent years, he was a private consultant who shared our most valued secrets but never tried to parlay them with competitors. Most people interpret life in a way which gives them the answer they want to hear. This wasn't Mike's style. Recently Mike was thinking of starting a new company. He realized that EarthSat had great need of him to solve some immediate problems, and although he realized he might have limited time left, he honored his first obligation to help EarthSat. Mike "set the bar" in ethics and loyalty too.

Finally, Mike "set the bar" in humility. Although he was brilliant, he never tried to intimidate the less gifted; rather, he tried to listen to other's ideas to identify and utilize their best thoughts and give them the credit.

Even if you never knew Mike, your life has benefitted by him. EarthSat owes much of what it is today in technical capability, in integrity, and in respect between colleagues to where Mike "set the bar."

But does Mike's approach really work in the real world? Just ask some of the people who worked with Mike and mourn his loss today. What greater legacy can one leave than the respect for him that we, his fortunate friends, celebrate today. Which of us will contribute as much in the short time we have on this planet? To understand the challenge, ask someone who knew Mike.

CHARLES SHEFFIELD, R.I.P.
A Remembrance
by Bob Porter

Charles Sheffield died of brain cancer November 2, 2002. It wasn't suppose to happen this way. Certainly not in my mind. In fact, I had designated him as the "decision maker" in my living will. I felt good about having him accept that responsibility. It would relieve the burden for my wife and children. Charles would ask the best questions and make the right choice. I'd bet my life on it. I had bet on Charles many times over the last 40 years and it had always turned out right.

I first met Charles in 1963 through our neighbor, Don kahn, with whom Charles worked. Charles was in a class with very few peers in which the word "brilliant" truly applies. I was charged at NASA with allocating funds for remote sensing to academic institutions and government agencies. I often found their tactic was to make the process as technically complicated as possible so they could snow me with technical jargon. My response was to bring Charles' intellect to my side-of-the-table. It worked. He kept them painfully honest and had a significant long-term effect on the development of image processing technology for remote sensing.

Charles was just plain fun to be with. In Iran, we had a voluptuous secretary named Vicky. One day she brought in some special teas and homemade cakes for our working group. Charles, after thanking her, volunteered to reciprocate by taking her to lunch. She blushed from head to toe (which was clearly evident in her mini skirt.) Charles wondered if he had said something inappropriate and pulled a Persian-Italian staff associate aside. "I have two questions. I asked Vicky to lunch. First, is that tantamount to a proposal for marriage?" Pulyani said, "No." Charles looked relieved, then asked, "My second question is, will she bring her mother?" Pulyani thought a minute, and realized that if Vicky were a voluptuous twenty-year old, her mother would be a voluptuous forty-year old, and replied, "I don't think so, but if she does, call me!"

Charles learned to speak Farsi in about 4 weeks and could read and write it in 8 weeks. His technique for learning was to combine Farsi with English, incorporating more Farsi words into a mixed language sentence until he eventually had one in pure Farsi. Occasionally, this caused confusion. One time, he was reviewing some work with Vicky and said, "that's alright as is." Once again, she blushed, for the Farsi word 'as is' means 'darling.' While Charles claimed this was a mistake on his part, I remain skeptical.)

Charles seldom did anything conventionally. For example, he obtained his Ph.D. because he was senior author on academic papers on the subject of "general relativity." Some prominent professor friends thought it "improper" that they had been relegated to junior author status on some publications in which Charles was the senior author. Charles didn't have a Ph.D. They corrected this embarrassment by stapling his papers together, calling it his dissertation and awarded him his doctorate.

Charles joined EarthSat in 1970 and has served in numerous positions, including Chief Scientist, Vice President and a member of the Board of Directors. Few people associated with EarthSat have done more to advance our reputation. In addition, while working full-time at EarthSat, Charles, in his spare time, served as President of the American Astronomical Society (then, the largest aerospace organization), served as President of the Science Fiction and Fantasy Writers of America, published his first twenty books, over two hundred science fiction stories, numerous technical articles, served on many national committees, spoke on numerous talk shows and made several presentations to congressional committees. When EarthSat sued EOSAT for breach of contract, their counsel counter-claimed "that EarthSat unreasonably charged us for some people who couldn't possibly be working full-time at EarthSat while they were pursuing many other activities" and specifically cited Charles. In fact, he was working at least 40-hour weeks on EarthSat business. They lost. Furthermore, Charles spent more "spare time" talking with and teaching junior employees and attending EarthSat social functions than any other officer or director. Many of the great names at EarthSat came and stayed to work with Charles. His dedication of his first LandSat book, "Earthwatch" to "Lee and Bob Porter, for non-obvious reasons" is one of our most prized possessions.

Charles was an excellent negotiator. He would get all the facts out on the table and carefully explore the limits of each clause, examining functional relationships and explicit limits of each term. Sometimes he would even express them in the form of a mathematical equation, and then translate this back into English for consideration by the rest of us. He always looked at himself in a humorous perspective. He played a major role in negotiating our contracts with the Iranian government (in part because they didn't know he understood Farsi). Once I told him that an Iranian with whom we negotiated said Charles was the best negotiator he had ever met. Charles responded that he interpreted that to mean he was the worst, and that was why the Iranian preferred to work with him.

Charles was dedicated to seeking the truth as much as anyone I have known, regardless of whether the truth helped or hurt his own position. On the other hand he realized that good friends tell their friends hard truths. Charles took the time to read each of the books I have written in draft and final form. While being polite he was constructively blunt in pointing out criticisms that were valid and very instructive.

There are few people I can truly say influenced and enhanced my life every day. When I read a story I liked, and wanted to test my own understanding, I imagined explaining it to Charles. I would try to anticipate the questions he would ask, and how I would respond. It's a mental exercise I have gone through almost every day and expect to continue the rest of my life.

Finally, as I stood by Charles' bedside in the hospice, saying my final goodbye, a quote from MacBeth came to mind, which was taken, in part, by Charles for the title of my favorite Sheffield book, Tomorrow and Tomorrow. It is a story about a trip through space and time in pursuit of love lost by death. The relevance struck me, so I recited the MacBeth speech to Charles just as I had heard him recite it on several occasions:

> 'To-morrow, and to-morrow, and to-morrow
> Creeps in this petty pace from day to day
> To the last syllable in recorded time
> And all of our yesterdays have lighted fools the way to dusty death. Out, out brief candle
> Life's but a walking shadow, a poor player that struts and frets his hour upon the stage
> And then is heard no more.
> It is a tale told by an idiot, full of sound and fury,
> Signifying nothing.'

It's a harsh view of mankind's antics but one I think Charles shared. I must disagree with its conclusion, and I believe Charles' life proves my point. He meant a great deal to me and to others. He was one of the most loved people I have known. Charles played a significant role in many lives, especially his children's, in the only world we know. Charles signified much more than nothing. Even Charles can be wrong once.

COMMENT: Call, write, e-mail or visit a friend, preferably an old friend

There are many seasons or passages that we go through coincident with others, although we did not communicate about it at the time. College is an excellent example. There you find classmates having many similarities as well as differences. My class at Dartmouth operates an e-mail listserve through which over a hundred of us participate and share opinions on any subject without censorship. It's an opportunity to hear a diversity of opinions on a broad range of subjects. Many of these I never knew in college. If there is one thing I've done right it has been to call up old friends. It's truly amazing how many casual contacts have resulted in strong friendships. These are a few of my contributions.

re: Iraq
January 19, 1998

The Iraq confrontation brings to the forefront America's greatest strength and weakness, i.e., its respect for human life and its reticence to react to potential dangers. As a culture, we abhor bullies and give the presumption of innocence to the point of absurdity. Document this by the fact that there are thousands of murderers convicted every year in the U.S., but very few executions (even the co-conspirator in the Oklahoma City bombing was not given a death sentence). We must address a threat, bacteriological warfare, which puts the whole world at risk. If developed in Iraq, it would be subject to the direction of a man who has already demonstrated a willingness to use chemical agents on his own citizens. Further, he mocks our ethics by surrounding his facilities with a human shield of innocent civilians. Clearly, he is one of the most "certifiable evil men" in the history of despots.

Wouldn't it be nice if we could just "take him out." Regretfully, that's not easy, and, even more regretfully, probably won't be the ultimate solution anyway. One must ask who will be next? Evil as he may be personally, he is not alone in his malevolence. Genocide and mass hate killings are still in fashion, whether executed with machetes in Zaire, bombs in Bosnia, or chemicals in Iraq. The capacity for genocide is, I fear, in our genetic makeup, as is the drive to develop ever more powerful weapons. The potential of bacteriological warfare (BW) could end civilization as we know it either by intention or error.

Over the past 35 years, I have been involved with the intelligence community and have seen a great deal of material prepared for the president and his advisors. Technology, such as spy satellites, certainly played an important role in the Cuban missile crisis, but ultimately, the personal decision not to "push the button," was based on much more nebulous considerations. I have reached only one clear conclusion myself: that no one conclusion is ever uniquely clear. There are always other well reasoned alternative plans or means of execution. Ultimately the difficult decisions of history depend on the leader's "gut feeling" under conditions of great uncertainties. Even though the Soviets and Chinese represented an awesome threat, they were well aware of the unacceptable consequences of a nuclear holocaust. The implication is that we have to depend on enemies to also make rational decisions.

The most noteworthy point about the Iraq/Biological warfare crisis in a historical context will be as a milestone from a cold war period during which only super powers had to be reckoned with to a new phase in which even terrorist groups could pose a credible threat to large regions. As "weapons of mass destruction" fall within the technological capabilities of ever smaller groups, even suicidal cults, what will be the chances of preserving the public good while at the same time preserving human and civil rights? Today may be "the good old days."

This is a response to an Investment Letter from Ron Roth '57 Dartmouth. Its main point is that whether one is giving or taking investment advice over the next two years, a dominate consideration should be the likelihood of acts by terrorist. This must become an open issue if one is to do "due diligence." In the "middle game" there is a wide differential in the effect of terrorist's events depending on the company, its business line and location. In brief, the rules are depending on the company, its business line and location. In brief, the rules are going to change and we must change our perspective. Bob Porter

Investment Letter

May 10, 2002

Dear Ron,

I received your investment letter today and it stimulated some thoughts I'd like to share with you.

I'm neither an economist nor financial advisor, but I do claim extensive experience in analyzing intelligence matters. I've been actively working in the intelligence community for 35 years, and, if I do say so, I've gotten so that I can read between the lines pretty well. We are on the verge of one of the greatest terrorist incidents in history. The probability that such an event will occur in the next two years is close to 100%, I believe. The Maginot Line philosophy of reliving the past will once again fail us. We are so bloody naive that we believe we will be confronted by an enemy who plays by our rules, i.e. concentrates themselves in one place and wears clear well-marked uniforms. The most likely cause of this event will be the sale of Russian nuclear backpacks, which will easily destroy a city the size of Washington DC or level Manhattan. This could happen anytime because the technology exists and only an illegal sale is required to initiate this course of action. One would not necessarily have warning. This will not be good for the economy.

Speak about conflict of interest. Our government has one which puts Wall Street's in the shade and makes ENRON seem simple. Granted there are arguments against yelling "fire" or "Nuclear attack" until you've actually seen the mushroom cloud, but waiting until it's too late isn't a good solution either. Finally, what politician is going to give the bad news that his administration may not be able to stop it. They just keep on repeating their "buy America" theme to keep the economy up. They are unwilling to face the reality of what their own analysts tell them. Our vulnerability is added to by our insatiable urge to offend old friends and further insult old enemies.

For example, it's insane to name the next generation of tank, the "Crusader." (Like we don't have enough fronts to fight on already.) All the while, the number of people/governments who have sufficient technology to build a threatening "dirty nuclear weapon" or bacteriological warfare capability is growing. We are virtually at a point where we have to go into Iraq in order to intercept their technology before it becomes too dispersed.

The stock market's rise comes from a willingness to make long-term capital investments. The converse is true as well. The chaos associated from terrorism threatens every strategy an investor has. It literally boggles the mind. People casually say, "I don't want to live in a world like that." They think denial is the solution. This government is going to change, the likes of which we have never known. I'm no different than the rest of you. I just bought a new apartment in Washington DC (ground zero?)

Is there nothing an investor can do? Is there not a priority list of industries which will be affected to different degrees? THERE IS SOME GOOD NEWS. Terrorism may be able to bring a government down, but it can not replace it. There is not the danger in the near term that all of civilization is threatened by a nuclear holocaust as there was during the cold war. There may be a spare weapon or two, but that can't destroy civilization. If we consider acts of terrorism, isn't there something we can do to protect our investments?

IS THERE A RATIONAL INVESTMENT PHILOSOPHY FOR IRRA-TIONAL TIMES? For example, should we sell travel and cruise ship stocks if large crowds won't congregate for fear of terrorism? Will the price of gold increase? Will the insurance companies be hit first? Will geographically dispersed companies be protected? Will domestic air transportation decline. Oil seems like a particularly promising commodity. It's sensitive to subtle political fluctuations. One can buy from a company that has predominately domestic production and would be bullet-proof if foreign oil was denied us. On the other hand, one could invest in companies which have large reserves of foreign oil, but could resist political pressures to cut off oil sales to the US.

There are a dozen ways to play the oil game. You can bet (hope) that the CIA and the Department of Energy are performing analyses like this right now. I'm not trying to reshape your career, I'm just pointing our that there is a rational "middle game" strategy. It seems to me that consideration of terrorism should be part of anyone's investment strategy for tomorrow.

If this stimulates any thoughts, I'd be interested in hearing them. If you are just inclined to pull the covers up a little higher and not write, that's okay too.

Best regards,

Vox Clamatis in Deserto

January 22, 1998

The potential of E-mail has barely been touched. It truly represents a revolutionary moment in mass communications history. My class at Dartmouth, for example, has set up a bulletin board which permits anyone in the class to "publish" anything which may be on his mind through the good offices of Dartmouth College. Approximately 100 subscribers/participants have signed up. It provides a fantastic opportunity for Dartmouth classmates to communicate on a wide variety of subjects which thus far have included a large number of jokes (generally in good taste); opinions about what traits should be sought (or avoided) in the current search for a new college president; some exchange of opinions about current political issues, such as proposed U.S. actions in Iraq; a few remembrances from bygone days of long-gone friends; and some sharing of wisdom or at least perceptual observations attributable to maturing. A classmate has served as "Webmaster" and overseen the compilation or editorial function, albeit limited. To date, I would say the harshest criticism which could be launched would be a paucity of substance.

But, hold on. Is a free press really what **all** the people want? The differentiation between "freedom" and "anarchy" owe much to the eye of the beholder. For some, it may be alright for a "voice to cry in the wilderness," but what if someone actually listens and doesn't like what he or she hears? What if some jokes are considered "offensive" or "insensitive"; some opinions about faculty and college administrators interpreted to be "mean spirited," perhaps some might say, "libelous"; political discussions, "biased by the 'evil Web Meister's' hushed censorship"; or what if a classmate's fond remembrance invades another classmate's sense of privacy. Is the college libel? Can the Webmaster be sued? Can't anyone be sued for anything, substance aside? Who will pay for his defense? Is insurance needed? Is a declaration of editorial policy needed? What are the rules for this brave new world?

Note: At least four new foundations were started as a result of this stimulus.

Some Reasons You Might Consider Starting Your Own Charitable Foundation
May 16 1999

Perhaps you realize you can't take it with you; perhaps you care more about what you leave behind for future generations. Certainly our college class is at an age in which the disposition of our estates becomes of greater interest.

Ten years ago my mother died leaving an inheritance that, when added to my own assets, covered my estimated requirements for living out the rest of my years and taking care of my family obligations. It became evident to me that I also had obligations to the community that had treated me so well, and reflected on the fact that many of the benefits I enjoyed in my life were made possible by people whose names I never knew. At first, I thought that I had too little funds to make it worthwhile to start my own foundation. I am now very pleased I did and would like to share some of my reasons for my conclusion on the supposition that some classmates might be considering the same issue:

First, estate taxes reach the 55% level soon after the unified exemption of $650,000 (currently) runs out. Thus above that point **you can either let your congressman determine where that 55% goes, or with a modicum of pre-planning, you can start a foundation and let the trustees (often family members) make that decision.**

Second, **profits are not taxable but are retained directly to build your charitable investment base.** Under tax laws you have to give away 5% of your charitable assets annually. Of course, you can always give more if you wish. For example if you had a good year in the market and made more than 5%, you could share your good fortune with an organization you want to support without markedly diminishing your asset base. Alternatively, if you saw a particularly worthwhile activity you could give any portion of the assets, or even all, and terminate the foundation.

Third, by just having funds set aside for charitable purposes, you think about your role in life and your responsibilities differently. As Dartmouth Professor Rosenstock-Huessey used to point out: The Greeks drew a distinction between "speakers, conversationalists, and talkers." Declaring your commitment in the formation of a foundation is a serious act. It puts you in the role of a "speaker," one who occupies a position of "responsibility" as distinguished from a "talker" or "conversationalist" who lack a formal relationship to the subject matter. This means that you are subconsciously looking for good causes to affirm and not just reacting to outside pressures to support what others want from you. You become a more educated and sophisticated "shopper."

Fourth, you learn to network with other foundations and individuals. This is a key for maximizing the effectiveness of your contributions. As a donor, you want to get the greatest impact for your contribution. One way is to provide incentives for additional contributors by requiring that your grant be matched as a "challenge grant."

Raising more money is one way to increase support for your causes. **But where does your money really go once you have given it?** You still have to protect your investment to insure its uninterrupted journey to serve the purpose for which it was donated. Often to accomplish this we have applied disciplines in which we had to be the "heavy," the "tough cop," to insure maximum use was to be made of our gift for the purpose we intended. For example, to insist that no overhead would be charged by a university or medical institute. (The recipient, or Project Director, can not argue this very effectively within his/her own institution, rather he usually "plays the game.")

Finally, it is unfortunate but true that **there are many more well meaning charities than well run charities.** None-the-less, effectiveness is a relevant part of the philanthropic decision. Networking is tremendously useful to insure that your contribution goes to the need with reasonable efficiency. Further, you should require a short follow up report on the project results. This is much more likely to be satisfactory if you are affiliated with a foundation. (We almost always require it)

One of the most frequently asked questions is, **"What is the minimum amount I need to put aside to make it worth the trouble** of setting up and administering a foundation? It's a little bit like asking, "How big of a garden should I plant?" The answer is that it depends on whether or not you're a gardener or just enjoy gardens.

If you're the former, you won't mind a lot of work and your outside costs would be minimal (one to three hundred dollars per year.) The basic bookkeeping is not very demanding, because you're not going to be processing a lot of information. IRS requirements are minimal. Naturally, the foundation pays it own expenses including trustee travel to board meetings and secretarial support.

One of the most important early decisions you will make is whether to consider unsolicited proposals or whether you will search out possible candidates and then "invite" a proposal. I prefer the latter approach, at least initially, because you maintain control, and it will probably take you a couple of years to set your priorities.

I think our case was fairly typical. We have a board of directors, which consists of our four immediate family members and one long-time friend. Our children are now in their thirties, and so we divide the responsibilities. Our interests are as diverse as our personalities, but we also share many common interests. One function of a foundation is that it makes its trustees aware of their financial limitations. You've got to choose between grantees. You can't support everything. **It's normal in the first few years to learn the lessons and benefits of diplomacy within your board.** I was interested in supporting geological and medical research. My wife is very concerned about problems of the homeless and the very poor. Both of us knew good candidates. Our children have sharpened their interests to include activities close to their lives today. In particular, we all believe the inner city poor need our attention. Fortunately, there are a number of good efficient organizations in Washington to address this issue.

In our case, **we have followed a typical route of progressing from being passive donors who respond to "invited proposals" to becoming a foundation which defines a specific project** which originated in major ways within our foundation. Specifically, we believe in helping people empower themselves (learn to fish not just to eat fish). The object of this program is to motivate teenagers to learn how to raise money, network, and to become aware of what they can do with a few skills and a lot of enthusiasm. We call the program "Make a difference." We're just completing the first year and are very encouraged.

In its second year, we are expanding the program and have prepared brochures that we are sending to about fifty schools and church groups from which we expect to select six to ten. We will match every two dollars they raise with one dollar. It puts them in a position to go to other foundations and individuals and say, "Someone already believes in us. If you'll help we'll get a match." The first dollar is often the hardest. Most of their funding comes from student organized activities.

Both of the schools we went to first already had active community assistance programs underway. **One school, Archbishop Carroll, had a major community program in which they prepared and distributed several hundred sandwiches per week for the homeless even though they were dependent on public transportation!** They needed a van, but couldn't afford one. With a match from our foundation they raised the funds they needed. **Another of their community programs stands out among all the ones we've seen. They collected 25,000 pounds of food from residents in lower middle class neighborhoods and distributed it to the inner-city's very poor.** Their organizational and logistical planning was awesome. Every child in the school participated in this Thanksgiving effort. Talk about self-empowerment!

There are many other issues a foundation addresses which are different from those faced by conventional donors. Privately, you are declaring a priority. The legal structure is simple; the administrative cost can be minimized. On the other hand there are additional activities in which you may want to participate for only slightly more money. For example, there are nonprofit organizations such as the Council on Charitable Foundations that hold several meetings a year and organize presentations by both large and small, established, and new, philanthropist on their experiences. Also, there are many local and regional groups who meet frequently to network. Even very small foundations can play an active role in these, if they wish.

There are many other reasons for setting up your own foundation, including the family conversations (including arguments) which stimulate the co-development of values with your children. The costs to set it up and to administer it can be contained, if you're personally able to do some work. The foundation experience is an education. It opens your eyes to new worlds. It provides a natural way to interact with other people, who have elected to be "part of the solution."

Some people say that you ought to have a minimum of $100,000 to a million dollars to make it worthwhile to establish a foundation. I strongly disagree. I believe that what the world needs most today are more people who have made a commitment within their means to "do something." I believe that we need people who know enough to ask good questions. I question why it is necessary to pay as much as we do to fund raisers for worthy causes (like the alumni fund). I believe we need families who learn to respectfully debate their preferences for different causes.

But I digress. **The lowest financial boundary for creating a foundation should be the point at which you would diminish the success of your moral agenda,** i.e., where you become less effective than if you hadn't created a foundation. There is no question in my mind that learning the ropes of the foundation world and how to network within it increases one's effectiveness as a philanthropist. Certainly you can work within a church or other community activity and attain great accomplishments. But establishing your own foundation is different. It's not necessarily better, nor, to my knowledge, more appropriate in your case, nor are they mutually exclusive means. The point of this commentary is simply to help you consider one option.

How low is low? Let's make an assumption that one funded it initially at $25,000 and earned 10% annually. That's one fortieth of an often voiced million dollar minimum. If he/she funded it subsequently by making a yearly $5,000 gift (deductible up to 20% of your gross income). It would have created a legal entity and got the process underway. Based on these assumptions, in just five years it would grow to approximately $67,000 and it would have already paid out $11,500 in grants. (A 20 year schedule is attached with examples of different levels of investment and different rates of return.)

One can make a difference even at that level. The following examples of the importance of relatively small grants is taken from the brochure of our "Make a difference" project.

HERE ARE SOME EXAMPLES OF THINGS YOUR SCHOOL COULD DO AND THE IMPACT IT WOULD HAVE ON THESE PROBLEMS:
YOUR SCHOOL CAN MAKE A DIFFERENCE…

\$4500 provides six months of housing and support for a formerly homeless and addicted person to gain employment and reestablish his life in a drug/alcohol recovery program ($3000 school, $1500 match).
* $1500 pays for three people working minimum wage jobs to learn computer and other marketable skills to be eligible for higher paid employment ($1000 school, $500 match).
* $2000 pays full medical costs for one day for 34 homeless patients at an infirmary for homeless men ($1334 school, $666 match).

$1698 pays for a student to have a year of tutoring to take the GED exam ($1132 school; $566 match).
$8000 turns a city lot into a garden ($5333 school, $2667 match).

Please note that the above figures were obtained from D.C. organizations that the Porter Foundation has provided grants to. We would like to thank the following organizations for providing these figures: Academy of Hope, Christ House, Good Shepherds Ministries, Jubilee Jobs, Manna, New Community Church and Samaritan Inns.

Establishing a foundation may be unreasonable in your case. Expenses and/or time may be too much. I picked the "$25,000 scenario" as an extreme example to make a point. More would be better but a modest amount can have an impact. I **am not advocating that everyone with $25,000 should start a foundation. I am recommending that more people look at their resources, then consider building a foundation with the establishment of an initial grant and subsequent grants. I am challenging the stereotype that philanthropy is just a rich man's sport.**

In summary, if you're someone who has the interest, the will, and a little extra money. You may want to have more knowledge and control over how it's spent. If you do form a foundation, it may change your life, as well as the lives of others.

ATTACHMENT I–EXAMPLES

There are numerous strategies to apply in setting up a foundation. In all likelihood one would plan to have it be multi-year and probably multi-generation. The following examples present initial funding levels of $25,000, $50,000, $100,000, and $250,000, all at a 10% rate of return. It is also assumed that $5,000 is put in each year in every case. The following details are given in case you want to set up your own spread sheet.

Column A "Year"

Column B "Foundation Capitalization" In year one this is the initial contribution. In subsequent years it is carried over from column G in the previous year. This presents the asset value as of the **beginning** of the each year

Column C "Year end Contribution" This assumes that one makes a supplemental contribution each year.

Column D "Year end Disbursements" Grants made over the course of the year.

Column E "Interest" The rate of return on investments. This is the tough one.

Column F "Year end assets" Calculated by multiplying (1+Column E) times Column B and adding Column C

Column G "Assets minus Disbursements" Column F minus Column D. These are the **year end** assets.

Year	Foundation Capitalization	Year end Contribution	Year end Disbursements	Interest rate	year end assets	Assets minus Disbursements
1	$25,000	$5,000	$1,625	10%	$32,500	$30,875
2	$30,875	$5,000	$1,948	10%	$38,963	$37,014
3	$37,014	$5,000	$2,286	10%	$45,716	$43,430
4	$43,430	$5,000	$2,639	10%	$52,773	$50,134
5	$50,134	$5,000	$3,007	10%	$60,148	$57,140
6	$57,140	$5,000	$3,393	10%	$67,854	$64,462
7	$64,462	$5,000	$3,795	10%	$75,908	$72,113
8	$72,113	$5,000	$4,216	10%	$84,324	$80,108
9	$80,108	$5,000	$4,656	10%	$93,118	$88,462
10	$88,462	$5,000	$5,115	10%	$102,309	$97,193
11	$97,193	$5,000	$5,596	10%	$111,913	$106,317
12	$106,317	$5,000	$6,097	10%	$121,949	$115,851
13	$115,851	$5,000	$6,622	10%	$132,436	$125,814
14	$125,814	$5,000	$7,170	10%	$143,396	$136,226
15	$136,226	$5,000	$7,742	10%	$154,849	$147,106
16	$147,106	$5,000	$8,341	10%	$166,817	$158,476
17	$158,476	$5,000	$8,966	10%	$179,324	$170,358
18	$170,358	$5,000	$9,620	10%	$192,393	$182,774
19	$182,774	$5,000	$10,303	10%	$206,051	$195,748
20	$195,748	$5,000	$11,016	10%	$220,323	$209,307

Year	Foundation Capitalization	Year end Contribution	Year end Disbursements	Interest rate	year end assets	Assets minus Disbursements
1	$50,000	$5,000	$3,000	10%	$60,000	$57,000
2	$57,000	$5,000	$3,385	10%	$67,700	$64,315
3	$64,315	$5,000	$3,787	10%	$75,747	$71,959
4	$71,959	$5,000	$4,208	10%	$84,155	$79,947
5	$79,947	$5,000	$4,647	10%	$92,942	$88,295
6	$88,295	$5,000	$5,106	10%	$102,124	$97,018
7	$97,018	$5,000	$5,586	10%	$111,720	$106,134
8	$106,134	$5,000	$6,087	10%	$121,747	$115,660
9	$115,660	$5,000	$6,611	10%	$132,226	$125,615
10	$125,615	$5,000	$7,159	10%	$143,176	$136,017
11	$136,017	$5,000	$7,731	10%	$154,619	$146,888
12	$146,888	$5,000	$8,329	10%	$166,577	$158,248
13	$158,248	$5,000	$8,954	10%	$179,073	$170,119
14	$170,119	$5,000	$9,607	10%	$192,131	$182,525
15	$182,525	$5,000	$10,289	10%	$205,777	$195,488
16	$195,488	$5,000	$11,002	10%	$220,037	$209,035
17	$209,035	$5,000	$11,747	10%	$234,939	$223,192
18	$223,192	$5,000	$12,526	10%	$250,511	$237,986
19	$237,986	$5,000	$13,339	10%	$266,784	$253,445
20	$253,445	$5,000	$14,189	10%	$283,789	$269,600

Year	Foundation Capitalization	Year end Contribution	Year end Disbursement	Interest rate	Year end assets	Assets minus Disbursements
1	$100,000	$5,000	$5,750	10%	$115,000	$109,250
2	$109,250	$5,000	$6,259	10%	$125,175	$118,916
3	$118,916	$5,000	$6,790	10%	$135,808	$129,017
4	$129,017	$5,000	$7,346	10%	$146,919	$139,573
5	$139,573	$5,000	$7,927	10%	$158,531	$150,604
6	$150,604	$5,000	$8,533	10%	$170,664	$162,131
7	$162,131	$5,000	$9,167	10%	$183,344	$174,177
8	$174,177	$5,000	$9,830	10%	$196,595	$186,765
9	$186,765	$5,000	$10,522	10%	$210,442	$199,920
10	$199,920	$5,000	$11,246	10%	$224,912	$213,666
11	$213,666	$5,000	$12,002	10%	$240,033	$228,031
12	$228,031	$5,000	$12,792	10%	$255,834	$243,042
13	$243,042	$5,000	$13,617	10%	$272,347	$258,729
14	$258,729	$5,000	$14,480	10%	$289,602	$275,122
15	$275,122	$5,000	$15,382	10%	$307,634	$292,253
16	$292,253	$5,000	$16,324	10%	$326,478	$310,154
17	$310,154	$5,000	$17,308	10%	$346,169	$328,861
18	$328,861	$5,000	$18,337	10%	$366,747	$348,410
19	$348,410	$5,000	$19,413	10%	$388,250	$368,838
20	$368,838	$5,000	$20,536	10%	$410,722	$390,186

Year	Foundation Capitalization	Year end Contrib.	Year end Disbursements	Interest rate	Year end assets	Assets minus Disbursements
1	$250,000	$5,000	$14,000	10%	$280,000	$266,000
2	$266,000	$5,000	$14,880	10%	$297,600	$282,720
3	$282,720	$5,000	$15,800	10%	$315,992	$300,192
4	$300,192	$5,000	$16,761	10%	$335,212	$318,451
5	$318,451	$5,000	$17,765	10%	$355,296	$337,531
6	$337,531	$5,000	$18,814	10%		$357,470
7	$357,470	$5,000	$19,911	10%	$398,217	$378,306
8	$378,306	$5,000	$21,057	10%	$421,137	$400,080
9	$400,080	$5,000	$22,254	10%	$445,088	$422,834
10	$422,834	$5,000	$23,506	10%	$470,117	$446,611
11	$446,611	$5,000	$24,814	10%	$496,272	$471,459
12	$471,459	$5,000	$26,180	10%	$523,605	$497,425
13	$497,425	$5,000	$27,608	10%	$552,167	$524,559
14	$524,559	$5,000	$29,101	10%	$582,014	$552,914
15	$552,914	$5,000	$30,660	10%	$613,205	$582,545
16	$582,545	$5,000	$32,290	10%		$613,509
17	$613,509	$5,000	$33,993	10%	$679,860	$645,867
18	$645,867	$5,000	$35,773	10%	$715,454	$679,681
19	$679,681	$5,000	$37,632	10%	$752,649	$715,017

WHEN "HOME" BECOMES "THE FRONT"

October 20, 2002

Attached is a letter sent to me by Joan Talley, wife of John Talley, Dartmouth Class of '50, and brother of Tom Talley, Class of '58. I first met John at the Dartmouth WRITE course and discovered we shared a common bond of both being from Oklahoma. Shortly thereafter, he visited his son who lives in Bali and was so captivated by the island that he moved his principle resident from Santa Fe to Bali. John is a practicing psychoanalysts. Today I received a copy of this letter from John to his friends. I think in the context of all the discussions we've had on whether or not to bomb Iraq, this represents an up close and personal insight into the war on terrorism. This letter speaks volumes and I will only submit a few initial reactions of my own.

First, this doesn't resolve unequivocally in my mind whether or not we should bomb Iraq, but it does reinforce the fact that war is hell and no matter how many proxies our president holds, the result of bombing is still hell and, eventually, what goes around comes around.

Second, that still leaves us with the issue of how much does it take to justify "sufficient provocation" to require "preemptive" military action? Presumably, to lessen the amount of misery ultimately unleashed on mankind (or does this just initiate it?).

Finally, dare I point out that man's inhumanity towards man as witnessed in Africa or Croatia or the Middle East doesn't make me very optimistic that man has the will to restraint exercising the option of unleashing weapons of mass destruction. If man has these weapons he will use them. In Washington DC, one madman or terrorist has generated enormous fear with his string of 12 shootings, how this pales when compared to the casualties in Israel and Palestine, Afghanistan and now, in Indonesia. It is said that there are only six degrees of separation between the poorest and most disenfranchised individual and the most reclusive businessman or government bureaucrat. For the Dartmouth graduate, the chain to the decision maker is usually much shorter. It is important that we

116

use such influences we have wisely and not glibly, as I think we sometimes do on the listserv. John Tally knows this now from the perspective of one degree of separation. Read it and weep.

Dear Everyone,

What to say to you all about our experience of the bombing here in surfers' paradise (and sin city also} called Kuta. Immediately, gloom and sadness. Sadness for the injured and dead, sadness for the invasion/rape of this island that has for so very long felt separate and different, sadness for the immediate and long-term added poverty that will affect everyone in one way or the other. The more than 20 workers who are building son Mark's new house next to us wore long faces and there was none of the happy chatter that makes living next to a building site here a delight. His project is of course in doubt along with the projects of endless others whom we know or can imagine. Everything needs to be rethought. Everything I can tell, America already knows.

The size of the task and potential for disarray can be judged by numbers. The biggest hospital in Denpasar, the biggest city and near to Kuta, has places in its morgue for 10 bodies, and within hours the dead were listed over a hundred; warm weather and no refrigeration but ice and running out of that and other resources, crowds of people looking for their dead, and many others as always drawn to the lurid scene. An American woman doctor married to a Balinese was saying the hospital did not have the needed facilities for burn patients but there was no plan as yet to send them to a hospital in Surabaya on Java where they could get the treatment they need.

As the newspapers will have told you the Australians flew out their dead and injured back home very soon, but many families arrived to report missing children and wait. As for who did it, well everyone under the sun has been named, including of course the Americans.

Our only sense of fear came when a rumor spread that a bomb had exploded in the main town near our small village, That really gave us pause for thought…as well as hearing that all Americans were being asked to come home. It would have been good to be forced to evaluate the need for and the price of safety but the rumor was quickly proven to be untrue and we continued with our volunteer work. None of the experts we know or saw have given any thought to leaving.

More interesting were the kind of omens that are taken seriously by important people here that appeared in the 3 days before the bomb: a huge turtle had come ashore and it took 20 men to get it back into the ocean, a smell of death had been noted around Kuta and was traced to a huge flower, "raplesia" one meter across and 2/3 of a meter high that actually grows on one on the islands but is never seen in Bali, and perhaps the most seriously considered of all was the appearance of a bright star in the

NW sky persisting three nights and through the Saturday night. This star had been seen only twice before, each time three days before terrible disasters: in 1942 the Japanese invaded and occupied Bali and in 1968 the sacred mountain Gunung Agung, the site of the great Besaki temple, the St Peters of Balinese Hinduism, erupted killing many and destroying many villages in its lava path.

Our young driver and manservant has had nightly dreams of dead person's spirits asking for or needing help. In one he and John are carrying a stretcher with a dead person to the hospital. Contrast this with his more mundane but really urgent worry about jealousy (which is endemic in the small tightly knit villages here) Often I ride on his motorcycle for short distances. But he would not take me as usual saying that he feared the jealousy of friends who now knew that they would never again have access to foreigners, while he was free to flaunt his lucky state.

John and I became a part of the major export organizational effort at the major hospital to properly list the dead, missing, injured and evacuated and serving the families, international and Indonesian who came to find what was mostly going to be bad news or no news. In what ways this astounding largely female organizational ability with its unabashed "takeover ism" was coordinated with what the Balinese/Indonesians were doing I will wait to find out later when the ladies from the trenches come home. But almost surely their efforts were needed for as Mark says and we know from experience in matters that are not traditionally Balinese such as art and rice growing they do things 25% and call it 100% and the missing 75 is simply of no interest. John was able to do some supportive work such as being beside a lone lady who had come from Australia to look for "the niece of a friend" Actually she was one of the lucky/unlucky ones for she found the niece through a picture of the body. Now she must go through an elaborate identification process before the body can be released. I was Coordinator of Councilors and that was a matter of spotting among the volunteers ones that could fill useful roles and getting them to the spot and working. As we all know one problem is too many volunteers who crowd the scene and confuse the happenings and yet this was in some way everyone's event so learning to deal with that was useful. We certainly learned a lot about crisis management and have now been called by one of the major helping organizations to do therapy if needed. We meet with them next week.

The afternoon before the horror Mark and Karen's 3-months-old-son was given a lovely Buddhist blessing ceremony in the down stairs of our house, which became a beautiful temple. The ceremony was done by a very good friend of Marks (who had once upon a time introduced Mark and Joan to the Dalai Lama). Our house was filled with the sight and scent of flowers and incense and tongkas and safron cloths and the baby, Chakra by name, (a not unusual name in Thailand) uttering fine sounds of agreement at the right moments.

As Dickens wrote in his story set in the time of the French Revolution "It was the best of times, it was the worst of times" and so it is here. The tragedy is multi dimensional, the positive part being in the rallying of the community, among the Balinese and between them and us. There is so much to tell, so much to mourn, so much to value. Thank you for your concern. We are well and will be careful.

John and Joan

Exchange at 4:30 in the Morning
December, 1995

He said he was working on the conclusion to his book.
She said she was working on her credo statement.

He said, "The Truth depends upon the questions."
She said, "There is no human truth, only understanding."

He said, "The Greeks seek the word, *logos*, and truth.
The Jews seek the law, *ethos*, and judgement."
She said, "The Greeks perverted understanding by
too much examination and intellectualization of truth."

He said, "Faith doesn't matter, it's what you do that counts.
Faith without action is meaningless."
She said, "Faith is what empowers man to action."

He said, "Death is life's greatest mystery."
She said, "The revelation comes in life,
through the living Christ."

He said, "I'm not so sure. What if revelation
doesn't come until death?"
She said, "I believe God reveals himself through life."
"I am who I am. I will be, who I will be."

He said, "Who said that?"
She said, "God, from the burning bush!"

He said, "That's pretty good. In fact, it's great. All but
the burning bush part."
She said, "You never know where God will reveal herself."

He said, "Touche. I like the way you're thinking.
She said, "I'm not trying to think, I'm just trying to understand."

Conversation with a Psalmist
December, 1995

She said,

"When you have your health for sixty years,
how can you help but praise the Lord?"

"When you've had 60 years of friends and wealth, how can you
not believe God is Good?"

"When you have a safe place to sleep and good food to eat,
how can you not believe God is just?"

But, I said,

"If the earth openes up and swallows your home and crushes your children, how
can you believe that God is omniscient?"

"If a terrorist explodes a bomb outside your child's daycare center,
how can you believe that God is omnipotent?"

Then she said,

"But the down and out find God first!
The closer you are to death, the nearer you are to God."

I concluded:

"It's hard to be a Psalmist,
if you don't know the rules of the game."

Waiting for Armageddon
May 6, 2002

Living in the "days following 911," I can't help but reflect on our last great crisis in which millions of lives were at stake and the strange set of circumstances which affected my personal behavior.

One can measure crisis by the level of readiness for war our armed forces are assigned. "DefCon4" (Defense Condition 4) is the highest level of military alert. We have only reached that level on one occasion: during the Cuban Missile Crisis when the Soviet union was about to break the naval barricade around Cuba, I was at Fort Monmouth, New Jersey, serving two years of active duty as a signal corps officer.

It was October 1962. The public was well aware of world events after Adlai Stevenson's compelling presentation at the United Nations. Everyone was on edge. At SAC headquarters, near Omaha, B-52's were loaded with nuclear weapons, engines on, ready for take-off on 5 minutes notice. In Washington, at the CIA and Pentagon, recent KH7 satellite photos were studied. Communication intercepts to assess Soviet intentions and actions were continually paraded in from NSA carried in by an endless cadre of bleary-eyed colonels. This was the time of the MAD (Mutual Assured Destruction) policy which meant the Soviets and Americans had far more weapons than anyone possibly needed to destroy mankind. Machine guns were set behind sand bags at major intersections bordering Ft. Monmouth. One New York City disc jockey tried to be light-hearted about it and gave his weather forecast as "5,000 degree centigrade downtown, slightly cooler in the suburbs." He was fired. I'm a pro-active person so I put a few cans of beans away in our home near Ft. Monmouth, where the military had built a great whistle/horn which could be heard for miles around. It was designed to pass on general conditions to knowledge starved troops. It had no doubt been the product of a military brainstorming sessions (an oxymoron). It was a twentieth century answer to the mediaeval town crier who would announce "ten o'clock and all's well." Naturally, the Army wasn't satisfied to copy mediaeval simplicity so they contrived to have it convey a vast array of information which ranged in significance between "The Corporal of the guard is at his post" to "Nuclear attack—take cover." Furthermore, whistle codes were assigned according to when they were introduced to the system rather than having to do with their importance. There were about 60 messages which could be conveyed this way, and each soldier had his list for handy reference. Finally, to make a bad situation impossible, living around a big horn, day in and day out, became like the train or church bells which keep you awake for the first week but get filtered out after a short time so it's barely noticeable.

It was a night in which the Earth was still while 2,000 feet above the ground clouds raced furiously. It was an ominous, surrealistic, "witches sky," which I'd often seen preceding a tornado when I was growing up in Oklahoma. I had gone to bed and just dozed off when I became aware of a whistle blowing far away. Quickly I sprang from my bed and ran to the dresser to retrieve the "signal recognition list." The problem I found was that there was some confusion as to whether they had just changed the guard (12 shorts, 13 longs) or we were at war (13 shorts and 12 longs). Suddenly, a way to resolve the issue flashed in my mind. "Connelrad, the emergency broadcast network" was especially set up to communicate instructions to civilians in case of nuclear war. I hastily pulled out my battery powered radio and turned it on. I thought I remembered about where it was suppose to be. A voice cut through the sleepy fog. It broke out with confidence building clarity reserved for a radio preacher's voice, who said, **"Now everybody stay tuned, we're going to read the Bible from beginning to end."**

It was too perfect. I was convinced. I turned off my radio and reviewed my alternatives. My mind was perfectly clear. There was no panic. The world was in no hurry. There was plenty of time for everything. There was no place to hide. No shelter to protect us. It was exactly like times I had been in bed in Norman, Oklahoma, and the weather siren announced that a tornado was sighted within the town limits. We had no basement so I just pulled up the blanket and hoped it went away. So it was in New Jersey that night: I had just heard an announcement either (1) the changing of the guards, or (2) a state of nuclear war. I pulled the covers up and wrapped around Lee. No need to even wake Lee up and tell her my story. Well, maybe I did.

COMMENT: Write or tell your grandchildren a story

It is said, grandchildren are the reward you get for not strangling your own children. A review in the New York Times Book Section is not a prerequisite for writing a successful story. The first in this section was written for my grandchildren, and it included them in the plot. My granddaughter, Alex, age 8, called me to say that her third grade class had read the story, and they thought it was "the best book they had ever read." What praise could be higher or more rewarding.

The Oklahoma Adventure
Jan 22, 2000

Granpa said, "It's hot enough to fry an egg on the sidewalk." Vincent, age 10, Alex, age 8 and Porter, age 6, started their trip with Granpa and "Gammy" to Oklahoma. Vincent was not sure this was a trip he wanted to take. Three long days seemed like an eternity to be in a car with his sibling, know-it-all brother. He was in the mood for an adventure, and this hardly seemed like the way a real adventure would start. How wrong he was!

At the beginning of the trip, Granpa gave Vincent a sealed envelope which he was only to open once they pulled out of the driveway. In it, Granpa said, "You will find your secret orders and understand your mission." Granpa used to be in the CIA, and he loved to play "we spy" with his grandchildren. He was funny about this and while they never took him seriously, he seemed to enjoy the game, so they joined in enthusiastically.

This time when they opened the envelope it read:

> **To Secret Agents Mustaf, Fatima, and Pierre** (Granpa had insisted long ago that they should not use their true names so Vincent, agent 1, had been code named "Mustaf" Alex, agent 2, code named Fatima, because it sounded like the name of a beautiful, mysterious spy, and Porter, agent 3, code named "Pierre") Agent number 1, will drive to Oklahoma with Agents numbers 2 and 3. You will look carefully out the rear window to make sure you are not being followed. You can use the side view mirror so nobody can tell you're looking, but if you look into the mirror the licence plates will be reversed. Write down the license plate of any suspicious car you think may be following you. Pay particular attention to try to identify the make and model of any suspicious vehicle especially if it's driven by a bald headed man accompanied by a younger woman. Report all sightings to the others. Take turns. One of you can help navigate and help

126

Number 1 follow the map while the others keep watch. IF YOU STOP AT ANY GAS STATIONS OR HOLIDAY INNS, REPORT IF YOU SEE ANY BALD HEADED MEN AS SOON AS YOU LEAVE TO NUMBER 1. REPORT IMME-DIATELY ANY CARS WITH DC LICENSE PLATES (ESPE-CIALLY ONES WITH DIPLOMATIC TAGS) AND ANY BLACK MERCEDES.

I have also included this spy camera for you to take pictures of anything suspicious. Agent number 3 will carry the camera but loan it when requested. Finally, we intercepted this coded message but were not able to break it. Try your hand at breaking it, and if you succeed, it may help you find what you're looking for in Oklahoma City. Good luck and be careful.
"Z"

5,4,22,14,17;21,18,5,13,17,22;

While they knew it was just one of Granpa's games, it did occupy the time and keeping a count of the number of bald headed men that could be spotted first was a bit of a challenge. For the first two days, the trip progressed pretty much as expected: Vincent was three bald men and one Mercedes ahead of Porter, but Porter had spotted the same car with diplomatic plates on two separate days which he considered much more significant. Alex was drawing pictures of the bald headed men and an excellent picture of the mysterious car. Then, they stopped for gas in Springfield, Missouri.

"Look," said Vincent, "There's that car we saw yesterday with diplomatic license plates. I wrote them down here…it's 'FC 125' in bright blue and red. What country is FC? France?"

"No, it's Russia," Granpa said. "The DC police assigned a different code to each country so they can recognize them, but the code is not related to the name of the country. It's not like a person's initials. 'FC' is the code assigned to Russia" Porter was impressed with Granpa's vast knowledge and chimed in, "Do you think they're really Russian spies Gramps?"

"It certainly isn't very likely, but it is unusual to see diplomatic tags this far from Washington. I'd think if they were going to try anything really secretive, they'd use a lot better technique than this unless…."

"Unless what?" the spies who had named themselves "The White Panthers," because they were so silent when they observed "the opposition," exclaimed in one voice.

"Unless…they wanted it to look obvious so the FBI wouldn't think they were up to something and therefore would just put a light surveillance on them. Maybe just one car. That way, they'd be easier to lose, and the FBI wouldn't think it was anything unusual. Have either of you kids seen other cars with Washington, DC license plates since yesterday?"

"I saw one this morning when we stopped for gas. We had been in the lead, followed the Russian car, and then there had been a third car with DC plates. I'm sure it was white. It had one bald man and one young man in it. I remember it perfectly," Fatima said proudly, "The older man looked like an ostrich. He had along neck and a bald head. See, I drew this picture of him." Gammy looked at the picture, and said, "I remember this man, and he does look like an ostrich."

"Let's get back on the road, Gramps. The Russians are about five minutes ahead of us. Let's go!"

And run they did. They paid the bill rapidly and literally raced to the car. So fast, in fact, that they would have left Gammy in the bathroom if she hadn't come out just in time to jump in the front seat, but she rushed so fast that the attendant didn't have time to give them their change. The car bolted forward and the chase was on.

Vincent was doing his turn as navigator. "They'll have to stay on this road for a while," he said, looking at the map, "there's no turn off for almost fifty miles, and we should catch up by then if we just go a little over the speed limit."

The next forty-five minutes for Vincent seemed to last longer than cleaning his room before leaving for hockey. Finally, they recognized the familiar shape of a white Ford Taurus traveling about fifty yards ahead of an enormous semi-trailer. In the distance, they could barely make out the black four door car of the Russians. Contact!

Then suddenly, before their very eyes, a horrible tragedy occurred. The semi-trailer truck sped up as though it was going to pass the smaller car, pulled along side and then jerked over into the right lane sending the smaller Ford hurtling off the road, down the embankment, only to explode in flames on impact. The last thing Vincent saw was the white DC license plates vanishing with the car. The truck pulled over to the side and stopped, but Granpa had already decided that he was more interested in the black car ahead than the two men who were probably beyond help in the flaming white car behind them and the truck driver who intentionally killed them. In the stunned silence that followed, no one questioned that decision. Granpa, Gammy, and the White Panthers all agreed on two things: First, those FBI men were murdered. That was no accident. Second, this was no longer just a game.

The next exit was Miami, Oklahoma. Granpa kept his car as far behind the black car as he could and still not lose sight of it. Vincent's advice as navigator reassured him that there was no turn off for twenty miles, so he played it loose, very loose. One fact was clear: There was real danger associated with pursuing this. On the one hand, he had to follow this car for he knew not even the KGB kills FBI agents unless it was scheming something extraordinary. This wasn't a desperate act committed in haste. It was carefully planned, and the FBI hadn't expected anything out of the ordinary. They'd been fooled completely. Family in hand or not, Granpa knew he had no choice but to follow the mysterious black car.

"I'm sure," he said, "they'll get rid of that car soon. Certainly they'll change the license plates as soon as possible. No doubt they've got special plates they can put on with magnets in a twenty second stop. I would have bet they'd have done it before they exited to make sure no exit attendant notices a diplomatic car, but maybe they're more afraid of being seen making the switch on the highway. They appear to be waiting for the next exit."

"Shit. This is really exciting," said Vincent.

"Don't use words like that," Porter admonished, "but it really is! Wait 'til I tell the guys."

Gammy could no longer be silent. "I don't think you know what you're doing, dear. You're putting the kids at risk. It's not worth it. Let's stop at the exit and call the police. Please, I mean it!" she added earnestly.

"Oh, come on Gammy," whined Vincent, "Granpa will be real careful. Won't you Gramps?"

"I agree, dear," said Granpa, "but I want to follow just far enough to see if they switch cars or license plates, and, if so, what the new car or new plates look like. I'm not planning on any confrontation. I'll just drive on by if they stop. But I'll tell you what to do. Write a short note saying who we are and what we just saw. Say what we're doing, and I'll give it to the exit attendant and have him call the FBI. We can't risk a delay at this point."

Gammy wrote the note and five minutes later clutched it tightly in her hand—as Granpa dug deep into his pocket looking for exact change to put in the unattended toll booth machine! Then, as he turned his car down the road identified as State Highway 35 west towards the town of Pond Creek, he turned to Gammy, smiled confidently and said, "Piece of cake—I'll be careful." He patted her affectionately on the knee, but to himself he thought, "an unattended booth. This was awfully well planned." He wondered if they also had a plan to deal with anyone following them.

Part 2—The Convention

"Let's figure how far they are ahead of us," Granpa said.

"How will we know that?" Porter asked.

"Easy," said Vincent. They're just going over the top of that hill. Let's look at our watches and see how long it takes us to get to the same point." Vincent looked at the second hand on his watch and started counting 5-10-15-20-25-30-35-40-45-50-55."

"We're there-stop counting," cried Alex.

"Perfect," said Granpa.

"Why is it perfect?" asked Porter.

"Because it will give them just enough time to change licence plates and for us to get close enough to see them without changing our speed, which might look suspicious."

About ten minutes later, the black car pulled off to the side and quickly put on the new licence plates: ABC 226 from Texas. Alex wrote the numbers down. At the town of Miami, Oklahoma, Granpa pulled into a gas station. "I know just the person to call here, Judge Sam Fullerton, my roommate at Oklahoma University graduate school. The police might not believe me but they'd listen to a Judge they know."

Granpa knew the way to his house. Judge Fullerton lived in a big white house located on a big ranch with lots of Black Angus cattle. Granpa said it was one of the biggest Angus ranches in the country. He said when they were in school, the judge had owned an airplane and would load up his plane with steaks to be eaten over a period of months.

"Sam," Gramps said, "We ran into a lot of trouble driving up here," and then he told him the story.

"The nearest FBI office is in Tulsa, and that's a hundred miles away. I know Special Agent Scott there," said the Judge. "Let's call him." He picked up the phone and dialed. Granpa told him the story.

"We knew our men were missing, but we didn't know this. We'll get right on it. Do you know what any of them look like?"

"Yes, Alex drew a good picture," Granpa said.

"Great, just wait. I'll be there in two hours."

"Miami has grown a lot since you've last been here. Would y'all like to take a tour? We're having a convention of 'radio preachers.'"

"What are radio preachers?" asked Porter.

"Radio preachers are like priests except the preachers here are on the radio," said Vincent, "and they often talk on the radio."

We agreed and got into Judge Fullerton's car and drove into town. "This country used to have the largest lead and zinc mines in the whole United States." The judge explained that lead is an element in the rocks. It's very heavy and is used to keep radioactive nuclear waste safe because it prevents the radiation from getting out and harming anyone.

When they got back to the Judge's house, Special Agent Scott was waiting. "We've got an all-points look out for that car whose licence tag you gave us. Now if I can just see the picture you drew." The FBI man looked at the picture.

Then Porter said, "I took a picture with my spy camera.
I'll get someone to take it to be developed and made into prints. Do you have a rapid photo processor in town."

"Of course," said the judge. "There's a new mall just about a mile away." As they drove to the mall, Granpa said, "When did you take that picture, Porter? I hope they didn't see you do it." Granpa didn't say so but he was worried Porter might be recognized by the killers. He was even more worried when Porter answered, "Just as we passed the parked black car."

Special Agent Scott went to look for the "Hour Photo" store. Granpa stayed with the secret agents. Then he suggested they go look for an ice cream stand and see whether the ice cream at the mall was better here than down in the town.

"What are all these people doing?" Vincent asked.

There were a lot of men talking in small groups. "They're talking to their follow-ers. Look over there, that's Billy Dee 'Keep Satan in Hell' Harper. And there's Johnny 'Judgement Day's Coming' Johnson."

"Are those really their names, Granpa?"

"Yes and no. They're known that way by their followers but in most cases, didn't legally change them."

Alex was fascinated with the preachers and wandered around listening to different ones.

Vincent had just received his single dip chocolate ice cream cone when Alex came running in, gasping for breath. "I just saw the Ostrich man, but he changed into a disguise. Now he has a mustache."

"Are you sure it's him?" Granpa asked.

"Yes," answered Alex." He's standing right over there," and pointed to Pat, 'Praise the Lord' Paulson's area. Now, he was gone.

"Let's get Porter and go find Special Agent Scott," said Granpa. Everyone looked around. Where was Porter?

Part 3—Kidnapped

It struck them all at once. **Porter was missing.**

Just then, Special Agent Scott came back and sensed trouble. "What's wrong?" he asked.

Granpa told him, and then he went to get help from the local police. "I want every main highway shut down and every car stopped and searched. Bring in the state highway patrol." He told them that they might be disguised with mustaches or wigs

"When it rains it pours," said Special Agent Scott.

"What do you mean?" asked Vincent.

"I mean, when one thing happens, a lot of other things that keep you busy happen at the same time. For example, we had a nuclear bomb stolen from a military airport yesterday, then today we had those agents murdered, and now Porter is missing. It's been quiet out here all year, and then suddenly everything happens at once."

"Do you think they could all be related?" asked Granpa.

"What do you mean? Why would anyone bring a stolen bomb up here to Miami, Oklahoma?"

"I used to work on detecting nuclear weapons at CIA, and you've got one thing that makes this the best place in the country to hide nuclear weapons."

"What's that?" asked a suddenly interested special agent.

"Abandoned lead mines. That would hide the radiation from any of the government radiation detection systems. Furthermore, I don't believe you're going to find those guys on the main roads. I think they're almost certainly on back roads headed for a rendezvous with the terrorist who took the bomb."

"But there's nothing out there but leached arid soil and abandoned mines for an area 100 miles by 100 miles. That's over 1,000 square miles," the agent said.

"Sir," said Vincent," I believe that's 10,000 square miles."

"Why, you're right. We can send some planes but they couldn't possibly cover that large an area in a reasonable period of time."

"So let's use satellites," Granpa said.

"But we don't have access to satellites that can see a car," Scott said.

"No, but CIA does, and I'm sure for this kind of emergency they'd take a few pictures and analyze them in a couple of hours. I'll tell you who to contact. In fact, I'll call and grease the skids. We don't have much time to spare. I'll call Linda Zall at CIA. She'll help us." Gramps dialed some numbers and said, "Hello, Linda. I need a big favor. You'll be getting a call from the FBI in about 10 minutes. It's about looking for the bomb the terrorists stole, and Porter Dowling, my grandson, has been kidnapped. It's a long story, but we need the highest priority for a 10,000 square mile area near Miami, Oklahoma. The FBI will give you the exact location. Will you call me back with estimated image collection and interpretation time?"

She called back immediately and said, "You're in luck. We have high resolution coverage that can see very small objects very well, but can only see a small area. It would take many pictures to look at the whole area, but we can get some of that area today and tomorrow. We can get today's pictures analyzed by tomorrow and also get some low resolution for the whole area tomorrow."

"Good," said Special Agent Scott. "We're afraid we'll spook them if we send out a lot of planes. If we did that, they'd just concentrate on hiding themselves more carefully, and we want them to make mistakes because now I doubt if they suspect we know anything. But we will use some drones like we used in the Iraqi war. They're about the size of model airplanes so they can't be seen easily from the ground, and they're very quiet. They have a camera which will send pictures back to our temporary headquarters that we've set up at Judge Fullerton's. We'll use the satellite pictures to guide the drones."

Of course, everyone was worried about Porter whom the terrorists had planned to kill as soon as they got to the mine, but Porter was very good and turned on the charm. In fact he had made a friend with the only girl among them, and she persuaded them to "wait until tomorrow." That night, Porter made some more friends, and this bought him a second night's reprieve.

In the meantime, the FBI and CIA had been working hard. Indeed, the low resolution satellite detected three different places where objects that could be cars or trucks were observed. High resolution satellite data then identified a car that looked like a Ford Taurus. Then the tiny drone flew up close to actually see the license plates with its powerful lens. The FBI prepared a SWAT team with special night vision glasses for an attack in the middle of the night when most of the terrorists would be asleep. The recon team snuck up very close and listened with a sensitive microphone to count how many were there and to listen to tell if Porter was there. They reported that some kid named Pierre was there. Granpa explained.
Clearly this was good that he was alive, but it changed their tactics, because he would be held as a hostage. Stun grenades would normally been the best approach, but then someone realized that they might damage the wall and have the mine cave in on everyone.

Porter was just about asleep when he heard two people arguing. One said they should kill him tonight because he could identify everyone. The other one believed he might make a good hostage in case they were caught. Porter decided he had better sneak away but, there was a guard at the front entrance. Porter looked up and saw a small ledge that led into a tunnel small enough for him to get into, but the terrorist couldn't. He was barely hidden when someone noticed he was missing. The man started yelling and waking everyone up. Several of them ran outside. The FBI man operating the listening device called his base: **"Condition Red. Request permission for Plan C. Porter is hiding some place, and they're looking for him. They're preoccupied with that—let's get 'em."**

"Permission granted," came the reply.

The SWAT team flew into action. The FBI only had to fire one shot because the terrorists were taken completely by surprise, and half of them were arrested unarmed looking for Porter outside. When it was over, a smiling face appeared peeping out of a small cave near the ceiling. The FBI man took him back to the Fullerton's where he was joined by a relieved Gammy, Granpa, Alex and Vincent and his mother and father, who had flown to Oklahoma when they heard Porter was missing.

After everyone settled down, Special Agent Scott gave them a certificate which named them **Honorary FBI Agents.** Then he said, "Those guys told us enough that we were able to piece things together. They had carefully planned the operation. They figured that by taking only one car they would only be followed by one FBI car. They planned to meet the terrorists who had the bomb. These Russians represented a group inside Russia who wanted the cold war to start up again. Just the fact that a bomb was missing would make the terrorist threats seem more valid and cause, they hoped, a negotiation that would favor the terrorists. They thought they were safe, and then they saw Porter take that picture so they followed you to the mall and kidnapped Porter. They took the camera which had a new roll in it, but they didn't have time to get it processed. They never thought we'd find them or even think of those old lead mine".

"Well, congratulations. If Vincent hadn't spotted something suspicious in the first place, Alex hadn't drawn that picture and then saw through his disguise, and Porter hadn't bravely hidden himself, things could have been a lot worse. You're clever young people," said Special Agent Scott.

"Call me Pierre," said Porter.

Code information

Hint: Each letter(L) is related to a number. There are 26 numbers (N) in the alphabet, if they were lined up with A=1, B=2 etc that would be a simple code in which each N=L. Now, If you started at A=4, B=5 and rapped it around at the end then Z would = 3 as in the third column. The forth column contains a very different code. It is called a "one time pad" in which one assigns unique numbers to each letter, and one requires an exact copy of a matching pad (or list) in order to break the code. This is a very simple code to break with a machine if you have enough numbers or if you have a copy of one coded long message in both code and translated text. From that one can reconstruct the original "one time pad". In the simplest code one must separate each number from the next with a comma or letter. For example if one wanted to write the word "cab" using the one time pad below you one might write "1005;117;26; or 1005,117,26," Now if he wanted to make it even more difficult he might use a letter which could refer to different list of codes such as a"b" for list "blue" and (y) for list "yellow". Done in this way the "a" letter would replace a comma, and "cab" might be coded as 630y117b1567y

letter	base	N+3	O ne time pad "Blue"	1 time pad "Yellow"
	number	(wrap)		
A	1	4	117	256
B	2	5	26	1567
C	3	6	1005	630
D	4	etc.	Etc	
E	5			
F	6			
G	7			
H	8			
Ii	9			
I	10			
k	11			
L	12			
m	13			
N	14			
•	15			
P	16			
Q	17			
R	18			
S	19			
T	20			
U	21			
V	22			
W	23	26		
X	24	1		
Y	25	2		
Z	26	3		

Uncle Tut, Uncle Boxie and the West Va. Clan

Mt.Hope, West Virginia was a town where I could greet any stranger with, "Morning, cousin," and have a good chance of being right. Further, everyone who wasn't family, was just about family, like Oakie Patterson, who lived across the street and was elected Governor, or the Capertons, whose son, Austin, married one of my New York wife's cousins. (We discovered this when we both submitted a name in common with the address in Slab Fork, West Virginia on our wedding invitation list.)

It took me 10 minutes to walk from my uncle's house past the one drug store, one barber shop, one bank and one movie theater to my uncle Tut's office and the New River Store where we got ice cream cones "on the house."

Dad had a very promising career in the coal business, and it was with great reluctance, when my great-uncle Robert, said, "John, I'm going into the oil business; that's the future. Are you with me or against me?" Dad voted that he was "with him" and headed out to Oklahoma and Kansas in 1919. He loved his roots, so every year, until I was twelve, we packed up and headed to West Virginia at Christmas.

This required a logistical effort comparable to Caesar's Gaul campaign. We would assemble the Porter family entourage at the old Rock Island station in Oklahoma City. My mother, father, my sister Mary Alma, and I would assemble with our allocation of one brown, cowhide suitcase each, and all our presents for the relatives. It was, like most Porter expeditions, well conceptualized, with one potential flaw—me.

My family will never let me forget the time we changed trains after our overnight trip to St. Louis. I became entranced with the giant station's supply of comic books. The family didn't notice the unnatural quiet until they had already boarded the train, bags and all. Then they noticed my absence. There was panic: Was I wandering around? Had I boarded another train? Had it left? It was a tight connection. Meanwhile, I was quietly afloat in a sea of Superman and Captain Marvel comics. They actually held up the train. Finally, my sister, Mary, who was seven years older, remembered that she had last seen me at the news stand, and I was swept into the Pullman car with my father's strong admonition to "pay attention." I replied, "Yes, sir."

I loved train trips. I loved lying in a lower bunk in the compartment at night and peeking out the window under the shade pulled down for privacy. I particularly remember the thrill of climbing up a ladder into the upper bunk which was pulled down out of the ceiling by the Pullman porter ("Pullman" was the name of the designer of the train car for first class travel which had a bed that pulled down from the ceiling).

Most of all I remember the long trips through many, many doors which connected the narrow platform between cars, where the staccato "clack, clack, clack" sound of the iron wheels on the tracks was mixed with the noise of outside air as we sped along, contrasted with the relatively quiet walk through the passenger cars. I would slowly work my way back to the "club car," squeezing by people going the opposite direction. It was always the last car on the train, usually just after the diner, where dad would have a cigar and quiet chat with other passengers.

Each car was named individually, like airplanes are today, usually with names of cities. Dad told me the names were chosen by the daughter of the President of the Pullman company, and that she was paid a hundred dollars for each name. I thought it must be the greatest job on earth.

We would open our packages at midnight on Christmas Eve. (One time my cousins covered my body with "measles spots" made with lipstick "to trick our parents." Needless to say, I was the only one fooled.) At midnight on New Years Eve we fired pistols and shot guns toward Turkey Knob, and then dad gave each of the kids a dollar so we would be starting the new year with money in our pockets.

My two uncles had large houses on the main street next door to each other. They shared a driveway. The driveway was on a very steep hill. I'll never forget it because, one winter, my cousins poured water on it so we could better slide down where the snow had been removed. This worked well for our purposes but was less satisfactory to my uncle who sat helplessly in his Buick Roadster as he slid down the hill and smashed into the garage.

Uncle Tut, also known as Edgar Tutwiler, was a memorable character. He had been a close friend of my father's before he married Dad's sister. He was about six feet tall and usually wore a single breasted grey suit and vest in which he carried a gold pocket watch. He also had a slight pot belly. Uncle Tut always had a gleam in his eye, usually because he had just played a trick on someone and was slyly waiting for its discovery.

When my mother and father were first married, they took the train from Newton, Kansas, my mother's home, to Mt. Hope. They arrived at 6:00 A.M.. They looked around the tiny station—no Tut. He hadn't met them as scheduled. Dad didn't want to call the house and wake anyone up or worry them about Tut—maybe he had a flat. Finally, he called a cab. Forty-five minutes later they arrived at the house. All my aunts and uncles were in their pajamas when my father and his new bride arrived. Tut just smiled when he was lambasted for not telling them when my parents were arriving. "You just would have gotten all dressed up and put on a big act. Why not let them meet you as you really are?"

Tut was the only person who had known Mother, so he was considered the family's unofficial adviser on her likes and dislikes—an invitation to disaster. They had a big dinner party and invited a number of prominent people. Tut told them that there was a matter of some delicacy he had to discuss. "Margaret is part Indian," he confided, "and always eats her steak raw." Unbelievably, they bought his story. Without so much as a side glance they casually served her a piece of virtually raw meat. She struggled with it politely while Tut looked on with a knowing smile.

Going out with Tut was an unpredictable experience. One day when I was about nine we went out to a coal mine. There was a little pile of coal, and I got some coal dust on my pants. Uncle Tut knew that Mother would be a little put out if I came home with coal smudges on my clothes. He decided to escalate the incident so my mother wouldn't be angry over something that trivial. He told me to get down and roll around in the coal. I did. When Mother saw me, looking like I had survived a mine disaster, she was so relieved that I hadn't been hurt that she barely made it an issue

Tut was manager of the company stores for the New River Coal Company. It had about 10 stores which sold goods for "script," money issued to company employees who could only spend it in the company stores. He enjoyed pretending to be a grouch. He had a few good cigars each day, and had a slight raspiness in his voice. He always left the lunch table at home for an hour's nap, whether or not guests were there. This must have paid off because he lived to about ninety. One of his joys was shaking me up by statements like, "Come on Robert, let's go out and shoot a dog!" He was just kidding, but I always accepted with the fear that this time he just might be serious.

Aunt May was his better half, and a kinder person never walked the earth. She was so giving. The day she died she had over exerted herself buying wedding presents—coincidental, but fitting. Her oldest daughter, Alicia, was three years older than my sister, was bright, imaginative and went away to school. This gave her an aura of worldliness she wore with a certain panache which made her appear just slightly wicked, or, as her daughter, Lissa, joked recently, "She appeared to know things she shouldn't." After I grew up, Alicia became one of my favorite relatives as is her daughter, Lissa.

Ed was their son and one hell of an athlete. His national fame came in golf. He won the highly competitive West Virginia state tournament many, many times at White Sulfur Springs and played in all the great tournaments in the country with all the great golfers of the world as his partners. Sam Snead was a very close friend. The press referred to him as "King Tut," because of his last name. He genuinely liked and respected all people from golf caddies to board chairmen. I remember that he always addressed his elders, as "Mr. or Mrs."

He lived with us in Oklahoma for three years. Our back yard ran right into a golf course where Ed would play at every opportunity.

Unfortunately there are two memories of Ed that still make me wince: When he would return from the oil fields he would very often give me a big hug, at which time he would intentionally give my cheek a playful scratching with his unshaven beard. The second trauma of my young life was when Ed attempted to teach me to swim by throwing me in the deep end of the country club pool.

Ed met his wife, Flo, through a roommate of hers who lived in Mt. Hope. My whole family went to their wedding in Waco, Texas. I spoke with his wife recently who said that dad had given them some shares of Phillips Petroleum as a wedding present in 1943. She said, "We've never sold a share, and it's worth over a million dollars today." I would bet it was only worth a few thousand dollars then. He probably would have stayed in business with my father if World War II hadn't come along, and he joined the Air Force. Afterwards he joined his father in West Va.

I particularly remember Ed from one of my escapades, 15 years later. My college roommate, Derby Wilson and I developed a "system" and planned to break the bank playing roulette in Cuba starting with our college student's budget of only $100. The final score was: The Bank of Cuba: $98.65, Dartmouth Students: $1.35. Fortunately, we had prepaid our plane fares plus, I had "this great cousin," whose wife was from a well to do Miami Beach family (owners of "Maxwell House" coffee) where "I knew we would be invited to stay because they no doubt have a lot of room."

I called Ed from the airport. To my shock, and near panic, he said, "You don't want to stay here. You'd feel constrained coming and going with Flo's parents around. I'll call the motel and reserve a room, and then we'll stop by and pick you up for dinner." I remember thinking how foolish I had been giving, reflexively, the bell boy my last quarter as a tip when he extended his hand.

We did not mention one word about our impecunious situation. After dinner, Ed dropped us off at the motel. As we shook hands to say good night, I felt the crisp feel of good old American cash in my palm. "I want you to spend this on something you wouldn't have, if I hadn't given it to you." It was fifty dollars. "You might find a girl at the Fountainbleau bar you'd like to buy a drink." I thought, "—or pay for our motel room and a bus to the airport."

Jennifer and Amy knew "King Tut" and remember his black lab, Blazer, very well. Blazer would jump into the pool to rescue them despite their protests. Ed died suddenly as the result of an infection he acquired after elective surgery. At that time he was ranked number three in the world among "senior amateur golfers." I remember Ed most warmly.

Dad's second sister, Aunt Alicia, was much more of a disciplinarian: kind, but more business like with me. Let me put it this way. She liked me, but couldn't wait for me to grow up. Her husband, Uncle Boxie, was a small man, but a ball of energy who loved all of life, including teasing me. His last name was Snyder. He was also a boyhood friend of dad's and had many living relatives in Mt. Hope, including his father and mother. They all had good voices, warm personalities and liked to sing. The Porter genes passed on a monotone singing voice and tin ears.

Their daughter was named Marylane, and we called their son by his initials, "P.M." His friends now call him Phil, and he made me swear a blood oath never to reveal what his second initial stands for, although I have no idea from whence it came. (I still remember it, and my continued loyalty is assured.)

Even now, he still has the easy school boy smile I remember from our childhood. Also, he still looks very physically fit. His physical strength impressed me on two occasions: When I was about 14, we went to Hickory Lodge, a private hunting lodge owned by Tut and several friends about 10 miles from White Sulphur Springs. PM took his car and shined a spot light on a small deer in a field. With the deer, temporally blinded and confused PM was able to tackle it and hold its feet together for a short time so I could get a better look. This is very hard to do. His second memorable feat may be attributable to survival instincts more than inherent strength. I'm referring to when his six groomsmen, including me, tried to hold him down to lock a heavy metal chain around his waist at his wedding. Our assurance that we would eventually give the key to his bride didn't weaken his resolve to resist.

PM and his wife, Johanna, and ourselves have kept up. During the past eight or nine years in Oklahoma City for my sister's daughter's wedding, then at their daughter's wedding, and in Washington, D.C. for my sixtieth birthday party.

His sister, Marylane, was the second Mt. Hope cousin to have a first job in Oklahoma. After she graduated from Mt. Holyoke, she came to work for the Shawnee Star, a newspaper of which my dad was a director. I met her husband Dave, who has the resonate son-of-a-preacher's voice, when he was courting her at Christmas time in Mt. Hope. Later, their family lived in Vero Beach, Florida which is near Cape Kennedy. We saw them often over the years, especially when I was at NASA in the late sixties and then again when our daughter and her husband bought a vacation house outside Vero in the eighties. She died from cancer several years ago. It makes me nostalgic now thinking about my many good times with her and her family over the past 50 years.

Mother and Dad spent a great deal of time in Vero Beach during dad's later days, and Mother continued going there after Dad died. Uncle Boxie was always enthusiastic and jolly. Just being around him picked me up. He reminded me of his pet wire-haired terrier, Jigs—smart, alert, and friendly, with a twinkle in his one good eye that made you think he had a secret which was the human equivalent of jumping on the sofa.

It's very satisfying that we remained in touch over the years. This was probably aided by the fact that transportation and communications developed as they did, and also was helped by the fact that we moved back East. But I think the most important factor was the fact that Dad, his sisters, and brothers-in-law really loved one another. It was truly an "extended family." The family invested in business deals together. Dad bought stock in Ed's business. They all bought stock in my company. We all invested in the newspaper and radio chain dad started in Kansas with Oscar Stauffer. I remember seeing my paternal grandmother in Mt. Hope briefly before she died. We've attended the many christenings, weddings and funerals. We've watched ourselves, our children, and now our parents grow up. It really represents a life long commitment which now includes the fourth generation.

When I look back on Christmas in Mt. Hope, I especially think of the car going thru the back of the garage, Uncle Boxie's enthusiasm, his wire-haired terrier, Jigs, visits to the Coca Cola plant, "free" ice cream at the company stores, and the time, when I was ten, and ran around a counter in the New River Store crashing right into a mannequin. Uncle Tut, sharply said, "Robert, you ran right into that lady. Apologize immediately"—**and I did.**

Score: Crows Six Million-Christians One
August 22, 1995

Crows have always been my nemesis. They're too smart to be a bird and too sneaky to be a pet. Dad used to say a crow can count to four, but five hunters would confuse it, and it would get curious and come close enough to shoot. Consequently, it took five men to hunt a crow while it only took one to hunt a lion or bear. I took my twenty-two caliber rifle out to the oil rigs to hunt crows. I was a pretty good shot against stationary targets, yet I don't recall ever even nicking one crow.

One day we went down to a farm Dad owned in central Oklahoma. Oil was dad's reason for owning the "farm". It couldn't be planted with any crops, because it was completely covered by sand and occasional scrub oak. Just getting there was a memorable event.

After my fourteenth birthday, I especially looked forward to our drives in dad's black, Buick "RoadMaster." That was when he started letting me sit next to him and operate the gas peddle to give me a feel for the road. He, of course, had control of the steering wheel, the clutch, and brakes. This generally worked well, but there's a first time for everything, and I'll never forget the first time I had to pass a car on a hill, and I froze when we were side by side. It was one of those long, low Oklahoma hills on the way to dad's farm.

The highway was a federal interstate, which meant it was just a standard two lane in those days. The car ahead of us was going pretty slow, and there wasn't a "no passing line" in our lane, so dad said, in a calm voice, "Give her the gas". I did, and we pulled along side—and there we stayed, and stayed, until there was a "no passing line" on our side, and I had maneuvered us to the point just ahead of the other car that if we slowed down, he slowed down, and if we sped up, we might not be able to get by him before we met head to head with a big truck coming down the hill in the opposite direction. It was the driving lesson from hell. Well, as you know since I'm writing this, we made it, but I'll tell you, not by much, and the next few times I passed a car, it was on a long flat stretch.

The roosting of the crows was really a stunning sight. Experts estimated there were six million crows per square mile at this time of year. When they all took to the air the sun was eclipsed, and a massive shadow spread across the fields. The crows posed a threat to farmers who tried to blow them up by putting dynamite in the trees.

Needless to say, their efforts didn't even dent the crow population; the smart old crows just moved out of the trees. My friend, Charles Mee and I could do even less with our 22's. They would see us coming and all move about 100 yards and just wait for us to run out of ammunition, which we did after about five long frustrating minutes without one crow causality. Once they realized this, they came as close as five feet, just beyond the reach of our gun barrels, to taunt us. I'm not making this up—it's true.

We were chasing after them swinging our rifles, but they just hopped out of reach. We were finally saved from further humiliation when Dad called to drive us home…but on the way out, we notched up my only victory in my long crusade against crows. One crashed into our wind shield. I think it died.

A Grandfather's Tale
March 28, 1998

Up to then it had just been too quiet, the kind of quiet that can stir a mother from a deep sleep. Slowly her subconscious correlated her 4-year-old's screams of glee with the repeated opening and closing of the garage door. An immediate investigation revealed that Porter had simply invented a new, as yet unnamed, form of amusement in which he would push the garage door button and then race to see if he could catch the bottom of the door with his hands and ride it up a few feet before dropping off. I agree "all's well that ends well," especially if a 4-year-old just added to his growing list of life experiences. But it does make one wonder how long the warranty lasts on (a) the garage door opener, (b) an inventive 4-year-old, (c) a young mother, and (d) an increasingly nervous grandfather.

Further reflection deepens my amazement as to how any child ever makes it through life's training maze. Consider, if you dare, a few common obstacles in his /her path: how many times, for example, does a child get dangerously near a busy street, alone near a swimming pool, river, or hot tub; there are household poisons, toys that have parts which can injure, and fire. I'll shudder and stop here. I'm convinced that between ignorance and curiosity, surviving thru age six defies the rules of conventional statistical probabilities.

Further, if curiosity killed the cat, how do human beings survive? How did a helpless baby ever survive those first tests? Animals learn to walk within minutes of birth. Humans take about a year. Certainly one can attribute some of it to a few hundred generations of genetic sorting employing the mechanism of survival of the fittest. "Fittest for what?" you say. A good question. The earth's battlefield for survival is littered with the corpses of many different species who were, for a brief time, conquerors. Paleontologists know that species are forever modifying as are the threats to them. Over-specialization is a species' harbinger of its death. Consequently, while one's defensive mechanisms must constantly adapt to survive, today's adaption may be tomorrow's death warrant.

But one argues, "The fact that the world is becoming rapidly populated suggests that surviving is becoming easier and easier." Good news, maybe? But bad news for some because survival usually becomes competitive, a "zero sum game," as scientists like to call it. Further, with modern weaponry, what God created one day may disappear the next. "Man's day" in geologic history gives us little opportunity to trumpet humankind's dominance on some future road to survival.

So what can one conclude from this one-page tour of risks, from my grandson's garage door to the horrors of modern warfare? I can only speak for myself after an ethereal sixty-three years. I am impressed by the fragility of humankind, the whimsical nature of reality, the limitlessness of human curiosity, and my inability to intuitively understand statistical probabilities.

The word "evolution" connotes an overall direction or path along which our species will travel. I recently reread, <u>The Beak of the Finch</u>. It's a great book about a study in the Galapagos Islands, and presents, in convincing detail, the conclusion that adaptive changes occur over much shorter periods than previously thought, i.e., within a single generation. The implications are enormous, for it implies that instead of observing the Darwinian evolution unfold in progressive segments, which may lend themselves to speculation about our future, rather they may only be telling us about the "last summer's weather."

My final conclusions are that it's unlikely my insights will save civilization, just as worrying about my grandson will hardly protect him from life. Quite the reverse. If I told him, "Don't do that" he'd probably say, "Oh, grandpa, you don't understand." I'd smile, because he'd be wrong. My mind drifts back to the times I climbed up the stairs to the second floor, jumping to the bottom from each one trying to set a personal record, then adding one more stair's height until I finally hurt myself and learned my limits. I smile again as I hear my father's voice from the past say, "No one ever seems to learn anything from other peoples' histories."

SINGING ALONG WITH FRANKIE AND OTHER NOCTURNAL EMISSIONS

December 15, 1993

It's 4 AM. Do you know where your mind is? Even if you don't, this essay answers that searching question in my own case on December 2, 1993. Sometimes I awaken in the middle of the night and find my thoughts on a desert island which I'll call "me." "Me," for better or worse, contains all the memories I have; all abilities for deductive and inductive logic; the five senses I uniquely possess; facts or theories I have with me; and a body and mind with which to run new experiments and draw new conclusions or reconsider old ones. In short, what one can take to any prison, or call on in the middle of the night.

Last week, one of the mysteries of life I addressed from my bed at 4 AM (while staring at the clock) was how my brain keeps track of time. How do I know, for example, that I did this before that, or I did or saw something "about 6 months ago?" This ability starts decreasing in all of us much earlier than other types of memory loss. This was addressed in a 1950's article in <u>Scientific American</u> on man's perception of time. It showed that man's ability to estimate the date of an event varied as a function of his chronological age. Stated otherwise, a person 10 years old may be able to place an event that happened several years ago, plus or minus ten days, while a person 50 might only be able to estimate an event plus or minus 50 days. Further, if the center points of the estimate are connected, one gets an almost straight line which supports the interpretation that there is a common cause and constant rate of deterioration in the general population.

This is of special interest because, in one type of quirk found in some advanced Parkinson's patients, tests have shown some PD patients have a peculiar time memory deficit so great that if they are shown the famous picture of the Marines raising the U.S. flag over Iwo Jima, they can tell you the content, including the location and the significance of what's going on, but will fail to even roughly place the event chronologically in time. This is not a normal type of memory disorder or dementia. It's not what you find in Alzheimer patients; it's unique to

Parkinson's. I conclude from this that there is more than one memory mechanism at work. (Charles Sheffield pointed out that one must separate a memory for dates from memory for events, i.e. one remembers a date by reading it, versus figuring out its sequence in a series of events.)

The second mystery of life I addressed as I tried deep breathing was "why so much satisfaction comes from the right timing or sense of being at one with something." Meditating and repeating a mantra in beat with your heart or breathing is one example. Another is singing a familiar tune.

Speaking of the ridiculous, recently I started singing along with Frank Sinatra on his new album "Duets." No, this is not lunacy, and certainly not my idea. Because of PD and my neck operation, I speak softly and slur my words, particularly at the beginning of the day. My speech therapist tells me to pronounce the vowels on the way to work and screw up my face in funny ways to stimulate the nerves. After that, I'm supposed to recite something and try to express emotion in my voice. (I gave up the face contortionist routine at stop signs after people thought I was expressing something personal directed at them!) I've learned several things from this: First, it helps, because when you hold a note you stretch your throat and face muscles longer than when you just speak. Second, although Sinatra is in his 70's, this is a new recording, and he holds his own very well because his secret is timing. The way he juxtaposes words and music is masterful. Third, it's very satisfying to listen to and very challenging to sing along with him, but very satisfying when you succeed, even though only part of the timing is similar at best. Fourth, there's something compelling about music so you can't easily turn off a tune in your brain once it's started until it's completed. Finally, a sense of humor is good medicine.

"Why do we need sleep?" is the third great mystery I wrestled with as I drifted in and out of sleep. One prediction that I can confidently make (at 4 A.M.) is that some day we'll find a way to communicate directly and more rapidly between a computer and the brain, and from brain to brain as well. Perhaps it won't be so different from the old movie "switch the brain trick." Really, all we do is go through a microphone, sound system, and reader scanner, i.e. a simple transducer system (voice, hearing and reading) to convert one form of information to another and store it. Instead of reading it in fax-like fashion, someday we'll find a faster way to transform it. Great technological revolutions are those which compensate for some human limitation. For example, the communication revolution from the tom-tom through satellite communications compensates for the limitations and distance and speed for vocal communication; industrial revolution from the wheel to the machine to the nuclear reactor compensates for limitations of man's muscular strength; cybernetics revolution compensates for our brain's weaknesses in storage and repetitive processing, etc.

But the subject is sleep, and the relevance of all this to sleep is that I believe we have a data transfer and storage problem that requires a sleep cycle to compress and distribute the data. One way of data compression is to throw out the unneeded data; that is, simplify it by eliminating the redundant and extraneous. This fits with recent studies scientists have performed using EEG's and EKG's to study brain waves and heart rhythms and chaos theory. Specifically, they have found that as we age, these electrical signals become smoother, more regular, less chaotic. This makes sense if you consider that longer wavelength, lower frequency curves carry less information per unit of time than shorter wavelength, higher frequency curves. The latter could be interpreted to represent the non-linear, chaotic information needed to fine tune our learning cycle and deal with information which doesn't fit in the carrier wave. In other words, I would speculate that dreaming reflects the attempt to store in image form some of the similar emotional information; that is, it's the result of trying to file current data in usable image form. Dreams almost always have meaning in the near-term of activities. Think about it; you don't have a stress dream unless you're under a <u>current</u> stress, and you reuse the same images in repetitive dreams.

Now, let's look at the other side: pleasure. Pleasure dreams are usually much simpler than stress dreams; for example, floating or flying dreams in which rules are not constraints. You're free to fantasize or fly. Another explanation might be an attempt to reconcile current data in memory addresses taking advantage of the storage facilities in both the right (more abstract) and left (more linguistic or literal) side of the brain.

The need to simplify is not confined to dreams. Religion, science and philosophy are the product of man's effort to reduce the chaos of the overwhelming non-linear events nature presents us to an intelligible form he can accept consciously. Dreams accomplish the same goal but simply require or induce a different state of consciousness.

What's the conscious bottom line? It is simply that, regardless what that person looking at me from the next car thinks, it is perfectly logical and normal that I should wake up thinking about time, Parkinson's Disease, dreams, chaos theory, computers, religion, Frank Sinatra, and God all at the same time, in my bed, in the middle of the night, or in my car, singing and making faces on my way to work, confined on the little island of "Me."

But there are still two questions I keep losing sleep over but can't answer. "What are all those other silly people thinking about in their cars? Look at them! Do they all have speech therapists?" And, finally, how do I turn off the voice in my head from singing, "One for My Baby and One More for the Road?"

Profound? No. The grist for Nobel Prizes? Hardly. The best I can do alone at 4 A.M.? Definitely.

Yorkshire Pudding

January 25, 2002

In 1960, I was having lunch at the Locket Hotel in Norman, Oklahoma. It was Sunday, and I really can't imagine what caused me to go to the Locket for lunch. I never did it before. It was a somewhat dilapidated hotel, albeit the largest in Norman. Janet Gurley, my date, and I perused the menu apprehensively. The first line held promise. I saw in red "Roast Beef with Yorkshire Pudding." The interesting part was the Yorkshire Pudding, which was clearly not a home grown product of the Locket Hotel. It occurred to me that there was probably some young English lad who had come all the way to Norman with his family recipe for Yorkshire Pudding. I ordered it. The waitress brought out my plate which had an over-done piece of roast beef and nothing else.

I inquired of the waitress, "Where is the Yorkshire Pudding?" to which she replied, "Isn't it there sir?"

I looked for the bread basket, but found only saltine crackers. I said, "No, it's not here. Now, please go get it from the chef."

Five minutes later, she once again presented me with the same plate, but no Yorkshire Pudding, and once again I asked where was the Yorkshire Pudding.

Once again, she replied, "Isn't it there, sir?" I said, "Would you please get the chef?"(I wanted to meet this young English lad.) Out of the kitchen a large black African man galumphed. "Where is the Yorkshire Pudding?" I inquired politely. "Isn't it there sir?" he said, looking at the waitress for psychological support. "No, it is not here. Now what is the story behind this?"
"Well, frankly," he said sheepishly. "We copy our menus from another restaurant, and I thought Yorkshire Pudding was like *au jus,* a name they added after the roast beef that doesn't mean anything."

A Dartmouth Tale
January 25, 2002

I've gotten my comeuppance on several occasions, but the events which unfolded at Dartmouth in 1970 take the cake. I had driven up from Boston early in the morning and made my first speech at Dartmouth since my graduation. I was addressing the geography class, and they had reserved a parking slot right in front of the building. I was feeling pretty good about myself. I felt like I had been recognized for my accomplishments. As strains of Pomp and Circumstance ran through my memory, I turned the rental car I had obtained in Boston into the reserved place. I opened the door and started to swing out, but my tie had been caught up in the safety belt retractor mechanism, and when I dipped my head lower to try to pull it out, it just got more strongly ensnared so my head was trapped until I took my tie off. In the meantime, many of the students I was about to lecture had quietly gathered near my car and watched this scene. I was much more humble as I began my speech.

POST SCRIPT: "PLEASE READ THIS"

As I was lying in bed this morning, the power went off in the neighborhood. It was 5:15. I had a flurry of thoughts which I wanted to write down before I forgot, but alas, I had even more problems than I first realized: Obviously, there was no power for my computer; there was no light to see my keyboard on my portable; it was the year's second shortest day. I wanted to turn over, assume the fetal position, and turn the electric blanket up, but it wasn't working either.

Suddenly I remembered astronaut John Glenn's comment just before lift off: "It struck me that I was sitting on top of an enormous bomb with three hundred thousand parts, each of which had to function perfectly, and that each contract had been awarded to the lowest competitive bid."

There is a compelling analogy here. This is our species' dilemma. We have grown to depend on artificially interdependent systems, and we, like the astronauts, don't realize until the moment of truth approaches how many vital support systems we have taken for granted. For example, I couldn't write this unless I had computer assistance because my handwriting is illegible due to Parkinson's. I maintain a functional level only because software keeps me from repeating letters; correspondingly, I need light, paper, emotional support, food to nourish me, medicines to preserve me. The list goes on and on. Furthermore, all of these essential luxuries virtually go unacknowledged. Without these crutches, I would be a severely crippled, helpless human shell with little outward value. I'm like an astronaut, dependent on instruments to avoid catastrophe from a hostile environment.

So where does this place our species in the eternal competition? It's "tool-making" capabilities permit it to compensate for many weak links. Does this make for survival, or create a house of cards in which the weak rule until a "power outage" shuts us down? Were our forefathers better standard bearers for our species than our current generation because their ambitions were more in conformity with their environment? Clearly, today's technically strong forces could take the military measure of any generation which preceded us, but our question is: "Can today's generation of species meet its challenges today?" Further, if we empower our members to destroy one another, perhaps the tools on which empowerment depends are not the right tools for our own preservation.

There are more systems than we know, many more than we can control. This is the human condition. We need a belief system that will vindicate our experience, provide us an appropriate value system and empower us, and one that will forgive numerous failures and foster humanity.

Please, someone. When the lights come on, do something.

IT WAS A VERY GOOD YEAR
July 7, 2003

To tell you the truth, I would rather spend time with wine taster legends Alexis Lichine or James Beard than George W. Bush. Wine has been responsible for some very good moments in my life and provided a common bond with many new friends. I first became interested in wine when we moved to Washington. Lee and I joined a wine tasting club called "Les Amis Du Vin." This was in 1962, and a few of our friends were into wines. In 1965, we took a trip on "The France" and met Tom and Sally Jordan. Tom was already a living legend in Denver. He worked his way through undergraduate and law school, became an owner of considerable oil in Indonesia, located major oil reserves in Nevada, and won a seat in the state legislature. Most of the readers of this will know one or two friends who planned their itinerary in Europe, based on where they would eat and drink. Typically, they would pick out a few three star restaurants from the <u>Guide Michelin</u>. A few of these readers actually planned their meals in advance in great restaurants, which are known for specific dishes (e.g. pressed duck at the Tour d' Argent), but Tom and Sally are the only people I have ever heard of who actually spent two years cooking the dishes they were going to order at home so they would be in a position to better discuss the meal with the chef at the restaurant of their choice. The last night we were on the ship they asked us to join them on their quest for the perfect meal. We accepted and spent the next several weeks at the great restaurants of France from Eperney to Beaune to Bordeaux. Dinner would seldom take less than three hours in which the first thirty minutes required a serious translation of the menu, including discussion of each dish's preparation and the selection of an appropriate wine. This was often preparatory for sessions consisting of respectful questions to the chef.

Our visit to Beaune stands out particularly for two reasons: First, Tom arranged for us to meet Marc Cheviot, the owner of the *Hotel de la Poste*. Marc is one of the most respected shippers of wine. He arranged for us to visit the cave in which they stored the wine for the entire Domaine Civile Romanee-Conti district and it was truly awesome. This comprised the product for three vintages. In one room, the greatest wines of Burgundy; La Tache; Richebourg Echezaux Grand

Echezaux, as well as Dom Romanee itself. We barrel-sampled each of the vintages from three vineyards. After this, we joined Marc and his wife, who prepared *les Oeufs Bourguignon*, made with a modest 1948 burgundy. The story does not end here.

After lunch, I bought two cases of 1947 Chambertin, which we lovingly carried in our laps in our new 1965 Porsche Cabriolet for the rest of the land trip (by this time we had added Lee's brother Jim Wallace to our passenger list). When we arrived in the United States, I carefully placed my prize in a cool closet and let it settle. After a propitious period for the wine to acclimatize and any sediment to settle, I opened the first bottle with great anticipation while gently savoring its gentle bouquet with discreet inhalations. Simultaneously, I raised the glass so as to appraise the color. The shock of all these senses in my mind converged into one startling crushing conclusion. It was "grapy," "young," "immature," "brash," "pretentious," wine. A mere child, not the mature woman I sought with all her complexities, subtleties and earthy qualities." Instantaneously, a second conclusion raced to my brain, the goddamn French had "freshened it a bit." What I had paid for, lovingly transported and patiently waited for was probably one teaspoon of '47 Chambertin (to make it legal), diluted with a much younger wine. Well, he had picked the wrong pigeon. He had selected one of the few men in the world who could mobilize sophisticated government resources and expose him as the fraud he appeared to be. He had selected me.

In my other life, I was employed at CIA, in charge of their assessment of worldwide nuclear facilities. As part of this effort, tens of millions of dollars were spent to develop a collection effort of fallout from nuclear tests and leaks from nuclear facilities. The physics and chemistry of each nuclear test was different and by measuring the fallout isotope by isotope, the intelligence community could differentiate the fallout from different weapons. It is frightening to realize that these effects were literally worldwide. Consequently, we could identify the date of a grape grown in France by characterizing the fallout. With bitterness in my heart and vengeance in my mind, I turned over one bottle for analysis to be placed in a 10 million dollar instrument and declared, "I want to find out the date these grapes were grown." Behind super-secret doors, using super-secret instruments, the results were determined, and I bristled with anticipation as the PhD who led the project reported the results. "Bob, I can tell you one thing for sure about this wine. It's all pre-1950 because in that year the first H-bomb was fired and the world's surface was coated with tritium. If any of the grapes were post-1950, the tritium would stand out like a sore thumb. Furthermore, the fission products are relatively primitive which is characteristic of the fallout in the late '40's."

So what was the explanation? The wine had been stored in a cave at the proper temperature, possibly a bit lower, and was slower to mature. It was probably all '47 Chambertin. This theory was substantiated because in my closet, which was warmer than a cave cellar, it started its normal maturation, and in a few years, we were drinking a fantastic wine.

Come to think of it, the CIA played a significant role in enological adventures. Lee and I had traveled to New York to have dinner with Pierre Bennerupt. Pierre was a good friend of Larry Heilman. He had told us the best cellar in the United States, perhaps in the world, was at the Round Hill Restaurant on Long Island. The restaurant was set back in the middle of a large landscaped area, a 30-minute drive from New York City. The son-in-law of the owner was our waiter and presented us with the carte du vin. The first wine on the list was the most expensive, Lafite Rothschild. It was $26.00 a bottle. It was too cheap; "there must be some trick," I thought so I probed further. "What year is this?" I demanded, almost discourteously. "You name the year, Sir. We have perfect continuity back to 1926." It was unbelievable. He then asked what I did for a living. I replied that I was in the CIA. He lowered his voice and took on a conspiratorial tone. "Come with me," he said abruptly. We entered a dark narrow circular stairway that led into a cellar, which held more than 70,000 bottles of wine. Half way down the stairs he reached behind a bottle of German Riesling and pulled out a small packet of papers, which he carefully unfolded to reveal the bold classification markings, SECRET. He looked relieved and unburdened himself by uttering the exclamation, "OSS." It turned out that he had saved those papers from WWII when he was in the OSS, tracking German battleships in the fjords. He had waited for years to find someone to whom he could confide. When we left his restaurant, our pockets were stuffed with complimentary bottles of wine. This is not the end of the story either.

Two years later I received a call from Pierre, who said, "Do you remember the owner of the Round Hill Restaurant? He just sold his restaurant for its real estate value. The buyer was oblivious to the value of the wine, and when my friend asked him what he was going to do with it, he said he thought it wasn't part of the deal, and the present owner could do what he wanted with it as long as he cleared it out by the next morning. He called his friends and said, "Come and take all you can carry for $5.00 a bottle." We formed a buying group, obtained a rental truck within an hour, and we were on our way. It was a wine connoisseurs dream. We obtained 100 cases of wines from the greatest vintages of the greatest Chateaus of Europe.

This cache became the basis for the wine cellars of Wilson, Kerr, and myself.
I used to visit the library in the Office of National Intelligence estimates at CIA.
One of my friends there was Ambassador Matthews. He looked like Santa Clause
in the Miracle on 34th Street, with a permanent twinkle in his eye. He asked me
my summer plan, and I told him that I was going to visit Switzerland and the
wine country. His face became even more animated as he declared, "I scaled the
Matterhorn in 1922." Then his eyes clouded a bit and he added, "It's like the
New Jersey turnpike today. I understand that even cows have climbed it." Once
again his eyes brightened and he added, "At the end of WWII, I was named
Ambassador to France. The finest wine cellar in Bordeaux was selected to house
the allied embassies. One table was the American Embassy. Another, the British.
He paused, with great reverence, "We drank the last of the 1901 Chateau
d'quem." He lowered his voice and sighed, "A great year." He gave me the name
of the wine cellar. It had been sold to a hotel, and we arranged to have dinner on
our last night in France. I ordered the 1947 Huat Brion and paid $19.00. The
waiter went to speak to the owner who came over to our table and subtly queried
us to ascertain if we were worthy of his last bottle. He then asked us to his office
for a little cognac. What a way to leave France.

I still retain a number of bottles from these adventures as well as many good
memories from all the wine drinking experiences they provided. Incidentally,
Tom Jordan and I have retained a close friendship. He was instrumental in raising
the financing for EarthSat and is the owner of the prestigious California Wine
Chateau Jordan. Pierre Bennerup is now the owner of one of the largest high
quality nurseries in the United States.

COMMENT: Everyone needs mentors. Include your children in adult conversations

Perhaps my father's greatest gift was developing the ability in me to communicate with older generations. He accomplished this by including me in his conversations with his generation. These are the recollections I have of my mentors that are excerpted from my first book, My Friends and Mentors, the First Sixty Years.

Mentors

I think in anecdotes. That's just the way my mind operates. I would guess that in a normal day, phrases and/or scenes from past associations come to mind ten to twenty times and influence me. Fifteen years ago, I carried a pack of 3 x 5 cards around to write them down. I found they came from jokes, student friends, co-workers, a lot of people I didn't know particularly well and wouldn't have thought of as mentors. I stopped after the first 160 and decided to concentrate on the dominant sources of these anecdotes, my principal mentors. This section is the legacy of those reminiscences. I also was interested to think back to the personal styles and traits of each of "my mentors;" to see what, if any, generalizations could be made about them as a group. I concluded the following:

First: When I asked their advice on matters, such as EarthSat, the more authority a mentor had previously exercised in his own right, the more deferential he was to me when I was the one making the decisions. He recognized that the man who signs his name takes the responsibility and often must make his decisions with incomplete or different information than the advisor has available to him.

Second: They all avoided unnecessary fights. Fighting is the mark of inexperience and weakness. The pipeliner in Spain knew to avoid fights because it was only a matter of time "'til you got yours" and as one pipeliner told me, "only crazy people start fights." People like Webb, Smart and Cabell had been in enough fights to know to avoid them whenever possible.

Third: They all made a great effort to listen to the opposition and to understand where the "right side of an argument" was, even if they weren't on it at the time. Then, they would take the least costly way to get there. Walsh was a classic, but this was true of almost every mentor.

Fourth: They had all reached an age and level of accomplishment in life that they were in the "generativity" stage as defined by George Valliant.

Fifth: They were all "responsible" people. They were willing to make personal sacrifices to accomplish what they considered a worthwhile goal, even against the odds. They didn't expect "final solutions," but rather "incremental gains." They were focused on the positive and didn't suffer negative thinkers kindly.

My Father

My father was my foremost mentor. He was born in 1890 and died in 1962. He was a turn-of-the-century man who believed that man was put on this earth for some reason, and that it was man's lot to seek out his role and accept the responsibilities which were his to assume. I had a very close relationship with him. This grew strong because he planned for it, and because of circumstances which made it possible. He always treated me with respect. He never talked down to me. He made me feel that I had a role to play, and that I was privileged and lucky, but that I had additional obligations as well.

He believed in "life audits," i.e., that you couldn't keep dark secrets because you have to expect to be audited in this life with regard to everything you do. He said, "Most people can live with adversity because they have to, but living with prosperity where you have choices, then you're tested."

He believed you had to be trained to take responsibility. For example, he knew that I would inherit a relatively large estate and started me out by helping me make investments in stocks at the age of eight. He did this by asking me what soft drink I liked most. I said, "Dr. Pepper." He bought me ten shares each of Coca Cola, Pepsi and Dr. Pepper. Each day we looked at how they each did in the paper, and we would debate why one would rise and another fall. This way I learned about strikes, distribution and advertising.

There were three ways we had quality time together. Every night he would get home at 5:00 p.m. and sit in his chair in the library. We would talk about the day and the news. These conversations centered on business and school activities. At 6:30, he would listen to Fulton Lewis Junior, an anti-New Deal journalist, and then the family would eat promptly at 6:45. After dinner Mother would come in, and they would talk and read until bedtime.

The second period of quality time came when we would drive out to look at an oil well. Dad (I called him "Dad" but would always answer questions with "Yes Sir" or "Yes Ma'am") was an independent oil man, which means that he did everything from buying the land to completing the well. He was what was called a "wildcatter" because he looked for oil that was remote (more than one township or six miles) from known fields and civilization, i.e., the boondocks, "where one found wild cats."

Dad drilled wells in Oklahoma, Texas and Kansas. He found one very good field in north Oklahoma called the Watchorn Field, which was named after my great uncle, **Robert Watchorn**, who was the owner of the company my father ran.

My great uncle was quite a man. Lee calls him the "family relative." He worked in the mines in England from the age of seven. When he was about fifteen he got in a fight with his foreman. The police were after him, and he borrowed pennies from neighbors and left England, barely one step ahead of the sheriff, in the middle of the night on a ship to the U.S. He vowed he would pay back his neighbors if he ever could.

He succeeded very well. He became one of the organizers of the United Mine Workers, and Commissioner of Immigration in 1901 at the peak of the refugee flood. At one time he owned twenty-five percent of Shell's U.S. stock and fifty percent of Union Oil of California. Unfortunately, he didn't trust stock, so they didn't pay off the way they might have; but he was very well-to-do (and survived the depression).

He didn't forget his roots or his promises. In 1926 he went back to his home in England and bought the entire district. He built single family houses for people who were living four families to a house and charged them $2 a month for as long as they lived. He built a Methodist church in his mother's birth place, the Abraham Lincoln Library and a park. His goal was, "A bible for every Chinaman." He would come out to the drill rigs dressed in starched collar, spats and suit. He insisted that there would be "No cursing, chewing or spitting on the drill rig floor." I knew my great uncle fairly well since he lived to be 87 (he died in 1945 when I was ten).

Generally our trips took about two hours of driving each way from Oklahoma City, and Dad faithfully drove a series of black Buick Road Masters. These were great times to talk. I always took my 22 cal rifle along with me (even at the age of ten), and I would shoot targets sometimes while Dad would be talking business on the rig floor.

One of the more interesting activities was the Osage Indian Sale in Pauhuska (about thirty miles from Perry). This was a live auction of leases (one of the only ones in the country). It was held under a giant oak tree. Bidders had to pay on the spot and frequently came with shoe boxes full of money. I never heard of anyone being robbed.

We got to know all the people who owned the little stores at the crossing of the section lines in the country. They had names like "Bill's Corner" (and yes, I knew Bill, and Bill knew me), where we'd get a lunch meat sandwich. When we did find a restaurant in a town like Perry, the food was likely to be a bit old. Dad always insisted that we get our meat cooked really well done, and he would occasionally order an egg because "you can't do too much harm to an egg."

When we did arrive in Watchorn, Oklahoma, we'd stop at a warehouse with a big sign which stated "NOTHING FOR SALE DON'T ASK." Dad had a guy named Andy Crow working for him. Andy was a Crow Indian and was semi-literate. This was an accomplishment for that period, and he was quite a character. There are a hundred great Andy Crow stories, and a few must be told: Like the time he bought some drilling pipe just before the price skyrocketed. Dad asked him if he got a receipt because the seller wanted to double the price. Andy proudly reached in his pocket and showed dad a copy of his receipt written "in my own hand," I EXCEPT (sic) THIS PIPE. Dad paid.

Another time Andy thought he'd play a little joke on some English friends of my great uncle who were coming to visit. He took them into this little cafe and told them that it was pretty dangerous there, and if any shooting started they should get down on the floor. He then gave a signal to his friend who came in shooting, six guns in the air. The Englishmen dove on the floor. Andy roared in laughter. The only problem was that they knocked over a kerosene lamp and burned down the cafe. Dad paid again.

My favorite Andy Crow story is when he ordered a new water pump from Sears Roebuck. It finally arrived, but he couldn't find the handle. He wrote Sears a letter using every four letter word he knew but then, after writing it, he found the pump handle. He just added a P.S. to the letter, "I just found your #@#&#@ pump handle," and sent the letter.

Andy, Ben, the "tool pusher," and Everett, the geologist, were all sort of family members. They worked for Dad over twenty years and told me stories about deals he was in. They genuinely liked Dad and made me feel proud.

Mineral Wells, Texas was the site of the first real gusher I ever saw. It blew the derrick right off the drilling platform and looked like a giant black geyser. The oil rained from the sky on our heads. I was only about five and thought it was strange that everyone was so happy when this black stuff was getting all over them. Even my mother, who was usually pretty tidy, didn't seem to mind. That really confused me.

Mother had a "Gracie Allen look" about her that made her the world's greatest straight woman. I remember after we went to a dude ranch and returned home, someone asked Dad how he and Mother liked it. Dad said, "Oh, all right, but Margaret had a little trouble getting adjusted." "What happened?" asked the man. "Oh, the wrangler asked her if she wanted a western or eastern style saddle and she asked, 'What's the difference?' He replied, "The western style has a horn on it." Margaret said, "I don't think there'll be that much traffic. I'll just take the eastern style.'" At that moment, Mom came in and just stood there wondering why all the people were staring at her. (Dad, of course, had made the whole thing up.)

Dad did have one bad habit. He consumed thirty cigars a day. He mostly chewed them, but that's how many he finished off. One day he got a call from the Federal tax people to come down to their office. Dad went and sat down in front of a very stern looking man. "We've got you," the man said triumphantly. "We have the records. Is it true you've been selling cigars for twenty years and not paying any taxes on them?" "I've never sold a cigar in my life," Dad replied. "We have twenty years of records which show you've been buying 2,000 cigars every two months. How do you explain that? Do you expect me to believe that?" "Well, that's the truth," Dad replied. "I'll have to call my boss," the Federal agent said, picking up the phone sanctimoniously. "Hello, Boss, I've got a John R. Porter in my office who...." On the other end of the phone his boss said, "John Porter, John Porter, isn't that the guy whose always got a cigar in his mouth?" Case closed.

I understand all the reasons for getting guns off the streets today, but I also understand the nostalgia one has for his own gun. I had a 22 cal pistol, a 22 cal rifle and a 16 gauge shotgun. Each of these were highly esteemed presents that I received as I took on more responsibility. I kept them in my bedroom, and, without thinking, automatically took them to Dartmouth with me. I never in my entire life ever pointed them at anyone, even joking. They were something that I considered a milestone of trust. Dad and I spent many hours at an old canal doing target practice. My dad had a Remington 380 semiautomatic, which he carried in the oil fields during the 1920s when he had the payroll.

The third period of quality time was when we drove to Board of Directors' meetings. Dad served on a number of boards and took me to a great many board meetings. Driving up, he would always talk about what he was trying to accomplish at the meeting. I knew that at the end of each meeting I would be asked one question by him, and that everyone would hear my answer. The question was, "What do you think, Robert?" At four, I'd laugh. At eight, I'd say,"very interesting." At nine, I'd say, "very interesting, sir." At ten, I'd say, "I was particularly interested in Mr. Jones' point." At twelve, I'd add a paraphrase of Mr. Jones' point. At fourteen, I would add a question back, "…but I wonder if…," and by eighteen I was participating, respectfully, in many sessions. I was ready to replace Dad on some of those boards when he died. I was twenty-six. Quite an education.

Dad did quite a bit of traveling and frequently one of his friends would ride with him. One dusk he was driving along a farm road with Jim Vickers from Wichita. They hit a pig, killed it and broke their radiator. They knew the farmer would claim it was a "world champion hog," so Dad walked up to the farmhouse and asked if the farmer had any pigs for sale? He said, "Yes." Dad asked, "How much?" "Five dollars, take your pick." Vickers said, "I'll take the one in the road, and here's another five to bury it."

Dad was always generous with his remedial time for me. I was a hyperactive kid and a pain in the behind to be around. Dad was a believer that if you make yourself knowledgeable and useful, a lot of other things fall in place. Consequently, he bought me a lathe and spent time teaching me woodworking.

He also bought me my first camera, a first generation Polaroid. He was an ardent photographer, and I had a knack for it too. We went to Europe in 1948, and I took a picture of a camera store owner in Milan. He had to have that camera and traded me a Leica IIf with a 3.5 Elmar lens for it! Thus, I started my photographic career in style. I was taking and enlarging over 5,000 pictures a year by my second year of high school. I also made my first own stock investment. I bought the

Polaroid camera for $187 and put the same amount into Polaroid stock, ten shares at $18 a share. I sold too soon at $2,700 per share before it went up to $6,000!

We went to Europe as a family from 1947 thru 1950 on board the Queen Elizabeth and Queen Mary. The 1947 trip was a brilliant stroke on Dad's part. No one was going yet; London was in rubble. Dad knew it was a moment in history which could only be caught if we acted now. We did, and a year later when we went back, it was entirely different. I had all the intellectual curiosity and energy of a twelve-year-old and absolutely soaked up Europe. Thus, when I came home I had something to say in which people were interested, and which put my opinion in higher regard. I gained a lot of confidence and made more friends.

On our 1948 trip, Dad became friends with Jim Farley, who was President of Coca Cola International. Farley asked Dad if he would like the Coke franchise for Belgium, but said he'd have to get a Belgian partner. He wanted only $30,000. We had a Belgian chauffeur, and Dad asked him if he'd like a free half interest and be his partner. Indignantly, the chauffeur replied, "I am from Belgium and people from Belgium will only drink beer or wine. Never Coke!" About five years later we heard it sold again for about ten million dollars. I'll bet our chauffeur never bought a one.

Dad was not the slightest bit racially biased. He had grown up in the coal mines with workers from every ethnic background. I never heard him gossip either, about anyone. If any of the rest of the family gossiped, he would just remind us about "that guy in Pennsylvania who made a million dollars—just minding his own business." In other words, pay attention to yourself and let other people pay attention to themselves. You've got a big enough job taking care of your own problems.

We never discussed it, and I don't know how far he went in high school. The one course he insisted I take in college was public speaking. He felt that was his greatest deficiency. In point of fact, he was a fantastic raconteur and excellent public leader (he was mayor of Nichols Hills just because he got the most votes of any council member). I remember asking him why he never went with a big company. He said, in a very low key manner, that too often big companies require a "loyalty" that conflicts with the path you might choose. He liked the freedom that only came with independence. Some of his closest friends were big company men, but he identified most with the small businessman.

Finally, Dad was a brilliant deal maker and negotiator. I'll never forget one nego-tiation when I was about twenty. The other side had offered Dad "a deal he couldn't refuse." Rather than accept it immediately, he started pointing out the flaws in the administrative process. He showed that as structured (although it would have been to his initial advantage) some of the support they believed he would be supplying, but hadn't specifically asked for, would be difficult for him to provide. "Remember, it has to be a good deal for both sides, Robert," he said afterwards," otherwise it's invariably a bad deal for both sides." Those words have come to mind many times, and invariably they have proven to be golden!

One of his most unusual characteristics was the strong moral and ethical overtone in his business dealings. He was almost unique in the oil business because he never took a promotional fee or commission on any deal he undertook, even if he put everything together. He absolutely wouldn't make a profit on a commission basis. This was his personal ethic. He spoke with great contempt of "promoters." He would never put someone else in a business deal he was in. If they were to be a partner, it would be on the same basis as he was.
Another recurrent theme I remember from Dad is, "You've got to give to get" and the reciprocal," If you get, you've got (ought) to give back." I remember Dad often saying, "**There is nothing lower than an ingrate.**"

I think Dad's most unique skill was his ability to glean a wholeness from dispar-ity and from what were generally considered unrelated parts. This required the instinct to look for and find new insights and wisdom from the most unexpected places. **His openness of mind, his expectation to learn from any source is unpar-alleled in my experience. For example, he would talk to the guy pumping gas and get back in the car and tell us what he had learned about the national poli-tics or the direction the economy was going. All these gems from the mouth of a guy who thought he had just been asked a few questions on the changes in the price of gas, or the recent local impact of the merger of two railroads.** I am sure watching Dad exercise this skill is the reason I became an intelligence officer at the CIA.

It is interesting that while Dad and I talked quite a bit, he never lectured me directly on what I should or shouldn't do. For example, he never told me not to smoke, although I knew he thought it was a bad habit. He never told me not to drink, although neither he nor Mother drank at all. (I didn't drink until Graduate school.) He was deeply influenced by the tragedy of alcoholism in the coal mines.

A great gift my parents gave me was to actively let me interact with their friends. As a result I became very comfortable as a real person with the older generations, and I learned to talk about adult subjects with them. This greatly improved my odds of finding new mentors.

One final piece of Dad's advice: "Just remember, Robert, **when the government wants money, it takes it, and it's not fair!**"

My Mother

My mother was also one of my greatest mentors. She was a wife of the 1920s, '30s and '40s. She kept the checkbook and had complete management control over the house, but normally said not a word about business. I remember one time she tried to enter the dinner table conversation and asked out of the blue, "What did AT&T do today?" My father, sister and myself just stared briefly in disbelief but kept on talking as though she wasn't there. (I'm not saying this is how it should have been, but that's the way it was.) In Dad's mind, Mother was an administrator, not an entrepreneur.

If you're getting the idea that Mother was intimidated by all this, you're wrong. She deeply loved my father, and she knew she was respected for her side of the family responsibilities. She was a determined lady with a lot of character and courage. She had over twenty major operations from 1953 to 1988, including strokes, broken shoulders, elbows, arms, hips, gall bladder removal, kidney stones, gall stones, intestinal blockages, and oh, yes, breast cancer and pancreatic cancer as well. She was just as persistent mentally.

At her request, I gave her a stationary bike when she was eighty-four. A couple years later I noticed it had 732 miles on the odometer. I commented on this to the nurse who said that "your mother rides that one mile every day come hell or high water." Some people really make you stop and think.

I always knew my parents loved each other, and me, and were proud of me. Mother was the "explainer of emotions" in the family. My father was much more of a Victorian character and talked mostly about business and politics. Looking back, I think it's vital that at least one parent be there to teach about emotions. Mother's secret was she loved her friends of many age groups, and, in return, Mother was deeply loved and respected by her friends who continued to visit her and enjoy her until her death at eighty-eight.

I remember one day when I was a teenager. I commented on how much my girl-friend enjoyed spending time with her ninety-year-old grandmother. Mother replied, "That's wonderful for Anne Sheridan, too." I asked why, and she replied,

"Because if she enjoyed her grandmother, she'll be more willing to accept a relationship with her own children and grandchildren when she's old herself." Real wisdom!

The line between sarcasm, which puts one down, and teasing, which builds you up, often depends on the environment in which you are brought up. I was taught never to tease people I didn't like, and I didn't. Consequently, I didn't easily take offense. Sometimes Lee, whose family never teased each other, thinks I "just don't get the message" when I'm not offended by someone's questionable remark, but I think my interpretation has served me very well. **I thank my parents for that very important component of my life—humor with love.**

Mother was a great raconteur and could charm her way out of a parking ticket as easily as she could back out of the driveway. Speaking of which, we had a garage door that was seventy-six inches wide. Mother's Buick was seventy-two inches wide. Neither car nor the garage door suffered very well when Mother tried to park in the garage. Her life was changed when she bought a "small Cadillac" which was sixty-eight inches wide. She more than paid for the new car by the house repair bills she avoided.

I think I got to know Mother best after Dad died in 1962. She was very good about seeing me for short periods of time and not monopolizing me, nor making me feel guilty about seeing my friends when I was in Oklahoma. She really looked forward to going out to dinner with them sometimes. Consequently, I made a lot of short visits (every time I had the chance) and saw a lot of her. (I hope I can be as wise when I get old.)

Lee's mother and my mother were two entirely different people, but they became truly close friends. My mother-in-law, Amelie, had been an early women's rights advocate, came from a truly brilliant family (her father was second only to Edison in the number of patents he held), and she was trained as a biochemist, but had virtually no sense of humor. Although Mother had different strengths and weaknesses, they each harbored a secret desire to be like the other one in some ways. Amelie had many strong points, and Mother knew just how to bring them out. One year they took a trip around the world together and had a spectacular time. Amelie loved the Oklahomans she met on the trip and visited Oklahoma alone on numerous occasions. "The difference between New York and Oklahoma," she said, "is that when a visitor, like me, comes to Oklahoma, Margaret (my mother) has five friends who call and say, 'I hear you're having a house guest; can I have a luncheon for her?' But when she comes to New York, my friends call and say, 'I hear you're having a house guest. Don't worry, I won't bother you until she's gone.'"

They certainly shared basic values and supported each child's spouse. Mother was assertive, however. I was a strong-minded child, and it was a good thing I was. When she tried to assert herself into our lives, I stood up to her. If I had been just a little bit weaker, it could have been a disaster. Mother never gave up on anything; she never stopped trying to convince me to "go to church, slow down, and don't take risks." At times she had a heavy, but loving hand on the throttle. I remember one time she complained to Lee that I was drinking too much. I told Lee, "She's right. It's because she's been on me all day."

In her later years, we grew to accept that was "just Mom." One of my last remembrances was a trip we took to the trust department of the bank. It was 9 a.m. and the elevator was packed. Mother addressed me in a firm voice, "Robert, what did you have for breakfast?" "I had a glass of orange juice and some cereal," I dutifully replied. "That's not enough, Robert. Your father used to say, 'You've got to put a fire in the boiler to get it going.'" "Mother," I said, "I'm fifty-two years old. I think I can fix my own breakfast." The people in the elevator burst out laughing.

It was nice to be loved (or should I say, despite) the way I really was. Mother was well aware that her son was not a fashion plate, but she always hoped for improvement. When we were in Iran, we had an appointment to meet with the Prime Minister, Mr. Hoveyda. We thought it was going to be a five minute meeting, but instead he said, "I have convened the entire Cabinet to hear your presentation. You have two hours!" I made my pitch. When I told Mother about this I hoped she would be impressed, but instead, she paused pensively for a minute and then said, "I'll bet you had on those old loafers." She had that one right.

One final note: When I asked Lee to comment on this section, she said I had trivialized my mother. If I sound this way, it is not my intent. I have great respect for Mother. She grew up in Newton, Kansas. She went to Knox College, which was rare for a girl at that time, and taught school for a year before getting married. Further, she was a great wife, mother and neighbor. My father was about fifteen years older. Their marriage would not be considered "politically correct" today because my father was definitely, or so it appeared publicly, the dominant partner. In private, she was a strong southern woman. This required skill, commitment and sacrifice. It was not a one-way street. One can argue with the roles, but there was a commitment to each other that was real. Mother believed in her marriage, her family, and her God. She could not have survived the way she did if it didn't empower her. Of course, one can tell her she ought to think differently, but to earn the right he, or she, should do as well for as long a period of time.

In any event, my mother was one of the most important mentors in my life. She taught me to get in touch with my own and other people's emotions. This is one of the greatest gifts any mentor can give.

Rex Pennington

(written in September 1994)

Every five years or so something nice happens out of the blue. Yesterday was one of those days for me. Rex Pennington called for lunch. He lives in South Africa and was in Washington to visit his daughter. A legend in his own time, we met at Casady School where he taught me Latin and even how to recognize an "ablative absolute" when I saw one.

Since that time, Rex has become a world-recognized leader in improving education for blacks in South Africa. He brings to mind the quote from *Catcher in the Rye* when Holden Caulfield is told, "The sign of a mature man is that he <u>prefers</u> to live humbly for what he believes rather than die nobly for it."

Rex is widely known. Of the twenty-five or so South Africans I've met, from strangers on the streets of Paris to World Bank officers and diplomats in Washington, I have never met anyone from South Africa who didn't know him or know of his work. It's like the joke about the nun who asked the visitor at the Vatican, "Who's that guy standing on the balcony next to Rex Pennington?" Now I use, "Do you know Rex Pennington?" as a way of testing if someone's really from South Africa when he claims to be.

People don't become legends without a reason. In Rex's case I can identify at least three elements: First, and foremost, unimpeachable integrity. Second, dedication to make his life count, a calling. Third, humility and prayer, to ask for help to know what's right. He's a legend because he's succeeded where others have failed.

I asked his daughter, Ruth, and son-in-law, Jim Shannon, if they knew why he came to Casady. Jim said he believed it was, in large part, the challenge of an adventure. On reflection, that makes sense to me, but my student stereotype of him as a teacher had cloaked this part of him from my conscious mind. In the early 50s, Casady was an "adventure." It had a charismatic headmaster who had already recruited some highly unusual and dedicated people who were each making a sacrifice to take the job. It was "the road not taken."

Ghandi listed as three of his *seven social sins*: religion without sacrifice, wealth without work, and education without character. I think Rex would agree very strongly with these. What Rex brought to Casady was respect for responsibility, a search for truth, and leadership which demanded personal sacrifice.

I think his unarticulated message for the relatively affluent Casady student was "learn, take responsibility, work hard and sacrifice." He never lectured, preached or talked down to his students. He treated them as persons who had their responsibilities, just as he had his own.

Perhaps why he left Oklahoma tells more about him than why he came. He said at the time that he left because he felt South Africa needed him, and he was becoming too comfortable. What he did not say was that even "adventures" require goals and sacrifices. "One personal example is worth more than a thousand sermons."

A conversation with Rex today has that same enthusiasm and energy I remember so well from Casady. We talked about squash (he still plays exhibition matches at age seventy!), but when I asked, "How is South Africa doing today?" a softness came into his voice, his face muscles relaxed, and he replied with slow, pensive exhalation, "So far, it's really a miracle."

<u>Rex doesn't ever try to tell you what he knows; rather, he's forever trying to learn what you know</u>. Yesterday was a great day. My only regret is that I did far too much of the talking.

"Red"

"Red" was my boss on the pipeline in Spain. He had fought professionally 172 times, mostly for under $100 per fight, weighed about 160 pounds, and carried his forty-five to fifty years very well. There were forty-two American pipelines on the job. **I was 6'2" and only two men were shorter than I.** Red, at about 5-feet-8-inches, was one of them.

He was from Oxford, Mississippi. Every time I'd do something stupid, Red would come over to suggest the right way to do it. He would start out by saying, "Well, as an old Oxford man to a Dartmouth man…." and then make me feel stupid and good at the same time. I think I learned more about people that summer than any comparable period in my life. We worked seven days a week, eleven hours a day, in which the temperature often got above 110 degrees, and we often walked fifteen miles a day putting up fencing to define the "right of way." These men worked hard and made about $100/day plus expenses, which was a lot of money in 1955. I used to go to get a professional shave every day because it only cost a nickel, and razor blades were more expensive! Several lessons I learned:

Pipeliners believed "real men" lived by a code of "live and let live." "Real men" didn't fight for two reasons: First, in a *real* fight, someone gets maimed or killed. Second, "real men" lived by their own code but didn't give a hoot how someone else lived as long as he didn't try to impose his views on them. If you bullied people, it just showed your insecurity and was considered effeminate. I was accepted because I didn't try to be something I wasn't (a "real pipeliner"), and I usually did my job well, and that counted.

Sometimes you can try too hard. One day I was digging a ditch with the Spanish workers. Red came along and said, "If you'll stop working and start watching, you'll get twice as much ditch dug. Otherwise, they stop and watch you."

You've got to match the man to the job. I was about to hire a new man. Red came up and asked me what was the job. I told him a ditch gang. "Who you gonna pick?" I pointed to a strong looking guy about twenty-eight years old. "I'll teach you a lesson, Bob. You hire your man, and I'll pick mine, pointing to the old man. Tell me which one is making the most hole tomorrow." The next day he came by and asked how they were doing? I admitted that the old man was digging about twice as much ditch. Red said, "I bet I can tell you what happened. I'll bet that young man took off his shirt and started beating the earth with a pick for a minute or so and then rested. I'll bet that old man just turned a half shovel at a time and never stopped. When you want to move a piano, get a sprinter, a young man. When you want to dig a ditch, get a distance man, an old man who is just proud to be able to keep on moving!"

"Never brandish a weapon you don't intend to use to its fullest capacity or you'll throw away the other guy's rule book." We were talking about the Spanish machismo, the Spanish habit of pulling out knives. Red thought for a minute and said that his experience had taught that if someone pulls a knife and flashes it around, he just has one less good hand than you. If he comes after you seriously, run like hell. This lesson may have saved my life.

We were having our house on Newark Street renovated, and the bottom of the house was open. We had moved back and were camping out on the third floor. I had set up a makeshift burglar alarm on the second floor in the event someone came in thinking the house was empty and would walk into a confrontational situation. Lee had gone to visit her family in New York, and I had a friend, George Smith, a retired Lieutenant Colonel, staying with me. About 6:00 a.m., I heard the alarm go off, and I reached to pull up my 45 automatic. I yelled, "Who's there?" A voice came up from the second floor, "The painters." I gave my gun to George and then, stupidly, walked downstairs, with George staying behind in a hidden spot where he could hear. I walked into the middle of them, thinking to myself, "It's Friday the 13th. How's my luck?" Moments later, I realized that it wasn't my day. In retrospect, I was sure of who they were, but not sure enough to shoot someone. If I had walked in carrying a gun, they would have known I was their enemy. Coupled with my uncertainty, it could have been a dangerous situation. As it was, as long as I was the least bit uncertain, I couldn't have shot them. I retreated back upstairs and called the police. They got away with some tools. I got away without injury!

I like to think back to when Red and I were sitting out on the hotel patio looking up at two young, beautiful Spanish women sitting on the balcony of a house that clearly belonged to some very important person. After two weeks of admiration, I asked Red, "Would you like to meet them?" I walked over under the balcony and took a chance in my best French. I said I was in the University and working at a summer job. One of them spoke French, and they invited me up. Red's last comment, in his deep southern drawl was, "Bob, that little girl's pretty enough to take to Sunday School." (I went out with her every night for the rest of the summer. I would pick her up at eight and take her home at midnight in time for her to have dinner with her family, whom I never met.)

Eugen Rosenstock-Huessey

Eugen Rosenstock-Huessey never knew my name, even though he was probably the most influential professor I ever had. He taught a course which was a study of pre-Socratic philosophers but really spoke to me at a very deep level. We spent most of our time discussing words and the difference between words. For example, "speech, conversation and talk." When someone "speaks" in ancient Greece, he has a formal responsibility to his subject, e.g., a governor speaking as chief of state. By contrast, if two people "converse," they have responsibility to their subject but are not formally representing it; rather they are colleagues speaking at the same level. "Talk" is different again. Talk is an exchange between two people who are discussing a subject for which they have limited knowledge and no responsibility.

Another distinction we made was between countries, governments and nations. Countries are defined geographically, governments are defined politically, nations are defined in the mind of man and are governed "by someone who looks and thinks like me."

Most of the course was discussing *Physis, Logos and Ethos* and how the perspective changed from one pre-Socratic to another and how this transferred to later philosophers.

We studied Parmenides and Heraclitus and debated the merits of man being viewed as the "city small" or cities being "man large." He defined "frigidity" as the "inability to disarm."

He attacked the sophists hardest of all. He said Socrates drank hemlock to prove he wasn't a sophist. Jesus died on the cross to prove that he wasn't a sophist. He said, "We are returning to the age of the sophist, who is personified by the lawyer who argues any case without taking into account (except in fee) whether he's on the right side or not."

Rosenstock-Huessey said that some questions cannot be answered and should not be asked. When you and two friends are in the desert, and there's only enough water for one of you to survive; rather than choose, you break the water bottle and then walk, no—rather **march**—out of the desert together. He said you should never ask who loves you more, your mother or your father.

He was a man with a giant ego and unbridled enthusiasm for his own ideas. His brain seemed to be on fire, and energy radiated from his "speech." Yes, he "spoke" to students from his *office as Professor of Philosophy.* He focused a beam of ideas, each idea a charged particle, straining to release its load, or confront, or combine, with an alien force.

Trying to ask a question in class was like trying to get a drink from a waterfall with a paper cup. The only direct communication I ever had with him was on my term paper. He said I was a "Pythagorean." Something in the way he said it led me to doubt it was a high compliment.

In sum, he provided a framework to put many modern, as well as ancient, ideas in perspective. He demanded attention. He provoked thought. He engulfed you in the rapids of his mind and took you over the falls with him. He was a great professor.

Ben Levin

Ben Levin certainly has been a strong father figure for me. He was my boss when I was a Lieutenant at Fort Monmouth, New Jersey. We worked on lithospheric propagation, which is using the crust of the earth as a waveguide for communication in the event of nuclear war.

I was very flattered when he chose to join EarthSat after he retired from the Department of Defense, where he served as the Acting Director for R&D and was in charge of all basic research in DOD—a very responsible job.

At EarthSat, he was officially Executive Vice President, but unofficially also, "Dean of the Faculty, and occupant of the Sheffield/Colwell Chair of Logic and Elocution." He taught our staff and clients radar systems, optics, geophysics, geology, economics, business administration, international affairs, French and Portuguese. He led field trips to Zaire, the Philippines, Brazil, Greece, Iran and Mexico. He traversed the Alps, Andes and Atlas mountains and was the quintessence of what we EarthSatters all strove to be. Always the gentleman, he still always asks the tough questions. Ben always had time for a question or explanation. His own explanations characteristically flow first from principles down to the specifics, every step being thoughtful, logical and measured.

The characteristic movement I remember most was when he would bring his chair around his desk to be closer, so he could be as available as possible. Comparing the outside of our heads, we had about equal amounts of hair, but his was grayer than mine, both in fact and metaphorically. Ben is a wise man, and everyone at EarthSat was bursting with pride when we knew Ben was going to represent us on any subject. It was also very important from a business standpoint that we had a grayer head representing us, particularly with foreign governments. Ben has the experience and real class. His technological knowledge is so broad and so deep that our brain trust of scientists came to Ben day and night for his counsel.

Ben's intellectual abilities can't be emulated by most of us human beings, no matter how hard we try. He is just a unique individual. **Most of all, what he represents to me is a role model for professional integrity**. For that especially, I want to express my appreciation for the inspiration he has provided.

John Wallace

John Wallace was for many years a great father-in-law and member of EarthSat's Board of Directors. He was a founder of First Manhattan Company in NYC. John was always there when needed. He sometimes spoke up (very passionately) at board meetings when I would have preferred he hadn't, but he really cared that I succeed, and that the stockholders (including his partners) would get a good return on their investment. I recently reread some of the thoughtful letters he wrote me and couldn't help but reflect that the company would have fared better had I paid more attention to his sagacious advice. He died in March, 1991. At that time, I wrote down these memories of John which still ring loudly in my memory:

JOHN WALLACE—SPECIAL MEMORIES
(23 March 1991)

- Systematically assigning probabilities of each guest attending our wedding (our estimate 176; actual 178)
- Caring eyes, filled with tears, as he watched us leave the church after our wedding
- His loyalty to his family and his partners
- His inability to let me pack the car haphazardly, trying to hold back but inevitably stepping forward and volunteering, "You know I packed ships in the Navy in WWII."
- His honest reflection after looking at our third annual report. "You know, Bob, most companies your size have a Board of Directors that consists of two dentists, a lawyer and maybe an accountant."
- His long thoughtful letters of business advice
- His advice to a new son-in-law: "Bob, when your father-in-law offers to pay for something, don't argue. The correct response is 'Thank you'."
- His advice to an older son-in-law: "Bob, when you call someone on the telephone and he answers, say 'Hello, John, this is Bob.'"

- Introducing himself to everyone within three rows and revealing in a stage whisper, "I'm here because my granddaughter, Amy Porter, has been chosen to pick up the nutcracker."

- His dignity even during the long process of dying.
- John Wallace had class.
- John Wallace cared.

Judge Lawrence Edward Walsh

Judge Lawrence Edward Walsh is one of the people I respect most among the people I have met during the last thirty years. The posts he has held are impressive; for example, he recently served as Special Prosecutor for the Iran-Contra hearings and previously as President, American Bar Association, Deputy Attorney General and a Federal Judge. I met him, however, through the good offices of my sister, his wife, and I have come to value that opportunity greatly.

Ed, which is what most of his friends call him, is as sincere and modest an individual as I have ever met. He treats all his friends with great respect—so much so that I have felt uncomfortable on occasion, when I would suggest we get together for lunch or dinner and he behaved as though I was the one with the busy schedule that needed to be accommodated.

I remember one time when he came to my house in the early 1960's. There were a lot of young CIA officers there. Ed listened with genuine interest as they told him about international events. They never guessed that he knew a fair amount about Washington matters himself.

He always gives me straight answers even if they aren't flattering to him. Before Watergate, I asked him what he thought President Nixon and John Mitchell thought of him when he was Chairman of the ABA Ethics Committee. His answer was most prophetic. He said, "They probably think I'm a good Republican, but too academic and too much concerned with the administration of the law to be politically reliable." Ed has faced some challenging protagonists, including Nixon on the Supreme Court nominees, Reagan and Bush on the Iran-Contra hearings.

He enjoys sharing stories on learning experiences he has had personally. One story that frequently comes to mind is when he first sat in on one of Governor Thomas Dewey's weekly meetings with the state legislative leaders. He said he spoke on several subjects. Afterwards, the Governor took him aside and explained quietly that "he had learned it was best not to speak out on subjects you aren't

186

responsible for, because you will soon find it hard enough just answering questions to which you must give the answer. After they come to respect your answers, they will ask your opinions on other subjects."

Ed is the best example I know of someone who works to "get on the right side of the argument," i.e., to confront the world as it is, not as he wished it were. I saw an excellent example of this when he debated a congressman from Michigan before the Women's National Press Club on the role of the ABA in screening Supreme Court nominees. Ed was Chairman of the ABA Standing Committee on the Federal Judiciary, which reported in these matters. At the debate, he surprised some by conceding his weaker points and then proceeded to move to arguments he could enthusiastically defend. He said that the ABA was testifying solely as to the judicial qualifications of the candidate, and it was not its role to judge the political correctness of a nominee's behavior. That was the responsibility of the Senate.

He then took the initiative and addressed the remaining issue, "Is ABA advice useful?" and concluded that it was, although it shouldn't be regarded as a substitute, nor an excuse, for thorough scrutiny by the press and Congress.

Finally, one of the most important lessons that he taught by his own example, is to insure you go to the appropriate level for the issue you have to address. Stated otherwise, even, or especially if, you have high level contacts, don't use them unnecessarily or inappropriately. Ed definitely believed in erring in the direction of understatement.

The lessons I learned from Ed amplified in many ways what my father had taught me: face reality—even if it hurts, it will likely hurt more later on; get on the right side of the argument, and be certain not to have your energy and credibility worn down by defending a weak position, especially an inherited position.

Breene Kerr

Breene Kerr once told me, "The most important thing about a fight is knowing when it started and whether you're in it or not." It reminded me of a quote by Mr. Webb of a comment he attributed to Breene's father, who was considered one of the most influential men in the Senate, "I'm against any conspiracy I'm not a party to!"

Breene lived only a few houses away from my home in Oklahoma City, but because he was a few years older and bought his house after I'd left for college, we only really got to know each other after he moved to Washington to serve as Assistant Administrator for Policy under Mr. Webb. When I first joined him at NASA, Breene sat me down and said, "There's one point you must understand at the outset. My title is a misnomer. One person makes policy at this agency and his name is James E. Webb."

Breene, a graduate, and now a Trustee of MIT, brought me into NASA, and he, more than anyone else, was responsible for my involvement with space and remote sensing. Without him there would have been no EarthSat (nor would EarthSat have hired Pat LoRusso, now an EarthSat Vice President whom I met when she was Breene's secretary at NASA)!

We've also had a heck-of-a lot of fun together getting an education in "cornering the cocoa market." Despite that reckless affair in cocoa, Breene is one of the wisest and most private people I know. He is a totally independent thinker whose opinion is never stereotypical. His opinions almost always reflect the weighing of what he's about to say against the advice he has received from his mentors. He often quotes his father and Mr. Webb. Many parts of the essays I wrote on Mr. Webb were stimulated by conversations with Breene. (Breene once observed that most people who knew him very well called him "Mr. Webb." Casual acquaintances call him "Jim.")

Breene has a good way of phrasing. Before he lays out a concept, he thinks it through from so many viewpoints that when he presents it, he sounds like he's just letting you in on a little secret.

He is also a master of understatement and droll humor. One time before a meeting we had with Mr. Webb, he told me what I call his **one wish hypothesis:** "Bob, Mr. Webb's not going to ask us what ten wishes he can grant us today. We have to have one wish and then try to support why we're taking up his time with that one."

Another statement that I recall was "Beware of do-gooders, because they're at the heart of most of the world's problems." When I first drafted this, I was prepared to challenge Breene as being a "closet do-gooder" himself. He certainly has a long-time interest in education in general and of looking for a melding of interest, where practical, between the public and private interest. On reflection, I acknowledge there is a great difference: the "do-gooder" is typically out of control, while the person who succeeds at "doing good" has his ends in perspective and his means under control. Breene fits very well into the "doing good "group. It shows I'm still mulling over his words and learning.

Parenthetically, my father was practically the only Republican in Oklahoma for a long time and was naturally unhappy with Senator Kerr's successful reelection record. Senator Kerr died just three days before my father, and one of the last stories Dad told me on the morning he died was how gracious Senator Kerr was to him at a recent occasion preparatory of the swearing in of the first Republican governor. I noticed Breene attended my father's funeral. Since they were never close friends, I presume he went out of respect to him and because he was a neighbor. I appreciated it very much, especially after such a hard week for him. If you ever wonder, as I have, if people remember things like that, they do. He's a class act.

James E. Webb

James E. Webb, was the Administrator of NASA who "put a man on the moon," former Director of the Bureau of the Budget, former Under Secretary of State, holder of thirty-two honorary Ph.D.'s and numerous public service awards, a gracious man who cared about space and cared about companies like EarthSat, a founding stockholder of EarthSat and a loyal friend and supporter. It is rare indeed that an opportunity presents itself, as it did in this case, for numerous EarthSat employees to have the opportunity to interact with and share the time of great men like Mr. Webb. The following is a piece I wrote nine years ago on some experiences I had with Mr. Webb. He read this and gave copies to various friends and biographers, including one from the Smithsonian, which made me feel very good.

TEN LESSONS I LEARNED FROM JAMES E. WEBB
19 February 1985

"Great men I knew all had one quality in common. They each had the ability to select just the right chord from the full scale of emotions they possessed. They could be gentle, even tender. They could be tough, even ferocious. They knew exactly how much power to brandish at any moment in time. They never wasted it needlessly. They knew their limits and their beliefs." Joe Fox, author of Executive Qualities, could not have spoken truer words. This idea sets the context well for the recollections of some lessons a truly great man taught me over the past 19 years.

First, KNOW WHAT YOU WANT. Sometimes the wait was long, sometimes short, before being admitted to the Administrator's office during the Webb era at NASA. But once inside, an enthusiastic question usually greeted the visitor who had requested an appointment. "What can I do for you?" Mr. Webb would ask. This simple question accomplished several objectives: It minimized the likelihood he would waste any more time than necessary on an agenda item he couldn't or didn't want to address. It politely urged the visitor to come to the point. It quickly and subtly established the relationship between the requestor and the grantor so that the official difference in their relative roles was made immediately clear. Finally, it sometimes had the effect of stripping a carefully contrived approach of its timing and style and instead let the presenter know from the outset that he would not be "in control" of this meeting. In short, Webb had known and accomplished what he wanted: to establish a structure for the meeting and indicate that he was a willing listener.

Webb demanded no less of himself or his associates. Breene Kerr, the former senator's son, was my boss and understood Webb's standards very well. Each week Breene would have an appointment with Webb, and on occasion he would ask me to attend with him. After one or two meetings in which I had made several suggestions for actions by Webb, Breene called me aside and quite politely set forth what I call the ONE WISH HYPOTHESIS. "Bob," he said, "Mr. Webb isn't going to ask us today which ten wishes he can grant; rather, in the first five minutes we must tell him what one wish we want him to consider. In the next 5 minutes, we must point out why it is timely he consider this now. In the next 30 minutes, we must show him that we have done our staffing well and understand the implications of a decision. If, in an entire year, one big wish is granted and implemented to the benefit of the agency, we will have the satisfaction of knowing we have been more effective than anyone who has occupied this position before us."

Webb was also very astute at knowing WHO TO INFLUENCE. One story which illustrates this is told by Julian Scheer, formerly his Assistant Administrator for Public Affairs. He tells the story of a speech Webb gave which Julian thought was a disaster inasmuch as half the audience fell asleep. Afterward, he as much as told Webb this. "How did Senator Smith react?" Webb asked. Julian replied that he had picked the only person who was on the edge of her seat all evening. "Good," Webb shot back, "because that's who the speech was intended for!"

Second, when he was at NASA, whether asking for advice, giving advice, or agreeing on a course of action, Webb was careful to ENSURE THAT COMMUNICATIONS WERE CLEAR. Frequently, several possible courses of action were considered which could result in different versions of the event. Consequently, at the end of many conferences, he would pick up his tape recorder and carefully summarize, in the presence of his visitor or staff, their respective views and the agreed course of action. He would then play back the tape and invite his visitor to suggest any amendment or ask for elaboration on any points. This would result in a memo which summarized the background, current position and future actions agreed on by both parties. It not only served as a record of the meeting, but also sharpened its focus.

When there was a difference of opinion within EarthSat regarding management and marketing priorities, I discussed the matter with Webb, particularly the proposition suggested by some that we have a company-wide meeting to let everyone have his say. While my staff's intentions were good, the proposed alternatives were as diverse as the number of employees.

"Bob," he said, after listening to my summary, "you've got a lot of tough questions to consider, but having a big meeting is not the approach I'd take. Clearly, it's important that you not be, or even appear to be, arbitrary. I would seek counsel from those whose judgements I trust, but I'd NEVER ASK ADVICE FROM ANYONE IF I WASN'T PREPARED TO SERIOUSLY CONSIDER HIS ANSWER. If I understand your appraisal correctly, some of the viewpoints are unrealistic. I'd be concerned that a large meeting will just embarrass your associates who don't have useful contributions to make and anger those whose positions are rejected. If it was I, I'd get together my top two or three advisors, put the hard questions out on the table, seek their advice, and summarize your conclusions in a memo to make sure you're all in agreement, and report the conclusions to the others. That way, you'll start out with your top men behind you, and you'll avoid unnecessary confrontations."

It is noteworthy that although Webb had vast administrative experience, when serving as an advisor himself, he provided honest advice when asked, but always respected the fact that I had to take final responsibility. It's been my observation that the more decision making experience a person has had, the more deference he shows toward the one who has to "sign his name and take the final responsibility." The mark of an inexperienced advisor is that he tells you what to do. The mark of an experienced advisor is that he "shares his thoughts and experiences for your consideration" and leaves you to make the decision.

Third, AVOID UNNECESSARY FIGHTS is one of the best lessons I learned working with Webb. Watching Webb go through the daily mail with his staff was a part of my NASA education. One of the problems each CEO faces is the proclivity of his lieutenants to spend his valued equity points. One such instance arose when a subordinate had drafted a letter for Webb's signature complimenting the Ambassador to the UN on a victory he had won on an intra-administration policy issue. Webb reflected first on the substance of the letter and then addressed the broader issue. "This was a hard fought battle. What if the loser reads this? What business do I, as NASA Administrator, have using energy and equity I need to do this job on something that's not my fight!"

Fourth, one day Mr. Webb and I were discussing a forthcoming negotiation with some potential joint venture partners. Both groups brought something essential to the table, but our opposite number was COMSAT, a somewhat larger company than EarthSat (albeit with a somewhat more limited name). "I'd let them know who some of your stockholders, directors and advisors are so they'll respect you, but I wouldn't be too explicit about their respective roles. WHEN NEGOTIATING, ALWAYS KEEP AT LEAST ONE HOLE CARD," he advised. "IT'S NOT GOOD TO LET SOMEONE THINK HE KNOWS YOUR FULL HAND. MAKE SURE THERE IS SOME DEGREE OF BOTH PREDICTABILITY AND UNPREDICTABILITY IN YOUR STRATEGY."

These were words spoken by a master of negotiation. Not a man prone to bluff, but a genius at expanding the dimension of an issue to include every resource he could bring to bear. At times, this ability made it appear that he could create new cards out of air! In staff meetings, when confronted by a phalanx of aerospace engineers whose logic was sometimes arrogantly technical, he would quietly query, "How do you think we can communicate that to Senator Margaret Chase Smith?" which would abruptly change a know-it-all group to a let's-work-together group. When testifying before hostile congressmen who were preoccupied with avoiding criticism for space program expenditures, he would shift the focus from "dollars and schedules" which had negative voter image to "jobs and mission objectives" which had positive image by dramatizing "the task of managing over 20,000 contractors, subcontractors and suppliers." These were not just verbal ploys to assert personal dominance; on the contrary, they had the effect of building a team effort.

It is important to note that being predictable (but not totally so) was also a sine qua non to this strategy. Clearly, if one were too unpredictable he couldn't be trusted or relied upon to be able to perform as a "good team member." But by not revealing all his cards, he causes partners and opponents with large appetites to think twice before considering his portion. By revealing some, without playing them, one demonstrates his ability to be a strong partner while avoiding some unnecessary confrontations that might cause wounds which may be hard to heal.

On personnel matters, Webb believed in being very predictable. During one period of EarthSat's development, I was concerned that I was coming to loggerheads with some of my staff which could have been exacerbated by having one or more threatening to submit his resignation. Webb's advice was firm. "Whenever I've taken a job one of the first things I would tell my staff when I gathered them together was that I would accept any resignation submitted without debate. In your case, Bob, a small company can't afford to be polarized between two groups. I suggest you let this position be known." It proved to be a very effective way to make sure there were no miscalculations (and no resignations were threatened).

Fifth, I was having discussions with a major aerospace company about their buying a minority interest in our company. I discussed it with Webb. His response was, "If you let GE to invest in you, do you realize that you're declaring war on TRW and Westinghouse and all the rest of GE's competitors? Are you prepared to make this choice now? Can you afford <u>not</u> to do business with these other companies? Will GE give you enough business to compensate you for the business you'll lose by taking sides?
Remember, WHENEVER YOU CHOOSE A FRIEND, YOU SET YOURSELF UP FOR A FIGHT WITH HIS ENEMIES! Senator Kerr once told me, 'I'm against any conspiracy I'm not a full party to.'"
Sixth, EarthSat had an early opportunity to get national coverage in LOOK magazine. I went to Webb and asked him his opinion on the advisability of this. He replied, "Just remember, Bob, the higher you go up the mountain, the better your view, but the more people can see you from the valley who might choose to take a shot at you. I'd suggest that you KEEP A LOW PROFILE until you get established and can protect yourself." This philosophy was reflected in an earlier time when we were talking about his approach to hiring consultants at NASA. "You must always view what you pay someone from the viewpoint of a taxpayer or stockholder, not just in terms of his value to you. For example," he said, "at NASA, I chose not to pay any of my personal consultants more than the regular government scale because above that amount the average man in the street might misinterpret our relationship."

On the other hand, Webb also knew how to use his considerable visibility to good effect by breaking convention and doing the unexpected. For example, he would make a point of visiting a limited number of subordinates in their offices from time to time rather than always expecting them to be summoned to his. This had the effect of not undermining the General Manager (Seamans) and avoiding the stereotype of being aloof, and also built up the image of those he visited with their own staffs. (It also, on occasion, caused them to invite their staffs into the meeting so Webb would get a look one echelon lower than usual.) Nowhere was image more important than on Capitol Hill where the traditional antipathy between congressmen and administration bureaucrats was legend. Webb addressed this problem by visiting congressmen at their offices whenever possible and avoiding the usual high profile perks. One classic story of the Webb administration occurred during a congressional hearing when he was testifying during a time the papers were attacking government officials in general for living "too high on the hog." Sure enough, one senator asked him, "How many chauffeur-driven Cadillacs do you have supporting your agency?" "None!" Webb answered. "Then what's your personal car?" the senator countered. "A Checker cab, Senator," Webb replied. The exchange was featured prominently in the paper the next day.

Seventh, as a manager, Webb was a realist. While many managers conceive of elaborate schemes which require that the employee adapt to the system at all cost, or conversely, manipulate the whole management organization to accommodate one individual, Webb felt it was his charge to provide the mechanisms to amplify the natural talents the manager had while accepting the person as he really was. "DON'T LET THE BEST BE THE ENEMY OF THE GOOD" he used to say. "Look for 80% of what you want in a person. Be happy if you get 70%, and don't replace anyone who appears to be providing 50 to 60 percent without an alternative in mind!" I saw this a number of times when he would take a good look at his objectives, then augment existing management methods to provide accommodation for the style of the employee. For example, George Mueller was in charge of Manned Spaceflight which was the largest individual line responsibility in NASA. Mueller worked very hard, was courageous and effective, and certainly gave his job 130% of his available energy. At times Webb realized that he had reached the limit of what he could expect Mueller to provide and consequently, when he had pressing additional duties he wanted Mueller to assume, he found a way to relieve him of some present responsibilities so that Mueller could reorganize his time to meet Webb's new priorities.

Eighth, I had prepared a speech for Mr. Webb which he was to give to the American Society of Cyberneticists. I attended with my wife expecting to hear my own words. Instead, he gave an entirely different, impromptu speech in which he said that he thought it was an important and worthwhile objective that the cyberneticists had set to pretend to the throne of the decision maker. In that context, he wanted to review for them some of the decisions he had been a party to so that they might better appreciate the magnitude of the challenge. He then recited numerous examples: the Marshall Plan when he was Under Secretary of State, the setting of the government's budget priorities when he was Director of the Bureau of the budget, the decision to send a man to the moon during his tenure as Administrator of NASA. His conclusion was simply that in each of these important decisions, THE SUM OF THE SECOND AND THIRD

ORDER CONSIDERATIONS WAS GREATER THAN THE FIRST ORDER ISSUE IN MAKING THE FINAL DECISION. "Therefore, he reasoned, "your task is going to require a very sophisticated data base which will be difficult, if not impossible, to prepare."

"For example, we had the technology to go to the moon. We had to pursue several routes in parallel, and we didn't know which would work, but we knew we could do it if we could get the national commitment. The technical decision, which many people considered primary, was in fact a foregone conclusion. On the other hand, the importance of image in world political and military affairs became a critical factor as did the management flexibility which was provided in the legislation setting up NASA, and the confidence both Kennedy and Johnson showed at critical times."

After the speech, Mr. Webb came over to the table where my wife and I were sitting and asked, "What did you think of my speech, Bob? I guess you noticed I changed it. At the last moment I got thinking that this group understood all the theoretical issues we had discussed in your version, but what they don't know is how people make decisions in the real world, and that's what they've got to know if they're going to succeed."

What he did not tell them that night was that acts of courage by individuals like himself also made a difference that would be hard to program on a computer. One example of this occurred when NASA was about to fire a regular "thin skinned" Atlas missile in a major engineering test of the Mercury capsule. Several days before the launch, Webb received a request from the Air Force that NASA not use the regular Atlas booster in an open civilian launch because it might jeopardize national security. If it failed, the Soviets might think that the Atlas, which was the backbone of our military defense system, was unreliable. The alternative would be to delay the test until the "thick skinned" Atlas would be ready and to use it. Webb considered the matter very seriously and asked Dryden, Seamans and Mueller to review the estimates of a successful launch. All replied that a change of system now would be difficult and costly in time inasmuch as the system integration had already taken place between the Atlas and the payload. Further, all three felt confident of success, having reviewed the matter with the technical team. Webb knew also that if he relied on outsiders rather than the NASA officials, doubts of his understanding of the engineering issues would arise in future decisions. He advised the Air Force officials that he was going forward with the current plans to launch. I understand that the matter was referred by the Air Force to the White House, which did not intervene. The test was a success.

(As a postscript, several months later the thick skinned Atlas was launched and blew up very soon after it left the pad!)

Ninth, during the time I worked for NASA, Webb asked me to interview several "wise men" and ask them the question, "When you look back, what did you do right, whether or not you knew it was right at the time?" Several years later, after he had left NASA, I asked Webb that same question. After some reflection he replied that he felt he had been able to PACKAGE DECISIONS IN A MANNER WHICH WAS UNDERSTANDABLE TO THE DECISION-MAKER AND WHICH WOULD YIELD RESULTS IN A TIME FRAME THAT WAS RELEVANT TO HIM. He elaborated further that different decision-makers have different time frames in which they expect results to be produced. "For example," he said, "a scientist could understand the importance of developing advanced technology, a philosopher could understand the importance of the United States becoming a "space faring" nation, while a senator with a six year term, or a President with a four year term could relate to the goal of 'landing a man on the moon within a decade!'"

Tenth, and finally, one of the most unusual aspects of Webb is his ability to confront the unvarnished realities of life. An example of his bringing reality to the table occurred when I first talked to him about our brain damaged son, John. At that point, most of the medical facts were quite clear; nevertheless, most people I spoke to perpetuated the myth of denial by reciting anecdotes which would hold out for an optimistic future. Not so with Webb. He asked about ten, basically, "give me the facts" questions: "What does your doctor think? What does your wife think? What do you think? After assessing these he looked up and said, "Well, Bob, you're just being tested. NO ONE IS EVER TESTED ON TERMS ACCEPTABLE TO THEM, TERMS THAT ARE 'FAIR,' OTHERWISE, IT'S NOT A REAL TEST. PEOPLE ARE ONLY TESTED ON TERMS THAT ARE UNACCEPTABLE TO THEM." He quietly continued, "John can't do anything about his condition. Probably the doctors can't either. Certainly you and your wife can't. Your test is to survive this and become stronger with the knowledge you can survive the unacceptable. Bob, when and if you get beyond this, you'll know more about yourself, your wife will know more about you, your friends will know more about you, and you'll develop a new strength."

I've reflected on this conversation many times and observed that this is what separates, and unites, the "Jim Webbs of the world" from, and with, the rest of humanity: They accept life as it really is. Instead of complaining about cards they don't like, they say to themselves, "You're just being tested. Now play the hand." This is the Webb I shall always remember.

General Jacob E. Smart

General Jacob Smart (Four Stars) represents the finest class of human being with whom I have ever been privileged to be closely associated. It wasn't just his four stars, nor the fact that he had been Deputy Chief of Staff in the Air Force that impresses; it is much more: His passion to attain excellence, his willingness to commit precious energy to solve difficult problems, his clarity of thought, his decisiveness and humility, his pursuit of the "right" answer and to be on the "right" side of the argument."

I first met General Smart at NASA where he served as Assistant Administrator for Defense and Inter-Agency Affairs. He was my boss after Breene Kerr. NASA had fifty-five generals and admirals. I got to know a great many of them and couldn't help but try to second guess the Department of Defense and see if I could characterize differences between a retired one star, two star, three star and four star general. There were a lot of fine people in the group, but the one virtue that stood out with the limited number of "four stars" was that when other people described them, the word "gentleman" always found a place somewhere. The other trait was a willingness to listen to new ideas, then act decisively. This certainly described Jake.

But there were other experiences in Jake's past that hardened his personal steel in the crucible we call life. He was a genuine war hero who had flown many missions in combat, had been wounded twice, shot down and made a prisoner of war. He had planned one of the most dangerous raids of the war, the low level raid on Ploesti, the Nazi oil refineries in Romania. He also served as a staff officer at the Washington, Casablanca and Quebec conferences with Roosevelt, Churchill and their military chiefs. After all of this, having witnessed and participated in history-making events, Jake is one of the most humble people I know.

The kind of experience represented by mentors like Jake is too deep to communicate in any number of words. This was a man whose wisdom and experience I was privileged to share and that far exceeds any other gold EarthSat could ever produce for me.

We had some good times together. In Iran, we went to visit the Minister of Agriculture, Rohani. His office was on the sixth floor and the elevator didn't work. The person who met us was about thirty years old and he rushed us up the stairs with the admonition that "we can't keep the Minister waiting." After racing to the top, Jake wryly commented that "he wouldn't have to waste money on an EKG for a few years."

Under the Shah, the military and civilian ministries were kept separate, partially as a security measure. I had been asked to address the entire Cabinet, and Jake had been in touch with the top military. We had unwittingly crossed a line which was a "no no" in Iran. Further, we had visited Ambassador Helms on various occasions and my history with the CIA was no secret. The upshot was that we must have been under tight surveillance and our room was unquestionably bugged. One afternoon Jake said to me, "Let me see those enhanced Landsat pictures." I told him they were in my briefcase. He looked at them and commented, "I'm certainly not going to show these to the military or they'll classify the whole project." A short time later, we left the room for twenty minutes. When we returned, the pictures were gone!

Although Jake is retired now, he is in good health, visits us for lunch a few times a year, and always volunteers "to be of help any way I can." There's really nothing I can say or do to reflect adequately the appreciation we feel for his service and support over the years.

Jake taught me by example. It's the only way he knows.

General Charles Pearre Cabell

General Cabell (four stars) served as Deputy Director at the CIA. Subsequently, he advised the Administrator of NASA on national security affairs. We met at NASA and developed a close friendship. General Cabell had one of the keenest analytical minds I have ever known, and he gave a new meaning to the word "staffing." The first time I prepared a letter for Mr. Webb to the President, I went to Cabell and told him about the assignment. "Who's receiving the letter, Bob?" he asked. "The President," I answered. "No," he replied, "Who is going to <u>receive</u> it before the President, and whose going to take action on it afterwards?"

Cabell continued, "One of his staff will highlight the key points. It's critical that we don't put anything in we don't want highlighted, or that will take the President away from our central point. When the President reads it, he'll probably circle one part and write someone's name to take the follow-up. We have to figure out a direction that we want him to go."

This was followed by numerous drafts, readings, twenty-minute debates over whether the tone of a word was right. The difference between "suggest" and "advise," asking for "comment" versus "opinion," "coordinate" versus "inform," etc. He knew very well that more than one general had been misled by his staff because of the poor choice of a word or for expressing one too many thoughts.

Cabell preferred not to play games; in fact, he was the opposite. He took negotiations very seriously and tried to get the principal issues on the table for discussion, but it wasn't for lack of skill or experience. He told me about one negotiation where his opposite number was none other than the legendary Sir Charles P. Snow. It was just after WWII and the subject was R&D development.

The Americans would have an advantage if they moved quickly, but the British benefitted by dragging it out until they could organize their commercial sector. Snow was always addressed as "Sir Charles," and he was accompanied by four British Majors who would nod every time Sir Charles spoke. "To be frank," Cabell said, "it was intimidating." What irritated him most was that the squadron of British kept tabling all the issues and sidetracking the meeting with time-wasting recitations on their position. Cabell went to the U.S. Personnel Officer and said, "I want you to assign me three bird colonels and one man over 6-feet-4-inches tall who has a Ph.D., whom I can legitimately call 'Professor,' and who will do exactly as I say!"

At the next meeting, the British were arranged in their usual "command post deployment" or the "British Square." They were surprised when four American colonels arrived late with their arms full of books and seated themselves in a fashion designed to discombobulate the British lines of communication.

Whenever Cabell made a point, they quickly looked at their private notes and skimmed through their big books. They would then nod vigorously. The next time Sir Charles suggested they "table that until it can be studied," Cabell said, "No need, Professor Smith can give us a quick answer on this." Then the professor stood up and stated in a booming voice that General Cabell was entirely right.

After the meeting, Sir Charles said, "It's become a bit crowded in there, why don't just the two of us meet with one aide each?" Cabell had his man one-on-one, which was just where he wanted him.

We did a lot of negotiating together. What impressed me most was the humility that characterized his preoccupation with understanding his opponents' strong points. He always gave the right side of the argument its due and worked hard to anchor his base in valid tenants. We talked about games and different personality types who were attracted to a particular game.

Was life more like poker, gin rummy, bridge or chess? How important is secrecy? One interesting contrast is the difference in communication. In poker, secrecy is very important; in gin rummy, information and limited communication is exchanged when one discards or rejects a card; in bridge, good communication and bidding conventions are central to success; finally, in chess, the board is open for both opponents to view, but strategy must be kept secret. We agreed that it was unlikely any one person would be a champion in all the games. In life, we concluded that secrecy is overestimated in importance and in personal relationships. We are all much more transparent than we think.

This subject of games and our roles in life has always fascinated me. When I first tried out for the squash team at Dartmouth the coach watched me play for the first time. "I'm sure you played predominantly team sports," he said. "If you're ever going to be a squash champion, you'll have to learn a whole new mentality—it's one-on-one. You have to force your game style on your opponent. If you adapt to his game, if you're a team player, you'll lose." He couldn't have been more right!

General Cabell played a vital role in my transition from the CIA to NASA. As a former Deputy Director of the CIA, he knew all of the key men in the intelligence community whose cooperation was required for the civilian space program to survive. NASA, as a whole, was and is considered by many DOD people to be the greatest effrontery to DOD. Cabell had both the CIA civilian intelligence background and the four-star military background. Because of my CIA background, he was able to use this to advance me in those circles. So, once again, **everything gets done through people.**

Len Jaffe

Len Jaffe was my boss at NASA when I took over the Earth Resources Program Office. Len has a series of different "looks." For example, sometimes he gets a serious look on his face "….maybe something I've done?" I'd think. Then, just about when I'd found something appropriate to confess, he breaks into a big smile, and I realize once again it's just his "serious look." I shouldn't take it personally. Len was one of the original group who had come up through the National Advisory Committee for Aeronautics before it became NASA. When I met him, he was Assistant Administrator of Space Sciences and Applications, which was the center of the unmanned programs, including meteorology, planetary, biological and earth resources. Len is honest, fearless and outspoken.

From Mr. Webb on down, everyone respected Len, and those who worked for him loved him. That's not to say he didn't have enemies, but even they respected him. No one could be as consistently honest and not offend some people. It should be noted, however, that Len welcomed being challenged as aggressively as he challenged others. What he disliked most, and showed his impatience with, were ill-thought-out over-generalizations, especially if they were just a chorus of politically correct hypotheses. **In short, "political correctness" is not his strong suit, but "technical correctness" is.**

When he retired from NASA, he became a Vice President at CSC, where he worked for ten years until he recently retired. I owe Len a lot. He supported me and my programs at NASA. I had come from "upstairs" in the Policy Office and had very good contacts on the "seventh floor." He was secure enough himself that he encouraged me to work with them to advance the program. There are very few people who would have been that trusting (or secure), but I think it served NASA well.

Len is a real friend in all the ways I described at the beginning of the book. We get together with Len and his wife, Elaine, once or twice a year to havae dinner and listen to jazz.

After a hiatus of a number of years, Len came back to EarthSat and helped me manage the company. He brought a breadth of experience we did not otherwise have and provided a level of wisdom I greatly appreciated.

Art Lundahl

Art Lundahl died about several years ago but once was the Director of NPIC (National Photo Interpretation Center), which is the central point for the inter-pretation of classified data from intelligence satellites. In that role, he briefed sev-eral Presidents. Art was a fantastic briefer and could, as one colleague put it, "talk the birds out of the trees." But even Art was humbled when he heard that, after he briefed the top National Security Council members on the missiles in Cuba and left the room, Bobby Kennedy asked several key advisors if they could see what Art had pointed out to them. They each answered, "no." Finally he asked the President. "No," he replied, "but I believe that man who just left the room could!" When Art told me this story, he breathed deeply and said, "To think that the decision to have the largest confrontation of all time depends on a briefer's credibility is an awesome responsibility."

I knew him first when I was a very junior analyst at CIA. When I was first named Chief of NASA's Earth Resource Program, he called me. "You have the most exciting job in the country, Bob," he said. "I'd like you to visit me and let me tell you all the things I've done wrong so you won't repeat my mistakes!" He was completely sincere. Art became a personal friend and valued advisor. We met many times.

I remember one story he told about when the Director of the National Reconnaissance Organization (NRO), who was an old and valued friend, came to see his new building. NPIC had been making do for years in some modified WWII temporary building on E Street. The NRO chief looked very sad, and Art asked him what was wrong? "It's the end of an era," he replied. "Don't get me wrong. I think you deserve the Taj Mahal, but so often when this happens, I see perfectly good people fighting for "turf." You've done so much making do with what you had, I just wonder what will happen next?"

One day I asked him what was the thing he had done most right in retrospect? He answered, "I made sure my analysts and spacecraft builders were never more than a beer apart."

The last briefing he gave personally before retiring from NPIC was, by his choice, to a group of cleared EarthSat employees whose future he identified with so closely! He was also a lifelong friend of our Director, Bob Colwell.

He played an unsung hero by welcoming NASA into the defense intelligence community. There was much opposition by the NRO and their contractors who didn't want to see the marketplace made more competitive. Art demonstrated great courage by taking me under his wing and trying to expedite the civilian program. We were also fortunate to have the support of Don Steininger, who was on the President's Scientific Advisory Panel. Had they opposed it, or even shown weak support, I believe the DOD would have killed it for a considerable number of years.

After I started EarthSat, Art and I worked together to try to help retiring photo interpreters from NPIC prepare for job interviews. Art would send them over for a "trial" interview, so they could get some experience and honest feedback. After his retirement, I visited him about once a year, and we'd discuss the promise he saw in civilian remote sensing. Art was always, first and foremost, interested in people. We all loved him and miss him even today.

COMMENT: Savor your passion

This section is about writing because, in my case, this is my current passion. The advice I derive from these three examples is to savor whatever is your current passion. Pursuing your passion keeps your mind off negative thoughts, improves your powers of observation so you get more out of life. It renews old friendships and encourages mentoring. Finally, it provides a modicum of immortality by expediting your communication with the subsequent generations. If writing is your passion, I particularly recommend Dartmouth's WRITE course in early August, but there are courses in many cities all year long.

MEDLICOTT LETTER

August 24, 1995

Dear Joe,

I've had a whole day to reflect on our WRITE course. "What did I learn?" which is different question from, "What was I taught?" The distinction is important. I'd like to share some initial thoughts.

First, I learned to appreciate that there is a "body language" or "proper distance" to writing which sets the relationship between the author and his or her audience. Lisa's writing was a prime example of how to do it properly. She dealt with a very delicate subject in a manner which conveyed sufficient detail to communicate the story she had to share without making anyone feel crowded. She might have created a barrier, either by providing too much or too little detail. She used just the right sprinkling of humor to say to her audience, "I want to share this with you, but I don't require your anger or pity to vindicate my perception."

Second, there is an "internal balance" which is determined by length, intensity and subject matter. Basically, it's the skill to pick the points to start, stop, and how many words are needed in between. Steve and Bobbi I's, The Hall, short stories were two excellent examples of doing it right. There is probably a necessary, but sufficient length for every story, and I think learning this will be one of my greatest challenges. This challenge is also a major quandary for Bobbie II and Jeanne who have very complex stories to set forth. Binky also faces the dilemma of what to include in her biography but so far, so very good.

Third, choosing "a voice" which allows writers to effectively present their work is one of the most important decisions an author faces. It must work for both the writer and the reader. Kitty's piece was an example of a "perfect" presentation which worked for her and her audience. Steven's piece was similarly perfect. Binky and John both had important decisions to make as to which relative was selected to tell the story. While their voices were very different, there was an ethnic quality to each. In my books, I found writing about my friends and mentors provided me with a posture to write a largely autobiographical piece without feeling like I was preaching. It was easier to say, "This is what I was told" rather than, "Let me tell you." The latter would have called for a more expository, defensive work, much longer and more difficult to write.

The question of voice is a particular challenge to writers of autobiographical-based fiction. What is the message or truth that one is trying to reveal? To what degree must this be validated by reality? For example, Bobbie I's characterization of the workers on her ranch did not depend at the core on whether her ranch was in Connecticut or Wyoming or whether or not Oscar plunged into the river or was arrested. These were not critical value judgements bearing on the message of the story.

On the other hand, I think it makes a difference in Bobbie II's story whether or not she really has the disease. I don't think it's necessary to validate her anger. It makes her victim into a special case. The real challenge is facing and dramatizing the actual case, which could include all fear of infection, which is no doubt a valid part of her pain, but not, I suspect, the principle part. My personal opinion is that she needs to identify the most central part and capture it, and the harm it does, in her own personal and very articulate voice. Jean has a interesting writer's problem. She could start her book at several points, such as the beginning of the trip to Brazil, the kidnaping, or the writing on the car, but her choice will have a role in posturing what is the message, even who is the victim, who is the heroine, and why.

One man's nostalgia may be another man's long, tedious march. For example, I wrote a description of some of my memories of an upper bunk on the overnight train. How do I make that interesting to grandchildren who have never been on an overnight train? Should I include it? If so, how do I represent it so it will be interesting (relevant) to them? It may be an acceptable piece of nostalgia for my generation, but in its present form, boring to my grandchildren.

John's piece does an excellent job of describing the frenetic scene of "The Run" and early Oklahoma, but it probably would be more real if one had ridden horseback and knew the West, than if his reader has only experienced New York City. It's an interesting question: "What additional challenges does the writer of a "period piece" assume?" Since all memoirs are period pieces, it's a relevant question for all of us who write "for our grandchildren," and it's humbling to look at how well the classics succeed. Kitty really wrote a classic.

So, Joe, what did you teach us? Why were you necessary, or even useful? It's the mark of a great teacher that we learned as much as we did without any of the apparent labor we associate with being taught. I thank you very much for making our experience all that a week could provide. I wish everyone in the Dartmouth community could have shared our experience.

Thank you,

J. Robert Porter, Jr.

P.S.   I know, Joe, "too many words."
Cc: WRITE class
      Lu Martin

So You Want to Write a Novel
November 7, 1999

Fifteen years ago I started a novel, a spy story. I wrote about 40 pages and then decided I couldn't think of an ending. Five years ago, I thought I'd figure out an ending and finish it. I wrote about 2 pages and decided that I was too old. Well, I started again this July, and I've just about finished. Here are some observations:

First, writing a novel is quite different from writing non-fiction, essays, memoirs, or short stories. I attended a short course on writing memoirs at Dartmouth. I self-published ("printed") three short books which I had a lot of fun writing and gave to a few friends. The best image I can use to describe what it's like to write a novel is to imagine a thousand piece puzzle with three thousand extra pieces. You build up islands of pieces and then eventually connect these islands into continents which eventually produces a recognizable picture. Stated otherwise, you have more ideas than there's room to present so you are constantly having to make choices. The high point of your week is matching and merging "island chains" in a manner which gives you more perspective on the big picture. It becomes very unwieldy trying to rearrange large islands of prose.

Second, when you write non-fiction or short stories, you are nudged by reality or working towards a punch line. Further, you can get a rapid sense of the quality of your work. You can show it to others without imposing greatly on their time and get the instant satisfaction or rejection from peer feedback. If someone says, "Rewrite this section or restructure the whole paper," it's not a life sentence.

Third, you don't have that much of your ego tied up in short pieces, and there's not the pressure to do something with it. Further, if you want to get a short piece published, you may not succeed, but it doesn't take three years of marketing to get a sense of it.

Fourth, I showed my novel's first draft to a friend who is a noted author. He gave me some excellent feedback. He pointed out some "indigestible lumps," pieces which reflect a preoccupation with my own interest which doesn't generally coincide with the interest of my readership. I call this the "Moby Dick syndrome" commemorating a book from which I learned more about whaling than I ever wanted to know. My friend then proceeded to tell me more things I needed, but didn't want to hear, like "you wrapped it up way too fast. You decided that you were through, but you aren't." I could hear the voice of literary justice saying,"For this crime you are sentenced to 40 more pages." (He was right, and I have since written 100 more pages.)

Fifth, one of the points I have come to appreciate most is the difficulty in learning the craft of writing. For example, in my case I need to consciously work to describe the scenes or context in which the action takes place. I never appreciated how important it is to describe a meal, a room, a house, or a neighborhood. The same care has to be given to the description of characters—their dress, smells, accents, breeding—all have to be compared and measured. If it doesn't flow to the page naturally, then you have to edit it in later.

Sixth, one of the biggest surprises I found was that I'm not really in charge of my characters, rather they take on a life of their own, and soon after I began to give them personalities and a history, my characters started asserting themselves, so much so that I would literally be going to my computer and be anxious to see how my characters were going to get themselves out of the crisis I, or they had created. This is the most exciting part of writing a novel. It's totally unlike any other writing form I know.

Seventh, there is a real drive to show your unfinished pieces to friends and well wishers. It's very difficult to show a single snapshot that captures a series of events. Consequently I found myself trying to explain what my reader doesn't know. This is simply impossible. The other problem with showing drafts is that unless you're willing to act on the advice you receive, you're better off not asking for it in the first place. I find with time I ask fewer and fewer people to look at my drafts. On the other hand, a number of my "final copies" turned in to "early drafts" after a little honest criticism.

Eighth, why would anybody read my, or anyone else's book? There are, of course, relatives and close friends. It helps if they like your genre. Other successful formulae are memorable characters, the right pace, or "how to" books. Doing even one of these well is damned hard. Fundamentally, I believe the readers want to be entertained and/or learn. If they don't get either they won't read your second book.

Ninth, accuracy and credibility is the hallmark of most accepted prose. In my first book I tried to write about subjects I knew first hand. In some instances I knew I was stretching current paradigms, e.g. brain chemistry. I couldn't write first hand about Moscow.

Fortunately, I thoroughly enjoy the process of writing and dueling with my hearty band of characters. As is the case in professional sports, the top pros make it look easy. It's not. But there's a more common feeling writing your first novel evokes—it's the simple excitement that comes from learning something new and being challenged, regardless of how well you succeed. And that's a great feeling.

What Do I Do If I've Already Quit My Day Job?
(The view from the second floor)
May 22, 2002

A year ago I wrote a piece titled, <u>So You Want to Write a Novel</u>. I wrote it at a time I had just finished my first novel. I was bathing in the adrenal juices that gush freely when you finally finish. Today I am writing in the aftermath of a second novel. I have not yet written the perfect novel, but I want to describe some cross currents I've sensed that can become a deadly rip tide if I don't learn to swim under those conditions. What follows is the advice I'd give myself after writing my second novel.

First, I have to do extensive research. If I don't pay attention to place and action details it will be noticed by a larger group than I expected. My readership has more expertise in a wider variety of fields than I initially gave them credit.

Second, concentrate on character development. If necessary, let character development occasionally override plot. This is probably the most difficult challenge facing a new novelist. Different accents, dress descriptions, and contrasting interactions with environment can be useful stepping stones. Avoid cliches and overly simplistic sterotypes. Make sure every character is accounted for by the end of the book.

Third, "take the time to let a scene develop." As one writer said to me, "Put in all the twists and turns you can but set up each one." Like a dancer or a bull fighter, you should move at a fast pace but not appear hurried. I still need to work on it.

Fourth, if I have more than a handful of characters, I put in a section at the beginning of the book and summarize each character in a few words. If done right, it won't give away anything that I want to keep as a surprise, but it will help readers to reorient themselves if they put the book down and don't pick it up for a few days. I've received high praise for this feature.

Fifth, beware, the computer is not always my friend. It gets confused in spell check and grammar check. It lets me cut and paste with abandon and, in doing so, facilitates my changing antecedents, or mixing tenses. These mistakes are particularly difficult for me to pick up editorially if I am the one who wrote it.

Sixth, don't expect final comfort from your reader.

Seventh, avoid English majors, and people who read with a pencil. Often they will critique the wrapping on the package more than they will value the contents of the box. They will be completely taken out of the plot by quotation marks which go the wrong way or, heaven forbid, if you mix tenses or leave out a "silent e." This is sometimes intimidating. As you may have guessed, not all English majors like this book, so I'm publishing a "second edition for English majors." You can write a good novel without conventional punctuation, just call it "stream of consciousness" or "free verse after Joyce" or "poetry after ee cummins."

Ms. Moorman is a friend who attended the Dartmouth WRITE class when I was there who wrote an autobiography which she sent me. This included a story about her parents who escaped with her from Austria just prior to WWII. She sent me this to cri- tique, and this was my response:

Moorman Letter
October 9, 1996

Dear Mrs. Moorman:

Thank you for the your untitled memoir. There are several minor changes which I think would greatly increase it's marketability. Let me speak frankly.

WWII is passe, "out." So's all Europe. We can get around this if we change it so that you were born in El Salvador. You were right to change your name the first time. "Liselotte" is too long to remember. "Lilot" sounds like an oriental porn star. I think "Lisa" strikes the right balance, ready but not strange. Of course to be consistent we'll have to modify a bit. For example, your father, Fritz, could be a plantation owner accused by the Sandanistes of cooperating with the CIA. He is sent to jail and the rest of your family escapes in the middle of the night taking an over-night bus from Monterey.

I like your refugee angle. Refugees are "in," especially ones from Central America. I also like the part about your family all living in the same apartment building. It also provides a great opportunity to introduce guest stars in character rolls when we sell the movie rights (Maggie Smith as Edith). Don't worry, as you can tell, I've got that covered too. I like the "other women" angle. (Love triangles are always "in.") There's a lot of "90's women who would identify with Nora, who "endures her husband's affair because of her commitment Her character needs a little rewrite. (I know the perfect guy.)

We'll have to search for the right Nora, maybe Sharon Stone. Steffi could be played by Meryl Streep (a little older, a few more times around the track but still assertive.) Picking the right Fritz could be difficult. Stallone's too big. Pacino's too pensive. Denzel Washington is too black. Michael York is too white. Michael Douglas, he's perfect or maybe Harry Hamlin. I'll bet you're wondering who I've got in mind to play you? It's a shame Audrey Hepburn's dead, but I'll keep thinking.

This could very well become a Sunday night movie, "REFUGEE FROM HELL. Based on a true story."

Keep writing. Let me do the thinking. Trust me. The first 30 pages were great. I'll get to the rest soon.

Your agent,

Hollywood Bob

INTERVIEWS
July 8, 1999

I had a "great idea" last night. It was one of those "great, in the middle of the night" ideas that almost always look stupid in the morning. I was dreamily thinking about what I could write about at Dartmouth's WRITE course. I was convinced that I'd wrung every memory neuron dry, when a question formed in my mind, "What should follow one's memoirs?" (I knew it wasn't "a preposition") Obviously, a problem with memoirs is that, in retrospect, you probably never asked the right question to the person you're remembering when you had the opportunity. For example, I knew my Uncle Boxie for 50 years, wrote about him in my memoirs, I was setting myself up as an expert on him, but never even asked him how he got his name? A skilled biographer, I clearly wasn't.

"It probably didn't matter anyway," I rationalized. All the good questions are ones I couldn't ask, or shouldn't ask because they might be awkward for the interviewee. Or ones I wouldn't, or shouldn't because they'd make me feel awkward. And then there are those people who are going to lie to you anyway. And those people who wouldn't know the truth if it hit them in the face. And those people who suppressed the truth–or repressed the truth. Finally there's the question, "Does truth maketh the man or man maketh the truth?" Clearly I maketh no progress.

I thought back to the memoirs I had written about friends and mentors. I asked myself the question, "If I could ask any one question to each person I wrote about and get as honest an answer as that person could give, what question would I ask?" THERE WASN'T ONE. I ask myself why? Perhaps it's because the image we have of someone is built on a trellis or scaffold which supports a number of impressions, and I just didn't want to change the shape and presentation of "facts" as I believed I knew them. Or perhaps, it was that I knew subconsciously that one piece of new information wouldn't change anything because my values of that friendship were based on so many data points. So much history. Perhaps it's because I believe it's not what people say about themselves, it's what they don't say, and what's said between the lines that matters.

On reflection I would like to interview each of the people I've written about, but no one question would suffice, or perhaps I should say, no one answer.

COMMENT: Time flies, memory lies, preservation thrives.

Even if you can't relive past experiences, you can preserve a sense of the moment in time. My approach has been to sum up once a year through my annual Christmas Letters. I tried to emphasize what we were thinking about rather than just what we were doing. These provide a context and a time line for a family's growth.

1987

Dear Friends,

Lee asked me to make a few brief comments on my view of the year, so here goes:

"Family event of the year" was clearly Jennifer's wedding. I guess it just proves that college reunions are more than just drinking beer and telling old war stories (while I was doing 'my duty' at the 25th reunion tent, Jennifer, I later learned, was out on the campus meeting VJ who was Dartmouth '82!)

Amy's had a great year at Tulane. She's majoring in 'political economics' and found a number of compelling academic reasons to attend school in Paris last summer. I said, "Alright, but only if you stay within a strict budget." She agreed and held to it with the occasional college student's complaint that "I'm really spending much less than my friends." I dismissed that until Lee and I went to Europe at the end of the summer and found out how little the dollar could buy now. In retrospect, I don't know how she got by!

Actually, Lee and I went to Europe twice last year: In January to London to see friends and enjoy the theater (6 shows in 7 days–fantastic); and, in September, to Paris (some business, some pleasure), Basel (visit friends, and Aga, a former au pair girl), and Provence, near Grasse (visiting the Lambert's, friends from Washington who had taken a home there).

Personally, I've not been bored this year: Business-wise, we pepped up things by suing Hughes and RCA (GM & GE) for breach of contract. This was pursued via the arbitration route, and we just finished the hearing so we expect a pre-appear answer any day (we assume they'll lose and appear!) Health-wise, it has been very satisfying. Lee and I played a lot of tennis this summer. My Parkinson's seems to be progressing at a slow rate and can still be controlled by mild medication.

Research in this area is very promising, and my doctor refers to it as "the brain disease of choice if you have to choose one."

Finally, Lee is having a great year (I think). While she is virtually camping out in her store, which is still open while they rebuild a mall around it, she is surviving. She is making a small profit. And, her "Oklahoma Oil Field" quilt, which she made for my godson, John Wilson, who graduated in geology, was accepted in a highly competitive jury selected show (it depicts a cross-section of the Oklahoma oil fields). This was her first competitive attempt so she's "one for one" and very pleased.

Merry Christmas to all and Happy New Year.

1988

Dear Friends,

Perhaps it's because of the increase in air fares, but we seem to be concentrating more of our family in Boston. Jennifer and her husband VJ have moved to Cambridge where he's attending Harvard Business School; Lee's father moved to a retirement home there last year; Lee's brother Jim and his family live near there as well. Naturally, we spent Thanksgiving in Boston.

An octogenarian once said, "When you get to be my age, time passes so quickly that it seems like there's just 15 minutes between breakfasts." At age 53 I'm beginning to know what she means. Jennifer's expecting her first child in February, and though she swears they've been married a year and a half, their wedding seems like yesterday to me.

Some people quietly set an example of how to live. I visited my 88 year old mother recently in Oklahoma City. Seven years ago I gave her a stationary bike. Since that time, she has had two strokes, two major operations, and lost most of her vision. She has nurses around the clock. Occasionally when I've called I've asked, "Do you ever use that bike?" She usually answers, "yes, and I just love it." The other day I happened to check the mileage: 731! Unbelievable!

Amy's now in her senior year at Tulane. Last summer she worked at the Kennedy Center in public relations and group sales. Could this be the direction of her professional life? With graduation quickly approaching, she's looking for a job. Naturally, she has her own style, i.e., first you choose a city, then you choose a job: Boston would be perfect if it weren't so cold. New York would be greater if it was warmer in the winter and cooler in the summer. Washington is terrific, but I've already lived there. New Orleans was ideal…for four years." "Baltimore," I suggested. "Really" she replied. Stay tuned.

Lee and I went to England again this fall. We saw seven plays in London (most noteworthy: "Lettice and Loveage" with Maggie Smith), drove around East Anglia and visited friends at Cambridge. We really enjoyed pretending we were history students: memorizing the names, dates and accomplishments of the kings and queens of England, reading relevant books, and even checking out video tapes on British history. Then quizzing each other before and after we visited famous houses and museums. It may sound awfully silly, but we enjoyed every moment of it.

Finally, Lee and my lives continue ever a pace. Lee closed her store after pleading with the Fire Marshall to let her stay open "just long enough for a going out of business sale" (the mall construction caused a few problems). Right now she's just "taking it easy" (from 6 AM to 10 PM): practicing the piano for two hours a day (she also takes lessons), doing curatorial work (quilt research) at the DAR museum, serving as a Director of the American Quilt Study Group, and now about to enroll at GW University to get a master's degree in American Studies! I continue to play tennis, work with my computer, watch television, or read while savoring a good port. I feel very well. I enjoy my friends and work; my family is well and happy; my dog welcomes me home every night; and I am very much looking forward to being a grandfather. What more can one ask?

Merry Christmas and Happy New Year,

1989

Dear Friends,

1989 was a sad year and a glad year for the Porter family: Sad, in that my mother quietly left us after a brief hospitalization; glad in that Jennifer bore us our first grandchild—Vincent John Gerard Dowling III. As much as we're surrounded by deaths and births in everyday life, when either event occurs within your close family there's a special completeness you feel that makes you stop what you're doing and appreciate the wonder of life.

I get exhausted just thinking about all the energy expended by other members of my family. Jennifer, after spending nine months submerged in "how to have children" literature, is now, in addition to attending to Vincent's every whim, taking computer courses in "Pascal C" and accounting (Yes, Virginia, there is a Superwoman). VJ, on the other hand, when not minding Vincent and taking six courses for credit in his second year at Harvard Business School, is auditing two others ("I'd rather optimize for courses than for grades…but the school couldn't operate if everybody did it") and running his business in Hartford by phone and fax!

Amy ("Aunte Ame?") has had a great year which was punctuated by graduation, a three month course at Katharine Gibbs to learn "survival skills" after which she observed, "it's amazing how much harder you work when you pay for school yourself" (yes, Amy, now about those phone calls and parking tickets…) and beginning her first job in an "entry level position" with Ketchum Advertising buying media time. She really likes her job, but her social life sounds like "the big apple" should be renamed "Tulane on the Hudson." Whenever I call Amy she's either "on the other line" or "just on my way out."

Lee continues her life ever a pace: Outside the home, she's spending a couple days a week leading the marketing efforts of Cana Industries, a subgroup of Jubilee

Jobs, which trains disadvantaged people to make the transition to the workplace by learning good work habits while gaining experience in a bulk mailing business. In the home, this is the "year of the piano" (most recently: Gershwin's "Preludes"), "the quilt" (most recently: a wall hanging titled "The Miracle at Cana," and "the audio book" (most recently, The First Elizabeth)! The combination of quilting and historic audio books has been a real discovery! Toss in a lot of tennis, aerobics, theater, a course in English History we took together at the Smithsonian, bi-monthly trips to visit her father (and grandson) in Boston, a week cleaning out and packing up my mother's house in Oklahoma, and you've got a pretty good picture of the year she describes as "easy, because I've learned to just say 'no'!"

Personally, it's been a very satisfying year: The kids are both thriving in their new roles; the medicine I've been getting in England the last four years has turned out to be the hottest new drug in neurology—the first proven to retard the progress of Parkinson's! Business is up. (In September, we celebrated EarthSat's 20th anniversary!) Tennis went well this summer. Lee and I have really been enjoying each other…and my dog seems to be adjusting to my grandson!

Merry Christmas,

1990

Dear Friends,

The nice thing about the ritual of writing this letter is that it permits me to slow down, sip, and savor many events of the year that I had just gulped down at the time they originally occurred.

For example, last May Jennifer and VJ took a 3 week trip to eastern Europe after he graduated from Harvard Business School. Lee and I were left in Vincent's charge (yes, that's what I meant to say). On reflection, it's a wonder any child or parent ever survives the unbounded curiosity of a newly mobile 15 month old. Happily, we all did, but I will never forget when Jennifer returned and went to Vincent's room. She watched his lower lip curl as he stood off just a bit resisting her hug, then with tears of relief slowly coming to his eyes, Jennifer softly said, "That's alright, you can be mad at mommy. I understand."

Amy is having another good year in the Big Apple. She is still at Ketchum Advertising in its media buying group. She has a steady boyfriend, Matthew, and while they don't live together, they did buy a dog together (which sounds like a stronger test to me). I've often observed that pet owners often look like their pets. Amy tells me she got a "Shitzu" which, when fully grown, is 13 inches long, 6 inches high and covered with hair like a mop. I haven't seen Amy recently but I'm wondering what to expect Christmas.

Lee is taking her quilt art very seriously. She is sharing a studio with two other women (a sculptor and a painter). I share the view of numerous artist friends that she is really doing first rate work. Naturally, she's also very involved in church work and dedicates much of her time to working with the homeless. Washington has a sad side. The crime rate and drug situation is even worse than the papers imply. Crime touches everyone directly or indirectly (for example, Theresa, our maid of 25 years, is a hard working, solid, church going citizen; yet last year, one grandson was murdered and this year another grandson has become a crack addict). There are just too many guns on the street. Frankly, I have mixed emotions, no doubt Lee has "a calling," but realistically, it's pretty dangerous where she goes.

I've had a great year. Business is going well, and we moved our office to bigger, nicer quarters in Rockville, MD. It's a 25 minute commute, but I just listen to recorded books on my car tape deck, and it passes very quickly. Parkinson research is progressing at a fantastic pace. I can honestly say that because of improved medication, I feel much better this year than last. I've been writing for fun. I wrote one paper called "The Parkinson's Card" about the advantage of being a "pro-active patient" which I may get published someplace. I still play a lot of tennis.

Lee and I really feel blessed with a good life. Washington is a great city in many ways. We often go to the Smithsonian jazz sessions (we saw Dizzy Gillespie last week), lectures on history (e.g., the French Revolution). We appreciate the diversity of views we get from our CIA and State Department friends as well as artists and people we know from the inner city. Clearly, no one group has all the answers. Certainly, we don't, but searching for truth is a great adventure whether you are 15 months or 55 years.

Merry Christmas,

1991

Dear Friends,

In March, Lee's father died from Alzheimer's at the age of 81. The memorial service outside Boston would have pleased him. Jim and Lee shared some remembrances. The Headmaster and some former co-trustees from Roxbury Latin School were there, as were John's former partners from First Manhattan, and lots of relatives. John had real class. I deeply value knowing him. He can't be replaced.

Jennifer's family increased by one, a little Halloween spirit called Alex (Alexanderson Jane Dowling). Jennifer and VJ live in Hartford, but VJ spends several days a week at his Boston office while Jennifer continues to manage a very impressive little company. I am sincerely amazed that they can do all this and give a clear priority to parenting demands, but they do, and Vincent, who will be 3 in February, clearly reflects the success of their efforts. (Vincent also benefits by the close proximity [1 mile] and loving attention of his Dowling grandparents.)

Amy and her boyfriend, Matthew, have moved to Washington. Amy is working as a coordinator of the Octagon Auction and for a designer. Naturally, she went to Hartford with us at Thanksgiving to check up on her future Godchild. She has always insisted on being Godmother to Jennifer's second child because, "I know what's its like to have hand-me-down toys, clothes, books, and teachers."

Lee's quilt art is just getting better and better. Her pieces usually relate to some biblical verse, such as "Thou setteth a table before me in the presence of mine enemies," Ps 23:5, which includes some menacing wolves in the background which would ruin anyone's dinner. Not surprisingly, they are often loaned to or purchased by churches. She did a terrific (non-biblical) one of Lake George which really caught the flavor of her family house and its Swedish heritage. It is on tour for a year. Also, she did several on commission, but now is completely focused on her first big show in April '92.

Professionally, this was one of my most satisfying years. Many activities (CIA, NASA, congressional relations) I had enjoyed separately in the past, merged in close step. The Persian Gulf War was the catalyst, and EarthSat was able to make a very significant contribution. Health-wise, it was a great year, too. I worked harder and enjoyed it more. The rate of brain research breakthroughs is astounding.

Finally, on a sad note, our dog, Ben, died. No doubt history books won't give the event the credit it deserves. To tell the truth, I don't dwell on it much, but I must say, I miss the pleasure of being met at the garage door and "making his day" just because I was home, and he knew dinner was coming.

Best wishes for a healthy 1992,

1992

Dear Friends,

Looking back, 1992 was sort of a "nondescript" year: Little people grew bigger.
The next generation grew closer to ours. Lee and I were pleased to find out there
is still a lot of room for growth left for us. All this occurred without banner head-
lines. Well, I guess I can try to find a few.

"JENNIFER BUYS FACTORY IN HARTFORD ENTERPRISE ZONE!" Yes
she did and in what has become her "characteristic fashion" of raising two children, running her company, and moving into a new house, all at the same time.
I've been very skeptical that anyone could do any, much less all, of these well, but
she continues to amaze me. She and VJ seem to undertake these activities in a
partnership mode which was almost unknown to my generation. She does have
some secret weapons: a great full-time babysitter (who just had a baby she brings
to work), an army of low priced, highly talented Portuguese workers (indigenous
to Hartford), some very proud grandparents 1 mile away, a husband who last
week took Vincent to work with him in Boston, and 2 very even tempered children.

"AMY'S ARCHITECTURAL AUCTION AWES ALL!" After returning to
Washington last year, Amy took an 11 month, almost full time, job with the
Architectural Institute of America (AIA) to organize an auction in the grandest of
styles: Prince Charles provided a water color penned by His Royal Hand, Lords
and Ladies opened up their manor houses and will take the successful bidders on
personal tours, many fantastic vacations and fabulous pieces of art (including a
quilt art piece of the "Tower of Babel" by Lee Porter) were to be had. They raised
approximately $200,000 from just over 200 guests. Tom Jordan contributed all
the wine! There were some real bargains. We bought a one-way, one person, first
class passage to England on the QE II for $825! (Jennifer and VJ are going to take
a short vacation to use it in the spring.)

"LEE'S FIRST ART SHOW" was very satisfying for both her old and new quilt art fans. Characteristically it seems, Lee's successes are also the source of her greatest problem; how to allocate her limited time. She is evern more active in her work with Christ House, a hospital and home for homeless men (many with AIDS), and she has been taking a very hard course on the Old Testament at the Wesley Seminary where she is slowly getting another degree. I am still awed by her energy, although I have stopped being surprised by her success. (I was just reminded by her piano playing in the other room of one more activity I left out.) If you wondered if all this is hard on me, it is. Especially when she wants to discuss Job at 5:00 in the morning!

"PORTER SUPPORTS GORE" is a headline it's best my staunch Republican father never lived to see (my other family members supported Perot). Actually, if he read the whole story, he would approve. It relates specifically to a project on which I spent much time last year called the "Gore/Gates Initiative." It resulted from a request from then Senator Gore to the Director of CIA, Robert Gates, to jointly see if a means could be found to exploit intelligence collection systems, such as satellites, to gather important information on the environment. Gates, presumably with Bush's approval, joined in this apolitical effort which is looking very promising indeed, and portends well for a fascinating 1993 given recent events.

Well, so much for the head liners. On further reflection, "It was a very good year." However, I am very concerned that Clinton and his successors face very difficult years with many daunting challenges. I'm afraid that to be a "super power," it requires "super humans," and only we Americans are naive enough to aspire to that role. It will certainly take super luck to take on the problems of Somalia, Bosnia, Moslem fundamentalism, the homeless, the deficit and AIDS, to name a few, while we try to keep control of 28,000 nuclear missiles which are not needed any more by the "loser" of the Cold War.

Finally, two much more positive notes: First, my Parkinson's is staying symptomatically about the same while research is forging steadily ahead with both pharmaceuticals and fetal transplants looking promising within five years (one more reason I couldn't give my vote to Bush); and second, after a two year test, I've concluded that my theory that pets look like their owners still holds! Amy really does look like Annie, her pet Shitzu. They both have big eyes and prance!

Seasons Greetings,

1993

Dear Friends,

To be quite honest I've dreaded writing this year's letter. There are some subjects that don't evoke glibness. On last New Year's Eve, I felt a lump in my neck which proved to be malignant. I was operated on February 16th in an 8-hour event, followed by radiation, but no chemotherapy. After asking all the questions I could about the fine print in the warranty, I concluded the overall prognosis was, "so far, so good, with a 50/50 chance of reoccurrence during the next few years." This means the glass is either half empty or half full, and I must admit, my perspective varies on this greatly from day to day. Some days I think that a "pain in my pinky" is the beginning of a cataclysmic event; other days I feel like Arnold Swartzenagger. If there's no bad news by next February, the odds go up to 75/25 in my favor. Keep your fingers crossed!

Our other medical cliff-hanger turned out an unqualified success: PORTER ROBERT DOWLING arrived in Hartford, June 26th, seven weeks ahead of schedule, a little skinnier than his proud namesake, but quite hearty, healthy and vociferous. His elder brother, Vincent, now a wise four and one-half, seems to be on the brink of a diplomatic career and whose favorite sentence is, "Let's discuss that later." Contrast this with his just-turned-two sister, Alex, who prefers the more direct pronouncement, "No way!", and you'll all share our flashback to when our kids were that age. We visited them at Thanksgiving, and what struck me most was the overwhelming communication advantage a two-year old girl has in charming her wishes to her father, her older brother, three uncles and two grandfathers. The thoroughly disarmed males just can't say, "no."

Parenting demands have asserted themselves more deeply into VJ and Jennifer's schedule. VJ now stays in Hartford four days a week. He just bought a small, historic bank building which was built in the late 1800's on the capitol green in downtown Hartford. After some renovation, he will move his office there.

Jennifer has had to cut back because of a difficult pregnancy but still goes at a pace which allows time for everything from running a company to a "moon bouncer" birthday party.

Amy moved to the City of Angels, earthquakes and forest fires in September with one of her best Washington friend's, Keeland Murphy. She has taken a temporary job with Dick Clark Productions, and as of this writing is on location in Las Vegas where they are producing the "Golden Globe" awards. This summer she went to Georgetown and earned a certificate as a Legal Assistant which provides her more options for job hunting in this very competitive job market.

I think Lee would say she has never been happier or more centered at any time in her life. Even with the unwelcome news of my illness, she has found great satisfaction, support and community in her quilt art, courses at Wesley Seminary and Christ House activities. She is preparing for her second quilt art show now and has just finished, what we both think, is her best piece.

Actually, the "full part" of the glass has been very refreshing this year: I've very much enjoyed working on the Environmental Task Force Vice President Gore set up to evaluate the application of intelligence community assets to monitor the environment; my series of essays on Parkinson's was published by the United Parkinson's Foundation under a grant from Dupont, and the feedback I've received has been very rewarding; and I derived a lot of joy from some activities our small family foundation undertook.

Finally, speaking of ridiculous, recently I've been singing along with Frank Sinatra on his new album, "Duets." No, this is not lunacy and certainly not my idea. Rather, in order to strengthen my speech in the morning, my speech therapist told me to pronounce my vowels on the way to work and to screw up my face in funny ways to stimulate the facial nerves. After that, I'm supposed to recite something and try "to intone emotion" in my voice. Singing along with Frankie was my brainstorm to accommodate this instruction. The only problem was I've had to give up the facial contortions routine at stop signs after several people thought I was expressing something personal directed at them! So now I just sing my way along between stop signs. My other problem is trying to turn off the voice in my head at night still singing, "one for my baby, and one more for the road." Humor which has its roots in real life is probably our best medication.

In summary, it's been a mixed year, but one with many pleasures and warm friendships, which we value more and more with each passing year.

Merry Christmas,

1994

Dear Friends.

This has been a long but good year for me: Long because I've been waiting for the time to pass without a recurrence of cancer, and the longer the cancer-free time, the better my betting odds for winning this round. So far, so good.

Jennifer now spends much of her time shuttling kids between birthday parties and other events, from their new house in Farmington, Conn.,just outside W. Hartford. **VJ** no longer commutes to Boston but has added the writing of a highly regarded weekly report on insurance stocks which is in great demand, but takes up much of his weekend. **Porter,** age 1.5 is very mobile and a real little competitor trying not just to make up his 2 month early birth but also vying with his elder siblings. His sister, **Alex,** age 3, is even more verbal than Porter is mobile. There is no question you can ask for which she doesn't have a perfectly acceptable (for her) answer. For example, Lee was trying to work the microwave, and Alex explained in a professional voice, that, first, she had to turn on the gas stove. **Vincent,** age 5, is now a self-proclaimed adult. They took a flight to Florid, and the stewardess explained to the passengers what to do if the oxygen masks came down and, in one part she said,"If you have a child sitting next to you, put your mask on first, then the child's." Vincent just heard the last part and, with a worried look, asked his mother, "What am I supposed to do? I have a child (Porter) sitting next to me."

This has been a good year for **Amy.** She loves her job with Sandollar, a production company which is on the Disney lot and produces numerous sitcoms and made for TV movies. She's lived in Los Angeles for a year now and has just recently settled into her own apartment. She likes her job, reviewing and evaluating scripts; her Boss, who is one of the real leaders in the field; finally, when asked what sports she pursues she says "doing and undoing lunches."

Lee's story just keeps getting better and better. She had a one women show of her fabric art at the Wesley Art Gallery in Washington. At the opening, the curator spoke for about 15 minutes on the significance of her works, then Lee spoke for about 30 minutes. The once shy, verbal mouse has grown into an erudite, articulate lion. About 100 guests were charmed and spellbound. (Lee will be embarrassed by this, but it's true.) Her sales were quite satisfying, and she now has pieces in a church in Vermont and a house in Switzerland. She has put aside somewhat her fabric art so she can take a full course load at Wesley Seminary for a Master's degree in Theology concentrating on the Old Testament. She does find it daunting that her fellow students view her as this "world famous artist."

For me, this has been what I'll call the **year of the book.** Ten years ago Jerry Lambert and I had a joint 50th birthday party, and we invited our guests to celebrate "100 years of gracious living." It occurred to me then that the guest list constituted a grouping of my best friends, and the idea was born to expand the list and write a book on Friends and Mentors. I also added another section which is a potpourri of miscellaneous poems and essays I've written over the past 20 years. It was a lot of fun to write, except for having to learn Word Perfect 6.1. Anyway I took all 190 pages to the printer today!

As one would expect I got more out of it than I put into it. It was a joy recalling some of the anecdotes. I was surprised by the unevenness with which I knew some friends. Not surprisingly it depended on what was going on in my life at the time I was around them most. For example, I knew more about divorces, than I did community activities, until I became more active in community affairs myself. Some friends are just there, all your life. They change. You change. But your friendship continues and your commitment to help one another persists through it all. It was also surprising how important the workplace was as a personal support mechanism. Lee made perhaps the most noteworthy comment. She said that I was a changed man once I started writing this book. That I changed from someone living in constant fear of cancer returning to someone with a zest for life. Sounds right to me.

Happy New Year!

1995

Dear Friends,

Simply stated, 1995 was a "year of bonding" and one of the best years of my life. It's also been a year of personal acceptance of both life and death: one in which I've come to appreciate more than ever that life's greatest gift is sharing love with friends and family, in sickness and in health, as we have this year.

Jennifer's greatest challenges this year has been in PTO activities at the Farmington, Connecticut public school Vincent attends. She led a successful effort to get an additional teacher for the school, so the size in Vincent's first grade classes was reduced from 24 in 3 sections to 18 in 4. She is also working with local businesses, foundations, and parents to provide computers for every room in the grade school. We're very proud of her.

Jennifer has also added women's soccer to her list of activities. She is quite a role model for Vincent, a mid-fielder himself, age 6, who proudly reports, "Mommy is a forward." Sometimes our parts as role models are assigned from circumstances we can't foresee. For example, over Thanksgiving, Lee took the grandchildren to the cemetery to see "if any pilgrims are buried there." Now anytime Porter, age 2, passes any cemetery he happily says, "Gammy." Alex, age 4, is more discerning. When she assessed my makeshift office in her house, her assessment was "Granpa is a real messy guy."

"I have to go" is about the longest conversation we ever have with Amy. Then she presses the hold button, the latest song from a Disney movie comes blasting on the line, and you know that you have just been assigned a spot in never, never land. (She works on the Disney lot and uses their telephone system.) Her boss negotiates contracts for scripts and personal services often by phone; Amy listens to every call and then takes the actions as required. This is fantastic experience, but very demanding time-wise. We visited her in Los Angeles on a "quiet" work day and were exhausted from just watching.

Lee continues to soar! She has concentrated on her courses at Wesley Seminary, especially the "*Book of Genesis*" and "*Politics and Religion*" courses. She is also able to find time for her art, teaching, and an occasional exhibition. (Oh, yes, she's working on publishing a paper for an academic journal on Baltimore Album Quilts.) She is looking forward to a trip to Israel in May and expanding her preliminary study of Hebrew.

I've felt well and have been writing about two hours a day in addition to Earthsat office work. The result was a second book, called, "Sooner Born," which examines the culture and people with whom I grew up through the prism of other cultures experienced later in life. Now, I am binding a third series of essays into a short book to be called, "Strictly Personal-1995." They revolve around the importance of identifying those values special in our lives and our responses to preserve them.

Another grand life experience occurred this summer at Dartmouth where I attended a class titled, "Writing Memoirs." There were 12 people in my section and a total of 65. Our teacher/tutor was first rate. The students ranged in age from mid-thirties to mid-seventies. Although none were professional writers, they each had a story to tell and sought the right "voice" to tell it. The depth and breadth of individual experiences was awesome. There was amazing bonding and shared good will. Many of us have continued to correspond. It will be offered next summer, probably the first week in August. It is open also to non-Dartmouth people. I couldn't recommend it more highly for a very low key experience in a delightful environment for one week. Half were women. I plan to attend again. If any of you are interested contact me for details.

Yesterday, I was with Larry Heilman, who recently broke his leg and ankle. He wears a cast and uses crutches. Martin Stoller has a very bad back. I went to pick them up. The back seat had some clothes in it, and the seat was back too far. We looked like the Keystone Kops falling over one another. I stopped at a parking meter. The big question was how many extra quarters should I allocate just to allow time to get in and out. The straining and swearing was eventually replaced by laughter as we saw ourselves for the joke we were and started laughing. I put on a car CD of Mabel Mercer, and we sang along to Cole Porter songs. It was male bonding time for senior citizens at its very best.

Best wishes for a good 1996.

1996

Dear Friends,

1996 was a year of tests and lifestyle decisions. The most difficult test was the discovery of a brain tumor in our three year old grandson, Porter. He was operated on in February. The tumor was on his left temporal lobe (a favorable position for surgery of a left-hander). Even though it was not malignant, we must wait until at least next March to see if they "got it all." Porter has held up the best of anyone. He never tires of jumping on you with a last second, "Catch me."

Jennifer and VJ are wonderful parents. What amazes me most is the way they seem to integrate this horrid event into their everyday roles of "soccer mom" (a coach on Vincent's team, and also a player on a women's team) and "hockey dad" (a proud supporter of Vincent's ice hockey aspiration, who still manages to run his own firm and write a highly respected business newsletter every weekend). Alex, age five, is never unsure about anything. When Lee asked her to identify "a low moaning noise" she was informed in a most authoritative manner that "It's the neighbor's burglar alarm." (It turned out to be Vincent practicing his cello.)

Amy has had a great year professionally and was given a good promotion, but she works horrendous hours which poses difficult lifestyle choices. Amy sometimes takes her dog Annie to work on the Disney lot. I can confidently predict that Annie will easily upstage a mere 101 Dalmatians. Watch for her at your local theater. Also, look for the soon to be written "101 Relatives." Amy is convinced that there's a story in our family history somewhere and is perusing her great-great uncle Robert's autobiography on his experiences from child laborer to oil magnate, great grandfather Alexanderson's contributions to early television, and Uncle Ed's forthcoming book on the Iran Contra hearings.

Lee, as always, wins the "Grandmother to the Rescue Award" with her rushed trip to fill in when Jennifer needed her. She is finishing up her degree at Wesley Seminary and took a month long trip to Israel and the Sinai. She has also written

242

a paper on "Baltimore Album Quilts," as well as working on several original pieces of art. We sold our house so in her spare time, she packed up the house and managed the move. I mainly kept out of her way (which wasn't easy). I was reticent to give up a house and garden, which I enjoyed (and Lee maintained), but it's about as large as the two floors we lived in before (2,700 square feet) with solid walls, built in 1929, and I am pleasantly surprised to find that I really like it.

I went to Dartmouth's writing course again this summer and had another great time. I haven't been writing as much this year but still find it one of my greatest joys. I have also been playing a lot of chess. My next lifestyle change will be retirement. I've concluded it's a lot like learning to ski: too much aggression and you'll break a leg; too much fear and you'll miss all the fun. Don't worry, I'll get there. Right now I'm at the ski lodge bar scouting out prospective "retirement runs."

1997

Dear WRITErs,

While neither "writer's block" nor "Christmas shopping" provide an adequate excuse for waiting until December 26th to send a "tailored" 1997 letter to my fellow WRITE classmates. I chose to think of it as not being "stampeded by holidays" and take pride in the fact that it's two weeks ahead of last year.

Two of life's greatest challenges are knowing what to say and then, whether or not to say it. The "Being-There-Without-Being-**Too**-There" award for 1997 should go to Lee, who earned it many times this year as a wife and mother. Also, culminating a six-year study of the Hebrew Bible, Lee was awarded a Master's of Theological Studies from Wesley Seminary. For her thesis, Lee, with some awesome design assistance from a friend, Marilyn Stern, produced an impressive retrospective book of her art. Finally, she finished the year by transforming our grandchildren's art into textile: Alex's (age 6) carefully crafted drawings of small girls and a rainbow's glow in Liberty cottons and gingham; Porter's (age 4) scribbles became intricate machine-embroidered designs which documented his earliest struggles to convert lines into primitive forms. It's truly a wonder to witness evidence of a child's neurons sprouting and interconnecting normally, especially after the terror we experienced just two yeas ago when this process went awry.

Vincent's (age 8) neurons are all in the right place, and rather than skipping a grade, he changed to a school for gifted students in science and math (eight in a class), which he likes almost as much as playing ice hockey. Alex, not to be outdone, is attending **two** schools: one in the morning, strong in art and music, followed by another in the afternoon, strong in neighborhood friends. Porter continues to progress as a robust, happy kid without any recent medical distractions. Jennifer, takes pride in their accomplishments, is having a hard time catching her breath while being a soccer and hockey mom, kindergarten chauffeur, and home construction administrator.

It might be said, "Amy, age 31, has put down the script and picked up the book." I asked Amy what I should say about her shift from producing TV movies to buying and selling rare books. She, in her inimitable style, referred me to an article in last week's *New York Times*. It said that while any copycat movie mogul can buy another Mercedes-Benz, it takes taste to select the right rare book. Apparently, the focus of this newsworthy activity is, of all places, Los Angeles. (Will this give new meaning to Hollywood's "Faustian bargains?") Although this is not her reason for going into this field, it may very well be the reason she can afford to stay in it. Confronted by the dazzling speed of the Internet, now added to by the energy of "AmyNet," I am anxiously awaiting to hear the reaction of Bill Gates (a well-known book collector). As always—stay tuned.

Then, there's me. I still look forward to going to the office in the morning (I also enjoy shortening some afternoons). We turned down an attractive financial offer to buy part of the company. I went to my third Dartmouth memoir writing course last summer. These have become very special reunions; ones which testify to the depth of new friendships made later in my life. I've finished my "memoirs of youth" phase and anxiously await the arrival of "middle age insights." On the medical front, I'm pleased to announce a breakthrough in the field of "home diagnosis." Specifically, my head tilts to one side, and I've debated for years whether to attribute this to Parkinson's or my cancer operation. However, recently I noticed that my computer monitor, to which I have been virtually glued, tilts the same direction.

Finally, Lee's changing her tune, literally. My study is off the livingroom, and the songs she practices herald coming events. Most of the year it's gospel hymns for church, where she plays bi-weekly. At Christmas, seasonal music. Now she's started practicing "Over the Rainbow," which means the grandkids are coming—gotta go.

Best wishes for a great '98,

1998

Dear Friends,

This was a "quick year." It was one that passed before I had a chance to do what I had planned at the beginning. I skipped a trip to London. I didn't go to Dartmouth's writing course. I didn't retire. It was over before I could get my act together.

This was not true for Lee. She celebrated her 60th birthday on a bike trip with Jennifer and her college roommate, Ginny Hawes and her daughter, from Prague to Vienna. She also entered one of her "Exodus" series quilts into a competition They selected hers, as one of only 45 to be in their traveling international show.

Jennifer and VJ were separated last January. I sort of hinted it was coming in last year's letter, but I had to face up to the reality this year. I have so many thoughts, so few words. I'm quite impressed, however, with the way she's making decisions and moving on with her life. I am also impressed with both VJ's and Jennifer's dedication to being responsible parents under sub-optimal circumstances.

Vincent, age 10, is moving on with his life too. He goes to a fantastic school which only has eight in his class. He's a very good student and has read 75 classic books, like *Treasure Island* and *Huckleberry Finn*, since last summer and plans to finish 100 by Christmas. I have to hurry to play chess with him while I still have a chance to win. His out of school passion is ice hockey and his mother spends nights and weekends transporting him to far flung ice arenas.

Alex, age 7, is the picture of composure and has a talent for drawing. She's definitely a young lady, except for an occasional "oops" when she takes a wild swing at her younger brother.

Porter, age 5, is a tower of power. He doesn't stop. Last March Jennifer was sleeping late. It had just been too quiet, the kind of quiet that can stir a mother from a deep sleep. Slowly her subconscious correlated her 4.5 year old's screams of glee with the repeated opening and closing of the garage door. An immediate investigation revealed that Porter was simply playing a new, as yet unnamed, form of amusement in which he would push the garage door button and then race to see if he could catch the bottom of the door with his hand and ride it up a few feet before dropping off. I agree "all's well that ends well," especially if a five year old just added to his growing list of life experiences. But it does make one wonder how long the warranty lasts on (a) the garage door opener, (b) an inventive five year old, (c) a young mother, and (d) an increasingly nervous grandfather.

"Listen to this" is a frequent exclamation I hear when Amy calls to tell about her latest find or sale. She has taken a job at William Dailey Rare Books in LA. She loves her work, which includes having a good boss and antiquarian book mentor. We drove around New England for a few days this summer looking for books. There are a lot of rare book dealers in New England, and Amy found several bargains which she bought for the store. The Hanover Inn at Dartmouth was our base, and we worked in some good meals with good friends.

"Retirement" is the big word in my vocabulary this year. I almost sold 75% of the company last year but the market crashed. They thought I wanted too much, and I thought they offered too little. When you're selling the company you founded, they're thinking, "If you're so smart why aren't you rich?" while I'm thinking, "If your so rich, why aren't you smart (enough to recognize what we are)." Of course, neither actually says that, and that's what makes it so tedious. Business is great. We just were awarded the largest contract in our history from NASA, to map the entire surface of the Earth in the 1980s and 1990s. We are looking forward to several new, exotic, high resolution satellites to be launched next year which should be good for business and a lot of fun. Actually, I'd be a lot more enthusiastic about retirement, if I could just go to work at the same time. Seasons Greetings.

1999

Dear Friends,

1999 was my "first year of partial retirement." I used to believe "retirement" meant "free time," and I've found that's not true, I have more activities. I have joined a cardiovascular fitness class which meets 3 days a week, After exercise I go to the office where I serve as "Chairman" but am not in demand in the day to day activities. I usually go home about 3 and work on my novel until 9 with time out for dinner and the news, play chess for several hours 5 days a week. I go to the office from 10 to 3 I really look forward to interacting with the people in my cardiovascular group. Three of my closest new friends include a two term Senator from Iowa who was captain of the Harvard football team, another guy who currently is the senior computer analyst for the Wall Street Journal and an MD with a Ph.D., a medical researcher in neurology at NIH who, coincidently, has offices next door to my Parkinson's doctor at NIH. It's not exactly the kind of random draw I expected in a fitness class. In fact the only thing we all have in common is having had heart attack or stroke.

Lee is even busier than I am. She has quilt (fabric art) shows planned or in progress at The DAR museum, Wesley Seminary, The Jewish Community Center, and Smith college(in association with her 40th reunion.) In her spare time she quilts and must be close to qualifying for a coveted black belt in Yoga.

Jennifer has still been playing soccer mom and taking two courses in social work. Vincent, age ten, is taking algebra in the fifth grade, Alex, age 8, continues to demonstrate her artistic aptitude, and Porter follows in his grandfather's footsteps of being a "holy terror" (venal crimes only). Amy is still in Los Angeles deeply submerged in rare books and the inter-net. It's amazing how the inter-net has revolutionized the rare book business.

Finally, for the last six months I've been totally absorbed in writing my spy story. I have attached a story which chronicles my efforts and offers free advice, titled "<u>So you want to write a novel</u>."

2000

December 24, 2000

Dear Friends,

In the second Millennium Lee and I continued our struggle to be "late bloomers."

Lee produced a new series of fabric art on the subject of "homelessness." She interpreted photographs in which she managed to catch postures of despair and resignation that are truly moving. She recently sold the largest number of quilts in a single sale to a prestigious not-for-profit institution and has been preparing for three exhibitions in the next six months. Demand is literally out pacing supply to the point that she has to caveat her sales opportunities with a request to "borrow them back" for a time in order to meet her display obligations.

My candidacy for being a late bloomer was submitted in the form of my first novel, not surprisingly a spy story, called <u>The Moscow Contrivance.</u> It hasn't been nominated for any literature prizes, but it's an undisputed fact that I enjoyed every moment writing it. So much so that I am already one hundred fifty pages into writing a second novel. The latest "novel" uses an event that actually happened to me as the point of departure for the fictional story.

Naturally, my children and grandchildren played significant roles in my year. We are told that, "You can't go home again," but I wondered if I could try "going away again." The test was a trip with Jennifer and her children, Vincent, 11, Alex, 8 3/4 and Porter, 7. We boarded the Queen Elizabeth II and sailed from New York to Southampton, England. This replicated six crossings of the Atlantic with my parents from age 12. It exceeded my hopes for bonding with the grand kids. We worked collectively on writing a short story titled, "Murder on the QE2", which was never finished, but Porter claimed to have written more pages than anyone else which he accomplished by increasing the font size of his letters. Vincent and I played a number of games of chess, and Alex kept a very nice journal with illustrated drawings. Incidently, I brought the journal book I wrote when

I took the QE1 in 1947 at age 12 and read it to the kids. After three days in London we took separate flights home.

Amy has left her job in Los Angeles and plans to move to New York early next year. She is currently knee deep in books in her LA apartment which she is selling off on e-bay to reduce her inventory before packing for the move. She and I are going into the rare book business concentrating on the higher end books which will minimize logistics and allow her to operate out of her apartment on the internet with an assistant. We recently went to New York to preview an auction at which we bought three items: a copy of <u>Pygmalion</u> inscribed to his secretary by George Bernard Shaw; a rare first edition in good condition of Steven Crane's <u>Maggie, A Woman of the Street;</u> and an eight page letter written by Queen Victoria enclosed in a book to a prominent American named Peabody, who had done the British government a great favor, inviting him to become a member of the Order of the Garter. Watching Amy on an internet hunt is like watching a first rate detective or intelligence analyst operate. It reminds me of CIA.

In addition to being a soccer mom, ice hockey mom and going to Europe with us on the QE II, Jennifer is having a busy year. She has taken two courses in Social Work and is serving as President of the Parent Support Group (the PTA equivalent) of Vincent's school.

When an author gives you a copy of his first novel, it's a gift that ranks a close second behind being given an elephant. By contrast, showing enthusiasm, and/or expressing criticism, is a wonderful gift to me. This is *a year of supporting friends,* for both Lee's fabric art and my writing. In my case, it may be a friend like my grand daughter, Alex, who called me to report on a short story I wrote about a fictitious trip to Oklahoma with secret agents Mustaf(Vincent), Fatima(Alex) and Pierre(Porter). She said, "It's the best story I've ever read. We read it in my third grade class. My teacher wants you to come up and meet my class"(Who needs a NY Times review?). Or friends, who delay a few minutes in the locker room just to give me a hand buttoning my shirt cuffs after our cardiovascular fitness class, or Lee who helps me edit these letters and memoirs even though she has many other things to do herself.

I feel greatly blessed as we enter the new millennium. My Parkinson's is stable after twenty years. I go to work everyday and share in EarthSat's enormous growth with employees who have been there since we started it 32 years ago. I also share time with our children and grandchildren. I write most days for three hours, and travel, mostly with my family. It's been a very good year from my viewpoint because of all of you.

2001

Dear Friends,

Unquestionably, my headline of choice is EARTHSAT ACQUIRED BY MDA. After 32 years, we have a binding Letter of Intent with MacDonald Detwiller, a Canadian company headquartered in British Columbia (details at www.Earthsat.com). I am very satisfied with the selling price and think of the many times we were tempted to sell at a much lower price. I also think of our struggles advancing new technology into a "show me," commercial world, which demanded short-term bottom line results. And we did.

We also had the honor of serving the intelligence community. This began with the need for accurate assessments of Soviet crops. Next, we located and estimated drug production in South America and the Middle East. We searched for SCUD missiles, hidden nuclear plants and produced over 90,000 maps of Iraq in less than one week at the outset of Desert Storm, an unprecedented mapping accomplishment. Now, we're helping in the war on terrorism. If you sense more than a slight hint of pride, I'm sure you can also anticipate a tinge of sadness. It's the end of a great segment of my life. I'm a lucky man who has looked forward to every morning of work.

Jennifer, Amy, and grandson Vincent, represented our family at Tim Coffin's wedding in Istanbul and with forty Coffin friends, including the wedding party, boarded two boats on the Aegean and spent five days visiting ancient ruins, swimming and soaking up the summer sun.

Of course, when there are three children in a family, a commitment to travel with one requires two additional trips to balance sibling egos. Jennifer subsequently took Porter, age 8, to Disney World and was taking Alex, age 10, on a trip to Cozumel the weekend after our fall visit. We were having a quiet Saturday morning when Porter with great glee rushed into the room to tell Alex about the killer hurricane that was waiting to strike the Mexican Gulf. Porter knew what buttons to press. Alex screamed, "I won't go." Vincent said, "I'll go instead." Alex retorted, "This is my trip and if I don't go, no one else does, for I don't want to hear what a great time you had." In the end, Porter's information was off by two hundred miles and three days. Alex had her own trip with Mom, and Porter had his moment.

Amy is settled on East 78th Street in New York City and has become very active in several historic preservation and rare book societies. She and her dog, Annie, frequently visit Jennifer in Farmington, and we enjoy seeing her more often.

The year 2001 will also be remembered as the year I finished my second novel FLYSWATTER, which will be published in about 2 months. It takes place in Athens, Istanbul, Iran, Washington DC, and Vermont and is based on a an incredible true experience. I've also finished a fourth non-fiction book, an anthology of anecdotes of personal experiences about our family. I want to tell you the naked truth, but must hold back a few secrets so I called it ALMOST NAKED.

Lee is "taking a sabbatical" from fabric art to concentrate on learning to draw. She is also working on embroidery using images from daily life and the national news as her subjects.

EarthSat deserves some further reflection. It has 165 stockholders, who are former or present employees, and personal friends. All three of the starting employees are still with EarthSat, and many have been with us for more than 25 years. We lost money in more years than we made money, and it took grit to stay the course. We had times when I picked up the phone and called friends like Rod Frates, Derby Wilson, Jon Longely or my father-in-law, John Wallace, and said, "Payroll's tomorrow," and all pitched in. I don't know of any stockholder who didn't think of EarthSat as something special. We were sharing history in the making. We watched the spatial size of an object seen by a commercial satellite go from 80 meters to less than 1 meter. We've watched the spectral resolution (the number of colors we could resolve) increase from 6 to 250. The satellites we use now control the balance of military power and, increasingly, commercial power.

"Everything gets done through people" is a truism I've seen validated at EarthSat. Together we've supplied crop forecasts to 120,000 customers, written 400 geological reports for over 100 oil and mineral companies, provided studies in nearly 100 countries. Finally, we mapped the entire surface of the Earth, twice (ten years apart) so a man could tell his location within 50 meters. It's been an exciting thirty-two years.

Happy 2002,

2002

Dear Friends,

The year 2002 could be called the "year of re-commitments" for the Porter family.

Jennifer recommitted herself to marriage by joining with Mark McKenzie, a father of Patrick (11), Riley (8) and Maggie (5). His children live with their mother in Nashville, and Mark visits them twice a month. Jennifer's oldest, Vincent (13) is busy selecting boarding schools for next year and recently completed a paper on the IRA struggle with the British government in the 1980's. Alex (11) is learning to play the clarinet and positively glows when she talks about the band sound resulting from the instruments playing together. Finally, Porter (9) is a soccer and ice hockey star and always has a story to tell.

On the studio front, Lee has re-dedicated herself to pursuing fabric art after a sabbatical year to concentrate on her drawing skills. Her travel itinerary included two foreign trips: Nicaragua in August with Judy Markley, who has recently set up the Global Education Fund, a foundation which provides funding to schools directly and teacher training in third world countries. (NOTE: Lee's current quilt series is about poverty and education in Nicaragua.) In October, she went to a women's house party in the Cognac district of France. Yes, our lives are a strange world of contrasts. When asked what she was doing today, Lee replied, "I'm going to the studio, then to participate in an anti-war demonstration at Farragut Square, tea at the club, home for dinner with you and then my book club this evening." Lee thinks her memory's bad because she frequently forgets something. Good Lord, I would think so.

Ten months after selling EarthSat, I am excited about re-entering the business world with the purchase of a minority interest in an electronics company in Baltimore that designs and fabricates devices used by the defense intelligence community in the war against terrorism. This is very synergistic with SpecTIR, a company in Santa Barbara, of which I also am part owner. SpecTIR makes advanced sensors to be used by the military and can also identify minerals and oil seeps from spacecraft or aircraft.

Amy continues to live in New York where she is looking for an apartment to buy to make her permanent home. She is very active in several non-profit activities, including the Morgan Library and The Central Park Conservancy.

I did not self publish a novel in 2002, but am about to go to the publishers with a series of mostly unpublished anecdotes and a few excerpted from earlier books. It is called <u>Almost Naked</u>. The logic for the title being that telling the truth, the whole truth, and nothing but the truth would be the "naked truth." This is asking too much of any autobiographer, therefore the title, <u>Almost Naked</u>.

I was shaken by the loss of a very good friend, Charles Sheffield, from brain cancer only two months after his first symptoms. Charles was the brightest person I have ever known and certainly one of the most loved by his many friends. Charles was sort of a "superman." He earned a "double first" in math and physics at St. John's College, Cambridge; learned to speak, read and write Farsi (Persian) in ten weeks, and published over forty-five books. It hits me hard when he went the way of all flesh without the need for kryptonite. It's all pretty humbling and makes me appreciative of how slowly my Parkinson's has developed.

Lee and I are greatly concerned about the pending war in Iraq and the ongoing war between the Palestinians and the Israelis. Like many American's, we have no sympathy for suicide bombings, but also have no sympathy for the Israeli settlement expansion, the accompanying road development and the land and water appropriation. We think it is counter-productive to only address the occurrence of terrorist acts without addressing the root causes. I am particularly bothered by the fact that our foreign aid perpetrates it. The arrogance of our foreign policy which shouts, "might is right," is loathed by billions of Muslims worldwide and many non-Muslims. It is a time one must speak his or her mind whether your name is George W. Bush or Lee and Bob Porter.

Peace,

John Robert Porter III was our third child and only son. He was born Friday, August 13, 1971 extremely brain damaged. He lived 11 years. The first two were at home. They were devastating for Lee who bore the major burden for John's care. She was very angry, then and even now, at me for not "doing enough." This piece is an attempt to say, "I heard you."

I kept this, unread, in my briefcase for a year and then showed it to two people: my wife, who thinks it's the best piece I've written and a psychologist, Bruce Bernstein, who said it's an example of Post-Traumatic Stress Disorder.

JOHN REMEMBERED
June 2, 2003

When a problem is just too big to contemplate, something in our brain obscures the unattractive problem from our mental view until we are prepared to confront it. This poses a problem in that to resolve the problem, you first have to find it; and if you've camouflaged it so it's not visible, it's hard to know where to start. It's there, acknowledged or not, and you can sense the problem's presence. This recently happened to me. My problem appeared in the metaphorical form of a "bull." We met, not surprisingly, in the china shop. He had been waiting undisturbed for thirty years, during which time he was simply not on my agenda. My excuses were many. Why give life to a dead issue? Why get to know an unknown problem? What good would it do to give life to a problem I couldn't solve? But I knew that day must come, and when I saw it face to face, I know that terror had found another victim.

He was a jet-black bull and of ferocious size. He so dominated the room that his shadow shut out the sun and his breathing sucked up all the available oxygen. My feet were frozen to the floor by fear. No space was safe. His nostrils gushed mucous and sweat permeated the room and made my eyes squint. The beast was indefatigable. He was a killing machine. His head was high, his eyes alert. Suddenly, I was startled. He spoke to me in a contemptuous, hostile tone. "Why did you come? You know you can only suffer by coming. I will introduce you to death and you will hate life because of me." HE TOSSED HIS HEAD AND A STACK OF CHINA WENT FLYING.

"I am here," said the bull, "to torment you." Once you have seen me your fate is sealed. You know now that I am too big to be killed, too impetuous to be understood. I was conceived in your mind and you gave birth to me. I will accompany you to your grave. I am everything, that means failure to you. I symbolize the loss of control. I have violated your wife and have planted the seed of retribution. I will foil your ambitions. You cannot possibly name one good thing that came out of my creation. But now you have entered my pen. I have split you and your wife forever. She blames you for the thousands of hours she spent caring for John. She hates you for not doing more."

"Even if 'more' could never be enough." I interjected hastily.

"More" might have made a difference. Now it's too late. You can never go back. You can never undo. You have given your wife a lifetime license to hate you which you will never undo." THE BULL LOWERED HIS MASSIVE HEAD AND RIPPED OPEN A LARGE BOX, THEN, TENSING HIS MUSCLES, THREW THE BOX, NOW IN SPLINTERS INTO THE CORNER.

"Your wife's anger is my feed. This fragile china is made from you and your wife's tears. It is the refuse of your hopes, dreams and excuses. Yours is not a crime of omission. It is a crime of commission. Ambition was your motive. A reach for perfection. As the song said, 'A girl for me and a boy for you.' Children to satisfy you. What arrogance. What inane stupidity. What mindlessness. What avarice. I reserved my fullest contempt for you."

"Me, why me?"

"Because you wouldn't even address the problem. You just turned your back on your wife and child and went your own way. You concentrated on everything else. You ran."

"I didn't run, I sidestepped. I chose to do those things I could do productively. I certainly wasn't going to look for you to fight. In my weakened condition, I was not match. Look at you."

"So you left your wife to fight by herself. That was brave," he snarled. "The two of you would have made it a better match."

"It wouldn't have changed the outcome, but you would have become closer to each other. There would be nothing to undo now. "The fact is, you ran, and your wife knows you ran. She knows she couldn't keep up with you, caring for John, and fighting with me. John is dead, but I have planted the seeds of failure. Don't you think she wanted to scream 'help' a thousand times, but she knew you wouldn't hear her. Eventually, she stopped crying and pleaded for help. Carrying the stiff crying child with half a brain alone in her arms."

"Okay. Enough of the past, what of the future? What can I do today to relieve her pain?" I asked.

"Some of the pain will always remain," the bull said, for the first time lowering his voice, "But some can be soothed. You can do 'more' even today. Admit that I exist and admit that you ran and that she didn't run. Give her due. And the next time a difficult problem comes along, share the burden."

The bulls' eyes narrowed as he disposed of a thousand excuses with the toss of his head. "One final point," the bull concluded. "You're damned the lucky you chose to run, because I would have ground you both to a pulp. Never forget that she made it possible for you to survive and she's never been given her dues for that."

"Thanks," I said.

"Don't thank me. Fear me." The bull replied. "I can come back."

POST SCRIPT

I had some trepidation in putting this in the Dartmouth listserv. However, I think that sharing personal insights are even more important in our lives than our political perspective. At the home where John lived after the age of 3, thirty-six couples had placed their brain-damaged children. It was a near-perfect alternative with much love and good-will run by a dedicated couple for more than thirty years. They told me that we were the only parents that were still married. Why did I decide to share this with you? It is because it helped me to recognize the intensity of the rage my wife felt and it occurred to me that some class members might have also underestimated a degree of trauma at some time in their lives and would benefit by having it put in perspective. **YOU DON'T NEED A WAR TO GET POST-TRAUMATIC STRESS DISORDER.**

September 16, 2003

In retrospect, two additional stories also related to the traumas surrounding John are presented in the chapters titled, "Rough Draft and Post Script to Rough Draft."

Twenty-five years ago, I saw Tennessee Williams interviewed by David Frost. Frost asked him if there was an underlying theme to his books. After reflection, he replied, "Yes, I think it is the importance of unreality." He continued that many of his characters coped well in a dysfunctional world, but when they were confronted by newly perceived, but pre-existing, realities, their strength was tested and this often precipitated tragedy. Such may have been the case here.

The bull has returned and Lee and I plan to get a divorce. This was totally unforeseen by me when this story was written a short three months ago. The role that was played by the actual writing of the story is speculative, but the revelations made by, and to, the bull elevated the issue into our consciences, which, no doubt, impacted this decision.

0-595-29685-8